CHINA
THROUGH THE AGES

About the Book and Author

Past studies of China have concentrated on specific events or have related a chronological history of the dynastic periods. These works have included aspects of cultural history but have under-emphasized the country's great social, political, and intellectual movements and their ultimate expression in the art and literature of the time. By focusing on such themes, Professor Michael provides a new framework for understanding the Chinese cultural tradition.

The author describes the evolving history of ideas in China, from ancient faith in powerful magic to more modern concepts of a logical moral order of the universe and mankind's place in it. He also explores the intellectual ferment following the dawn of the age of reason, the integration of Buddhism into the Confucian social order, and the social transformations accompanying the rise and fall of the centralized state. Throughout, he illustrates how the changing society's beliefs, values, and aesthetic sense were embodied in its art and literature. This portrayal of the Chinese cultural tradition not only puts Chinese history in a new perspective, it also illuminates the process through which China constructed a modern society from a non-Western foundation and serves as an essential tool for understanding modern-day China and its prospects for the future.

Franz Michael is professor emeritus at George Washington University, where he was associate director and director of the Institute for Sino-Soviet Studies from 1964 to 1972. Dr. Michael's publications include *Rule by Incarnation: Tibetan Buddhism and Its Role in Society and State* (Westview, 1982), *The Taiping Rebellion*, 3 vols. (1971), *The Asian Alliance: Japan and United States Policy* (with Gaston Sigur, 1972), *Mao and the Perpetual Revolution* (1977), and many others.

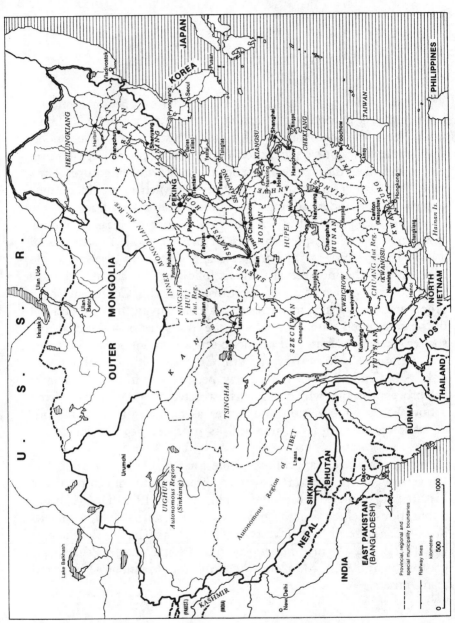

China

CHINA
THROUGH THE AGES

History of a Civilization

Franz Michael

Westview Press / Boulder and London

Copyright © 1986 by Westview Press, Inc.

Published in 1986 in the United States of America by Westview Press, Inc.; Frederick A. Praeger, Publisher; 5500 Central Avenue, Boulder, Colorado 80301

Library of Congress Cataloging-in-Publication Data
Michael, Franz H.
  China through the ages.
  Bibliography: p.
  Includes index.
  1. China—Civilization. I. Title.
DS721.M57 1986   951   86-11090
ISBN 0-86531-725-9 (alk. paper)
ISBN 0-86531-726-7 (pbk.: alk. paper)

Printed and bound in the United States of America

The paper used in this publication meets the requirements of the American National Standard for Permanence of Paper for Printed Library Materials Z39.48-1984.

10   9   8   7   6   5   4   3   2   1

CONTENTS

ILLUSTRATIONS

FOREWORD

THIS THOUGHTFUL BOOK, surveying the essentials of Chinese history from its prehistoric beginnings to the social changes of the 1980s, reflects the half-century of its author's involvement with China. The first chapter begins with a personal anecdote: The young Franz Michael, in self-imposed exile from his native Germany in the Hitler years, had become a professor at the National Chekiang University in Hangchow in the late 1930s. Along with the Chinese faculty and students, he experienced the great migration from Japanese-occupied coastal areas of wartime China to its far western interior. Along the way, pausing with that university group for some weeks in a village in Kiangsi, he shared their labor on a task of hydraulic engineering—building a dike to protect homes and fields from the summer floods, one of the ancient and significant involvements of the Chinese people with their environment.

That opening anecdote is the only point at which the author inserts his own story directly into this book, as he takes up the millennia-long account of the Chinese experience in history. His final paragraph, however, again reminds us of his personal involvement. There he expresses the hope that "the great humanist tradition of the past may still provide the moral strength on which to base a freer order for a people who have suffered so much in our time." Throughout his account of that great humanist tradition his scholarly mind searches for the most meaningful elements of the Chinese experience, those aspects of history that modern readers will want to know about as they visit China, or visit museums where Chinese art is displayed, or read Chinese literary works, or think about our world.

Franz Michael has the world, and particularly our world in our time, very much in his mind as he guides us through a Chinese past that is distant from us, but nevertheless of consequence to us. The problems he brings into our view are basic human issues: How did the Chinese adapt their lives to their immense land; how did they preserve their Chinese identity through the longest of all national histories, through the high and the low points of their often troubled past; how did they express themselves and transmit their vision in thought and art; how did they work out solutions to daily-life problems within the distinctive structure of their society? Professor Michael's discerning eye for human values, combined with his social scientist's perceptions of the social process, contribute the qualities that give this book its special flavor. Above all, he disdains the unexamined assumptions of formula history, and writes his own, very personal assessment of the route by which China reached the present moment in its history. At some points his sense of Chinese history differs from my own, as is often the case when two historians compare their larger interpretive constructs. That is another way of saying Franz Michael could not write a dull book.

First and foremost, Franz Michael is a student of Chinese government, and in surveying history he is ever mindful of its meaning for the political life of China today. His view of the stark political changes of this century sets his book apart from many others. He rejects the facile labeling of the People's Republic as a new imperial dynasty, one more in the long succession of imperial regimes. The Ch'ing or Manchu dynasty that ended in 1911 provides the base from which our understanding of the present must proceed, but Mao Zedong was not a new emperor, and Chinese Communism is not, either in intrinsic or in functional terms, just an updated version of "imperial Confucianism." His sense of the past is more accurate than that of the analysts who use those labels, and his characterization of the present cuts through those mists with greater clarity. He rightly points out that the political forms adopted by the Communists could not have been generated from within, using the concepts and the institutions of the Chinese past. The political forms of Soviet Leninism imposed upon the Chinese social base are culturally incongruous with China's political past. Nonetheless, something of the old Chinese pragmatic spirit and of its traditional humane values have persisted, and they condition the way all new elements from without are received, understood, and used. The Chinese experience in today's world can only be understood by drawing deeply on our knowledge of its long past. We are often tempted to explain all human behavior in terms of parochial-minded analogies to what we know best—the rather recent experience of our own society. That will not suffice; China, as Professor Michael states in his preface, was sui generis. That, however, makes the comparisons with our own past and present the more interesting, and if we make such comparisons well armed with sound information, they become the more revealing about the Chinese and about ourselves.

Another striking feature of this work is its attention to the art of China and the long history of the development of Chinese art under its own motivations. Franz Michael never indulges in superficial comments that attempt to "explain" the artistic genius of the Chinese as a by-product of social tensions. He does, to be sure, elucidate some of the philosophic ideas that accompanied the developments in the arts and in the high crafts, especially painting, calligraphy, architecture, and ceramics. But his intent is to urge the reader to look appreciatively at the objects, to observe them thoughtfully, and to gain his or her own sense of their beauty.

I first came to know Franz Michael, whom I should address more respectfully as Professor Michael, when I returned to this country in 1950 after some years in China and took up graduate studies at what was then known as the Far Eastern and Russian Institute of the University of Washington in Seattle. That institute's director, George E. Taylor, had assembled what I felt must be the most exciting faculty for East Asian and Russian studies in the Western world. At the center of its China studies was the Colloquium on Modern China, directed by Professor Michael. He chaired its weekly meetings, scheduled for an entire morning, but which often spilled over into the rest of the day, meetings that wholly dominated the scholarly consciousness of the entire faculty and student group until the next session the following week. The focus of the colloquium, formally speaking, was on the turbulent nineteenth century, especially on the Taiping Rebellion of the midcentury, for which the definitive treatment is Professor Michael's The Taiping Rebellion, in three volumes, published in 1971. But despite that focus, the range of the colloquium was as broad as Chinese history itself. Thirty or more years later my enduring impression of it is of Professor Michael in the moderator's chair, open to all manner of fact and interpretation, interested in whatever touched upon China, yet absolutely meticulous in his unfailingly rigorous examination of the ideas under discussion—what was the evidence, how was it being interpreted, what implications did it hold for other issues? Despite his awesome ability to be the critic, and despite the passion with which he sought the best possible understanding of the facts, he always performed that task with warm good humor. The present book is the mellowed synthesis of a thousand such intellectual engagements. Professor Michael's acute perceptions and the warmth of his feeling for his subject—and his acceptance of human foibles—come through to me as echoes of those remote student days. Those same qualities will be apparent to the readers of this book.

Frederick W. Mote
Princeton University

PREFACE

CHINA HAS THE longest continuous history of any civilization, reaching from the Neolithic—indeed the Paleolithic—age into our time. To explore this great human tradition as a comprehensive and interrelated story, assessing each phase of cultural development within the framework of a uniquely Chinese institutional and intellectual system, is the aim of this book.

For the Western historian familiar with the Judeo-Christian tradition, it is of vital importance to accept the notion that China follows a separate historical course, making its own great contribution to the common human heritage. The Chinese civilization is sui generis, and although the concepts and terminology of the discipline of history are universal, their applications in a non-Western tradition must be tuned to a world that has shaped its own mold.

Two points ought to be made prior to any narration of Chinese cultural history: one, that of all great cultural traditions the Chinese is perhaps the most historically minded. The volume of Chinese accounts of all facets of their history is massive. Aside from the twenty-five dynastic histories, there is a wealth of annals, chronicles, accounts, and descriptions, covering everything from dynastic events to the stories of local affairs found in the thousands of local gazetteers that provide extraordinary and still largely unexplored materials of daily life, economic and technical matters, and literature and art in the regions and districts of the realm. There are innumerable individual writings on all imaginable topics: The record of Chinese culture is indeed immense.

This historical tradition begins before the Christian era, and the pattern set in Han time by the great historican Ssu-ma Ch'ien placed its stamp on all later historical writing. It is an honorable tradition, based on the belief that man could learn from history; the emphasis was on Truth (what Ranke meant when he wrote that the task of the historian was to tell "wie es eigentlich gewesen"—how it truly was) so that the rulers of each Chinese dynasty could learn from the past. Eventually the dynastic histories were written directly from the records of daily affairs as taken down at the court by an archivist. These records were used by each successor dynasty for compiling the history of its predecessor. In recording events the archivist, at least in principle and mostly in practice, was free from the supervision of the ruler, who was not supposed to peer into the record.

The other point to make, however, is that this tradition provided facts and data, a chronicle of life and affairs, but did not attempt to analyze these data within a conceptual framework as a modern historical disciplinary approach would. This poses a problem for the modern historian of Chinese history, who has to apply modern analytical concepts derived from Western history to a non-Western culture.

Actually, there has been very little modern conceptual inter-pretation of ancient and imperial China. There is, of course, the unilinear Marxist-Leninist doctrine that all human history follows the same course, leading from "primitive society" through "slavery," "feudalism," and "capitalism" to the millennium of "socialism" and, finally, "communism." Its application to China by the Communists is particularly grotesque and is today in a few cases debated even among high-ranking Chinese Communist academic specialists, though continually and strongly reasserted by the party line.

The attempt to develop Karl Marx's dictum of an "Asiatic mode of production," based on control of water works, is today again debated within China. Its main Western protagonist is Karl August Wittfogel, whose concept of "Oriental Despotism," does not, in this author's view, do justice to the complexity and institutional as well as ideological greatness of China's cultural tradition.

The Chinese imperial past, which so impressed the eighteenth century European writers of the Enlightenment, Leibnitz, Rousseau, and many others, was indeed hard to fit into terms and concepts taken from Western historical writings. To deal with the Chinese cultural tradition from early prehistoric time to the problems of today, the author attempts therefore to describe and analyze each evolving phase as a non-Western story in terms that, though drawn from the Western historical vocabulary, take on a non-Western coloration. Indeed all historical concepts and terms should be global and universal. It is in this way that the following, largely chronological account of the various periods of China's cultural history is to be read. To see this civilization in its entirety, the author attempts to relate all aspects of its political, social, economic, and intellectual evolution to its art and literature and to link these various expressions of the whole culture as they evolve together, to recreate the spiritual bond that characterizes the unity of a civilization.

Chinese history narrates an evolving story—from the powerful magic of early antiquity to the great concept of a logical moral order of the universe and of man's place in it. The intellectual ferment following the age of reason manifested a struggle with concepts of the social order at a time when early Greek philosophers and the historical Buddha wrestled with parallel philosophical problems of social transformation. A centralized Chinese state, unique in character, all-powerful in its limited sphere of authority, rose and fell, while a viable social order provided the continuity and the platform on which the state was forever rebuilt. Buddhism, the one great alien rival to the Confucian social order, was overcome as a political challenge, domesticated and amalgamated, and used to widen the Confucian horizon. The result was not only a bureaucratic state, but also a bureaucratic society dominated and managed by professionals who were qualified not by birth but by education and the attainment of academic degrees and whose beliefs and aesthetic values were projected into art and literature.

The issue of today and the future is the problem of modernization under the handicap of a failing Communist system, aggravated by the economic, social, and intellectual decline created by the late Mao Tse-tung's utopianism. Under the surface, we trust, there is the moral strength derived from the past that may revive and carry on the great cultural tradition in as yet unknown form.

In writing about Chinese history in English, one faces the special problem of transliterating Chinese personal and geographic names and terms. The Wade-Giles system, which has been the traditional transliteration for the past century, has its unnecessary complexities, especially in the usage of consonants with or without aspiration (t stands for d and t' stands for t; p stands for b and p' stands for *p*, etc.). This system has been used in all academic and most popular English works on China until recently. The new transliteration introduced in the People's Republic of China avoids this double usage of hard consonants; but the new version, called *pinyin* has problems of its own (*x* stands for an aspirated *s*, formerly *hs*; *q* stands for a *tsh* sound, formerly *ch'*, *zh* stands for a *dj* sound, formerly *ch*, etc.). The quandary of the differing transliterations has been dealt with here by using the Wade-Giles system for historical names and terms, and *pinyin* for names of the present leaders, with the Wade-Giles form added in parentheses for clarification. In addition the usage of generally accepted postal terms (i.e., Peking, Canton) is continued.

Condensing the events and interpretation of a history of more than 5,000 years into some three hundred pages raises a problem of documenting each point of the theme. Only direct quotations have therefore been footnoted, although a selective list of works at the end of each chapter gives recognition to the studies from which the author has most profited and that he recommends for further reading.

To Lyman Miller and Ernst Wolff, whose comments have been most helpful in clarifying points and preventing errors and who have shared many ideas, the author is deeply grateful. He is most beholden to Dr. Thomas Lawton, the director of the Freer Gallery of the Smithsonian Institution, whose relevant comments and intellectual support have provided continued encouragement and who has selected the illustrations that give this study its visual character.

The Earhart Foundation provided an initial grant for the study, and the confidence and support of its former president Dr. Richard Ware, in this as in other studies by the author, have been deeply appreciated.

Franz Michael

INTRODUCTORY NOTE

CHINESE CIVILIZATION HAS been a source of fascination and a challenge to scholars for centuries. Why and how did a major culture emerge some five thousand years ago in the north-central region of what we now call China? Complete answers to these questions remain to be given, but as archaeological findings accumulate, our knowledge of the prehistoric period grows. Gradually, fact and myth are separated, and a more accurate picture of ancient Chinese society emerges.

From the time fairly complete written records were kept, the raw materials from which histories are compiled become richer than before, but various obstacles to balance and objectivity remain: ideological biases that preordain the way in which the available data is used; overreliance upon accounts by the winners in the great struggles that determined the rulers and the ruled; and the paucity of certain types of material such as those pertaining to the life-style and thoughts of the ordinary individual. The social scientist dealing with the contemporary world faces some of these hazards, but in comparison with the historian of the premodern era, the social scientist at least has a wealth of data drawn from every level of society.

For these and other reasons, history will constantly be rewritten, using new materials, new interpretations, and new combinations of the data that must be selected out of those which are available at the time. One of the virtues of Franz Michael's present study is that although it is correctly titled a brief history, it seeks to deal not merely with the broad political and economic trends of China from the still misty Shang era to the post-Mao years, but it also depicts the cultural and intellectual developments that accompanied these trends. We are thus treated to a picture of Chinese society in its larger dimensions, with the geopolitical, economic, and cultural components woven together in a single tapestry.

Some scholars may interpret certain events differently from Professor Michael. There has never been and there will never be unanimity regarding the conclusions that are drawn from the data with which we work, even when the data are identical. Yet even those who hold to different interpretations will be stimulated to reflect upon the central themes so skillfully presented in this lucidly written, succinct survey.

Certain issues of critical interest to historians and social scientists reoccur throughout Michael's account. How did the Chinese leadership and state acquire legitimacy, and how was legitimacy lost? To what extent and in what period is the term *feudalism* applicable to China? More generally, how well does Marxist theory fit the course of China's development? What was the organizational basis for the Chinese state and for Chinese society, and to what extent were state and society compatible or in conflict?

Few individuals are as qualified to undertake the very difficult task of digesting and synthesizing the whole of Chinese history as is Franz Michael. His long academic career has been characterized by distinguished scholarship. His work on the Taiping Rebellion, for example, is valued by every student of Chinese history. His extensive command of languages gives him a command of a wide range of sources. And the catholicity of his interests enables the presentation of the broad picture. As a senior scholar in the field, he gives us his interpretation of both the universal and the particularistic factors that combined to fashion Chinese history in its broadest dimensions. Many will profit from his effort.

Robert A. Scalapino
Robson Research Professor of Government
Director, Institute of East Asian Studies
University of California, Berkeley

One

BEGINNINGS:

The Geographical Setting

IT RAINED HEAVILY on that day in early March 1938, as a group of several dozen middle-aged Chinese college professors left the walls of the village of Shangt'ien—"up the fields"—in Kiangsi province to start the work on diking the river Kan, which flowed by the village. For them and the only foreigner among them, who had moved inland with their university in a retreat from the Japanese invasion, life in the Chinese countryside was a new experience, and the coming day's work was going to confront in practice one of the most important age-old problems of Chinese history: the necessity of water control.

During the last few years the Kan River, a southern tributary of the Yangtze River, had changed its course, and when the students and faculty of the National Chekiang University arrived by boat at the village a few weeks earlier and scrambled up the sandy bank, they could clearly see the marks of last year's flood upon the walls of the farmhouses. In a few months, when that flood would return, the villagers would be forced to take refuge under the roofs or on the nearby hills and wait for the waters to subside. For the several hundred members of the university who had crowded into the village, such a cramped existence was not enticing, and since the university had a department of hydraulic engineering, the decision was made to build a dike for the protection of the village. That day the professors who carried shovels, bamboo poles, and baskets were to give an example that Chinese intellectuals were no longer above physical labor; and even the dean, small and elderly, came along,

1

too frail to dig, but holding an umbrella over the shoulders of one of his physically stronger, laboring professors. The next day the students took over, but the real work had still to be done by the local farmers as paid corvée labor as it had been done in China throughout imperial history.

Indeed, Chinese history is inseparably linked to the problems posed by the rivers that had to be tamed to prevent the ever-threatening floods, and to the skill in building canals for drainage, irrigation, and transportation. This skill logically developed from the experience in managing the river waters. Chinese civilization had its origin in Northwest China, in the valleys of the Wei and Fen rivers, tributaries of the Huangho, and in the North China plain, formed by the alluvial sediment of this large and turbulent river, named after its muddy color "Huangho"—Yellow River.[1] Throughout Chinese history this river has posed China's greatest engineering problem.

The Northwest and the North China plain, the cradle of the Chinese way of life, are covered by a special soil called *loess*, which occurs only in a few minor areas of the globe outside of China. Within China loess soil is of windblown origin, formed over centuries and indeed millennia by the strong seasonal winds that blow each spring from the high pressure areas of the plateaus of Central Asia toward the Pacific Ocean with its less variable temperatures. Passing over the Gobi Desert and the steppe lands of the Northwest, the winds collect sand and move on as sandstorms over the northwestern mountains and the North China plain, covering the land with layers of loose sandy soil that over time have reached varying depths of hundreds of feet.

This loess soil retains the minerals of the surface growth it covers, is fertile and porous, and although hard baked on the surface, is easily worked with simple tools, a fact that greatly facilitated primitive society's shift from hunting and food collecting to agricultural cultivation of the soil, provided enough water could be supplied. It was therefore for good reason that in this area Chinese civilization began.

Yet the very looseness of the soil created in the Yellow River system problems of water control that became a key factor in the development of Chinese civilization. The muddy waters of the Huangho and its tributaries carry an extraordinarily high percentage of sediments, far higher than any other large river. This sediment is collected and carried along in the rapidly flowing current of the upper course of the Yellow River. But when the river breaks through the mountain barriers of the Northwest and levels off in the alluvial plain, slowing down its course, its sediments begin to settle, forming sand banks and raising the bed of the river, which easily overflows into adjacent land. To protect the land and confine the river to its course were therefore from earliest time major tasks of the early kings.

According to Chinese historical myth, the Great Yu, who was the founder of the legendary Hsia Dynasty, dated 2205 to 1766 B.C., gained his reputation by taming the floods. He is said to have accomplished the monumental task of confining the rivers to their beds in thirteen years, traveling constantly, allegedly passing his home three times without taking time to enter it. This legend of the Great Yu and his extraordinary accomplishment, recorded much later by the philosopher Mencius, may well bear a kernel of historical truth.

As an engineering problem, the control of the Yellow River has never been permanently solved. All along its lower course the river had to be diked. But when the accumulation of sediments in the riverbed eventually raised the water within the built-up dikes above the level of the surrounding countryside even at the river's normal stage, any further rise or any neglect of dike repair would bring disastrous floods and the loss of millions of lives. During historical times, the river has changed course often over many sections of the North China plain, flowing into the Yellow Sea at places from Tientsin in the North to the Huai River estuary close to the Yangtze River in the South, each time devastating vast areas over long periods until its new course could be diked again.

Such catastrophic floods occurring throughout history into modern times earned the river the name "China's Sorrow." With its stupendous flood problem, the Yellow River has remained a testing ground for Chinese skill in hydraulic engineering, a skill that, once acquired, was applied to other rivers with various problems in drainage, irrigation, and canalization throughout the country.

In the Northwest and the North China plain, the spread of early agricultural settlements, denuding mountain slopes of their forest growth, contributed to the change of climate, which in turn altered the flora and fauna and aggravated the problem of lack of moisture, resulting in insufficient rainfall. To the necessity of diking and drainage was added the need for irrigation, as evidenced by the impressive irrigation canals built in the Northwest in early Han time in the second century B.C.

The pattern had been thus set by the time that Chinese civilized life spread to the system of the other great river of China, the Yangtze and its tributaries, and southward to the triangle of the West, the North, and the East rivers with their confluence in the Pearl River delta at the city of Canton. Southward was the logical course of expansion for the Chinese agricultural and centrally governed way of life, shaped in the Northwest and the North China plain.

Along the northwestern border, the arid climate of the high plateaus and steppes set a natural limit to Chinese agricultural incursion. This was the domain of a different form of life, steppe nomadism, organized in steppe empires that recurrently invaded the Chinese settled agricultural areas and at times established conquest dynasties over parts or all of China. To fend them off, Chinese emperors built the Great Wall and in turn, when they were strong enough, extended military control over the steppe people. Whichever side predominated, the line between agriculture and nomadism followed the climatic border. And in peaceful times the two different ways of life complemented each other through trade or tribute missions. The Inner Asian frontier thus became one of the major political, military, economic, and cultural factors in Chinese history.

While seeking to guard the northwestern frontier, the Chinese expanded their moving frontier southward. The geographical setting in Central and South China differed in various ways from the conditions that had to be met in the North and the Northwest. South of the Tsinling Mountains—an extension of the Kunlun range, which divides North and South China and terminates in the foothills near the city of Naking—the loess soil that so decisively affected for better or worse Chinese life in the Yellow River system does not occur. The Yangtze and its tributaries and the rivers further south had their own flood problems, but they were of different origin. The centuries of agricultural use had denuded the mountains and the hills of much of their forest growth, creating flood problems of a differing order. If heavy rains occurred simultaneously at the upper course of the Yangtze and in the valleys where the tributaries originated, the flood danger at the confluence of these rivers became particularly severe. Lessening the risk, two lakes, Tungting Lake and

Poyang Lake, formed at such points of confluence, served as water reservoirs in time of flood danger. But most of the riverbeds had to be diked as the modern example of the Kan River demonstrates. Without the high sediment content of the Yellow River system, the Yangtze, its tributaries, and the larger rivers to the south, although occasionally flooding, retained their beds and served as major arteries of communication. Indeed, once developed, the Yangtze system provided cheap water transport for twelve out of the eighteen provinces of imperial China. In time, the Yangtze system became the richest agricultural area in China, particularly after centuries of neglect of existing irrigation systems and recurring invasions from the steppe had weakened the agricultural production of the Northwest and the North China plain.

The experience with water transport, gained in the South, was in turn applied in the North when later dynasties, retaining their political capitals in the old cultural areas of the Northwest and later at Peking, wanted to obtain access to the rice tax in kind of the fertile new area of Central China. From the seventh century A.D. on, great canals connected the Yangtze basin with the capitals in the North, culminating in the Grand or Imperial Canal, as rebuilt by the Mongol ruler Kublai Khan in the thirteenth century A.D. expressly for transporting the tax rice from the Yangtze area to the capital Khambalik—today's Peking.

With Chinese agriculture expanding into the Yangtze basin and southward, irrigation became even more important because a different staple crop was grown in Central China and the South. The northern staple had been chiefly wheat; in South and Central China it was rice, a crop that necessitates the flooding of the rice fields for long periods, from the time the seedlings are planted and transplanted until the crops ripen. The Chinese became masters of intricate irrigation systems in the lower Yangtze basin and the terraced rice fields that so characteristically cover the hills and low mountains of much of the center and the South of China.

This Chinese system of settling the land, developed in the North and adapted in Central and South China, depended on large- and medium-scale public works. In preindustrial time these required both the massive use of human labor, drawn from a dense population, and the intensive cultivation of the land. This combination made possible a rate of production per agricultural unit sufficient to feed such a dense population—larger in fact than that of premodern European rainfall agriculture. Socially, this pattern of agriculture encouraged the Chinese to settle in villages, not in isolated homesteads, wherever they spread their civilization. The effectiveness of this system also helps to explain to a large degree the vast population figures reported in China from earliest historical time on.

Of the territory of this traditional Chinese development, Central and South China is geographically more dissected by mountain ranges than the more compact North. The regions of the Center and the South were at times harder to control than the more cohesive northern plains, and this factor may help to explain why for most periods of its history the political center of China remained in the North, even after the key economic areas had shifted to the Yangtze region and the South. As North China's alluvial plain had few harbors along its coast but an endangered frontier toward Inner Asia, China remained inland oriented. In the North, the provinces of Hopei and Honan—north and south of the Huangho—the peninsula of Shantung and the northwestern provinces of Shensi, Shansi, and Kansu are the modern administrative divisions of the old heartland.

The regions of the center and the South formed recognizable units of their own that were more or less marked by political, i.e., provincial, divisions. The lower Yangtze region, from the city of Ichang to the outflow of the Yangtze into the East China Sea has long been the richest rice-growing area of the country. The rice fields are interlaced with irrigation canals and waterways, and the readily available and inexpensive transportation system has encouraged along its rivers the development of commercial cities and, in modern times, industrial centers. The steel city of Wuhan, the onetime capital of Nanking, and modern Shanghai (located at a tributary of the Yangtze, the Huangp'o River), the largest city of China and an important modern commercial and industrial center, flourished on the basis of this communication system within the rich hinterland. This central region of China, organized in the provinces of Anhui (Anhwei), Kiangsi, Hupei, and Hunan, is the area where the Western contact with China had its main impact.

Separated from the lower Yangtze through high, narrow river gorges known for their dramatic scenery is the highly irrigated fertile plateau of Szech'wan province, formed by the upper Yangtze and three tributaries. It is known also as the "Red Basin" on account of the red color of the sandstone and soil of the province. Divided from the other regions of China by high mountain ranges, this province has served during several periods in history as retreats and safe bases for autonomous governments. During the Japanese invasion in World War II it was the seat of the National Government with its capital at Chungking.

South of the Yangtze estuary, the coastal region of the provinces of Chekiang and Fukien forms an indented coastline with excellent harbors but is separated from the inland areas by mountain ranges that run in a northeast-southwestern direction, thus limiting communications with the interior. The harbor cities of these coastal provinces have therefore never gained the importance of Shanghai or even Canton in modern time. Although this was a major area of tea and silk production in addition to ocean fishing and coastal navigation, its overall impact on Chinese development remained limited.

Across the Taiwan Strait from Fukien, separated by one hundred miles of water, is the island of Taiwan (Formosa), the seat of the National Government after its retreat from the mainland. Its Chinese population migrated originally from Fukien and Kwangtung provinces. Primitive proto-Malay groups remain in the mountainous areas. Under the National Government Taiwan has enjoyed an extraordinary economic development and prosperity.

In the South the two "Kwang" provinces, Kwangtung and Kwangsi, form an economic unit, centered on the city of Canton at the Pearl River delta, the chief overseas trading center in imperial time. The semitropical climate of the region makes possible two or three growing seasons per year.

To the south of Kwangtung province, across a narrow channel of the South China Sea, lies the island province of Hainan, as yet only in the beginning of its economic development. Hainan is rich in minerals, coal, and forest resources, and its semitropical climate provides a great potential for cultivation of coffee, cocoa, coconut, hemp, and other tropical products.

The southwestern provinces of Yünnan and Kweichow were the last to be penetrated by Chinese settlement. High plateaus and a moderate climate provide good agricultural conditions. Pre-Chinese minority groups, living in the less accessible mountain areas, form almost half of the population, which includes a large Muslim group.

What linked together these varied regions, with their diverse climates, geographical conditions, communication systems, staple crops, and coastal access, was the application in different settings of the same basic concepts for civilized life. The beliefs and value system that have evolved in this geographical setting prevailed throughout time into the modern world.

This was the China of the Chinese way of life. Bordered by the ocean in the East, by high mountain ranges and plateaus in the West, a narrow passage between oceans and mountains in the North, and deep river gorges and tropical forests in the South, this Chinese geographical setting of roughly one-and-a-half million square miles has been called "China Proper" or "China within the Wall" (the Great Wall)—the territory where the Chinese way of life was formed and developed. It is an eastward sloping, vast bulge of the Asiatic continent, dominated by its rivers and the agricultural life affected by them.

As a political and cultural entity, however, China extended its realm beyond the area where the Chinese people formed their civilization. Having established their social order, the Chinese came to regard their system as the most civilized form of human communal existence. In the interplay between theirs and neighboring cultures, Chinese order came to influence and dominate the adjacent countries of Central, East, and Southeast Asia, with the result that China's military and political sway extended through much of historical time beyond China proper over the neighboring peoples of Inner Asia, Northeast Asia and Southeast Asia.

Imperial China was not a nation-state but an empire that was regarded by its rulers and its people as the only true civilization, very much as the medieval Holy Roman Empire was regarded as the civilized world by its inhabitants. According to this concept, China was Chung-kuo, the "Middle Kingdom" in a world of barbarians who, if enlightened, would recognize the role of the Chinese emperor, the ruler of T'ien-hsia, "All under Heaven"—the human world—and would submit to his authority.

In practice, Mongolia, Chinese Turkestan, and Tibet in Inner Asia, Manchuria and Korea in Northeast Asia, and Vietnam (formerly Annam) in Southeast Asia were bound to the Chinese emperor through much of history in differing dependent, tributary, or patron-client relationships. After the Revolution of 1911 and the end of the empire, Chinese governments reinterpreted these relationships in modern terms: belonging to a unified Chinese nation of different nationalities. In this modern Chinese state the ethnic Chinese formed a vast majority, ruling not only their own areas, but the regions of the "minorities" as well. Some other countries of Southeast Asia occasionally established tributary relationships with the imperial court, which provided them with commercial advantages and political prestige for their rulers. Burma, Thailand, Laos, and Cambodia, small Himalayan states like Nepal and Sikkim, or even the island states of Sumatra and Java, once in occasional tributary relationship, have long since cut any such ties. Some of the former dependencies, Outer Mongolia, Korea, Vietnam, succeeded in breaking away from Chinese control; Tibet tried but failed and has remained like others, an "autonomous region" within the confines of the modern Chinese state, today the People's Republic of China. Including these former dependencies, chiefly Manchuria, Inner Mongolia, Chinese Turkestan (Sinkiang) and Tibet, Chinese territory today encompasses about three-and-a-half million square miles.

Some of these non-Chinese territories and their people have become amalgamated or outpeopled by the Chinese in the twentieth century. Manchuria is a case in point. Its southern tip, the Liaotung Peninsula and the Liao River valley—even though outside the Great Wall—have been Chinese cultural territory since prehistoric times; but the Northwest, the Hsingan (Khingan) mountain range was Mongol steppe country, and the northeast forest land along the Korean border was the preserve of the Tungus tribes from which the Manchus originated. Because Manchuria was opened to Chinese immigration from China proper in the first decade of this century, its population of sixty million today has become almost entirely Chinese.

In Inner Mongolia, the Mongols have become a minority in their autonomous region. In Chinese Turkestan (today the Xinjiang Uighur autonomous region—the former Chinese province of Sinkiang) the Uighurs, some of whom still maintain aspirations of independence, have been numerically matched by Chinese immigrants. In Tibet, where after 1959 Chinese attacks against Tibetans and their culture were most violent, the quarter million Chinese civilians who govern the region are still a minority. The size of today's "Tibet Region of China," proclaimed autonomous, has been greatly reduced by the transfer of large territories to the Chinese provinces of

Chinghai, Szech'wan and Yünnan. The Tibetan population, originally six million, has shrunk to fewer than two million in the autonomous region of Tibet, in part by the division of the land, but also by the death of more than a million people as the result of Chinese policy and the suppression of all Tibetan resistance to it.

In the past, these non-Chinese components of the empire, with the exception of Manchuria under the Manchu Dynasty, were not part of the social and political structure of China as it was established in China proper, but rather linked to it through their bond with the emperor and the dynasty, a bond that differed fundamentally from the system of the emperor's rule and the Chinese way of life in the area of China proper. When we speak of Chinese culture and its history and evolution, we have therefore to distinguish between the China of the Chinese and the China of the expanded empire. It was China proper where Chinese culture was shaped.

Two

THE AGE OF MAGIC:

Legend and Archaeology

CHINESE MYTHOLOGY HAS adapted from India a unique story of the origin of the world and of mankind. P'an Ku, primal man, a giant figure, had created the space between heaven and earth for mankind to live in. He supposedly lived for eighteen thousand years, and his remains formed the Five Sacred Mountains of China. He was followed by the Three Sovereigns, the lords of Heaven, Earth, and Mankind, who ruled tens of thousands of years and were fabulous figures with several heads, bodies of serpents, and feet of beasts. Later there were other mythical rulers, such as Lord Big Nest, who taught people to build homes in trees in times of flood, and later still another group of culture heroes, Fu Hsi, Queen Nu Wo, and Shen Nung. Fu Hsi was credited with having taught man the domestication of animals, hunting and fishing, and having introduced the institution of marriage. He also was the inventor of musical instruments and of the calendar. Queen Nu Wo, who like Fu Hsi had a human head but a serpent's body, overcame with her magic a great conflagration. Finally Shen Nung, the "Divine Farmer," who had a human body and the head of an ox, was the first to teach people how to till the soil and use the plow. He also introduced markets for trade and discovered herb medicine. Taken together these legendary rulers and mythological figures, recorded by later historians, provided a fantastical explanation for the origin of China's landscape and the beginnings of civilized life.

More rational are the legends of the culture heroes who allegedly followed these early mythological figures: the Yellow Emperor, a

11

number of other legendary rulers, and finally the "sage rulers," Yao and Shun, and the Great Yu, the last already referred to. The Yellow Emperor (Huang-ti) was said to have defeated barbarian tribal neighbors, the Miao, then living in North China, and to have established government institutions. He invented the use of money and even the compass, successfully used in battle in the then foggy forests of Central China. His wife was credited with having originated silk culture and his minister supposedly introduced the first written signs. Yao and Shun were in Chinese tradition paradigms of virtue, in fact so virtuous that they overcame all problems of their times chiefly through the appointment of brilliant ministers and, especially, successors—Yao selecting Shun, and Shun selecting the Great Yu.

Confucius in his teachings referred to the three as model rulers whose period was China's golden age. Some modern Chinese cultural historians have indicated their speculative belief that these legends may well refer to historical persons, perhaps tribal chieftains who could have been elected, in the view of one writer, as heads of a tribal confederation.[1] Others conjecture that they may rather have epitomized periods and stages of social development.[2] Whatever the reality behind such speculations may be, the importance of legend as a source for the historian became evident when twentieth century archaeological findings provided proof for some accounts that had been regarded until recently as pure mythology.

The early Chinese historians, in particular the famous Ssu-ma Ch'ien (who lived during the second century B.C.) wrote not only about the sage kings but also about the first dynasty, the Hsia Dynasty, which supposedly ruled from 2205 to 1766 B.C., beginning, so we were told, the system of dynastic rule that lasted until the Revolution of 1911. He gave us the names of the rulers of this dynasty, seventeen of them, and continued with an account of the Shang or Yin Dynasty that overthrew the Hsia Dynasty and ruled in turn from 1766 to 1122 B.C. It had twenty-eight rulers, whose names were also recorded. Since these accounts were given about 1000 to 2000 years after the epoch they described, little credence was accorded by modern historians to these names and the data described in these chronicles. From some samples of magnificent bronzes it was known that a Shang Dynasty had existed, but the details about its rulers and the historical events of the time were discarded as pious fables. Anything earlier had to be pure legend.

All this was changed by an extraordinary discovery whose full historical significance was only slowly realized. Legend became history when archaeology provided data that confirmed the historicity and the details of the legendary story of the Shang Dynasty. In 1899 farmers in Hsiao-t'un, a small village in the district of Anyang in northern Honan province, found some extraordinarily shaped bones that had come to the surfaces of their fields after rain and plowing. They were mostly small pieces, smooth and polished on the surface with some unusual cracks. One ingenious farmer decided that they had to be dragon bones and would therefore contain special powers. Animal bones and especially horns of deer had always been regarded in Chinese medicine as aphrodisiacs and cure-alls, ground to powder and sold by traditional pharmacies as medicine. The magic of dragon bones would be an additional, psychological healing factor. Local pharmacies bought the bones, ground them to powder and, as it was, a whole library of historical documents seems to have disappeared in the stomachs of local patrons in search of renewed youthfulness. By chance some of these bones fell into the hands of a Chinese scholar who recognized that the incisions on the bones represented an early form of Chinese writing, in fact the same type of characters that evolved into the Chinese writing of later time, and it eventually became clear that the bones had been used as oracles by the Shang rulers.

The first decades of the twentieth century were a time of decline and revolution, and knowledge of the discovery and its acceptance spread only slowly. In the meantime an excited search began among specialists for more samples of these "oracle bones." When they became more valuable, imitations appeared on the market, rapidly and in large numbers. It took modern methods to distinguish between the genuine specimens and the forgeries. Eventually, in 1934 under the National Government through the National Research Institute of History and Philology, systematic excavations were undertaken at Anyang under the direction of the leading Chinese archaeologist Dr. Li Chi, ending the grave robberies and uncovering in a scientific way not only thousands of specimens of oracle bone records but also the whole capital of the late Shang Dynasty. From the fourteenth century B.C. on, the Shang Dynasty had been located at Anyang— a period in which the dynasty was also known as Yin. The oracle bones were found to be the royal archives of this Shang or Yin dynasty. These archives, deciphered at first by the leading specialist, Professor Tung Tso-pin, confirmed the story of the presumedly legendary accounts of the Shang Dynasty from the fourteenth century B.C. Names of the emperors, dates of events, and other information coincided remarkably with accounts of the ancient historians.

The materials used in the oracles were chiefly tortoise shells and oxen scapula bones that had been smoothed and polished. During the ceremony of the oracle, heat was applied to the bones until cracks appeared that were then interpreted as the answer of the oracle. For the record, the diviners who conducted the oracle inscribed on the bone the question that had been asked and answered, and it is this record that enables us to know more about major events of the time and specific rulers than is often transmitted from periods of such antiquity. The questions directed toward the deity were factual and can be regarded as even more reliable than common historical records. Taken together with the records they have provided a documented history of the time and life of the later Shang Dynasty. (See Plate 1.)

But what about the Hsia Dynasty, or even earlier periods, the time of Yao and Shun? Could the growing number of Neolithic archaeological findings fit together with the legends recorded by early historians and philosophers? The documentation provided by the oracle bones was, after all, a lucky historical accident. From the high level of development of the characters found on the oracle bones and from some marks on Neolithic pottery, it has been assumed that these signs of writing had an earlier history. But any earlier ancient writing, in order to survive, would have had to use similar time-resistant material; bamboo or wood, the most likely base for early writing, would not have survived into our day. It would be a very fortunate circumstance, indeed, should any earlier writing not only have existed, but also have been preserved through the millennia.

Nevertheless, recent excavations have unearthed many Chinese settlements of the Neolithic period, often as a result of construction projects undertaken by the government of the People's Republic. And, indeed, in 1976–1977 Chinese excavations near Loyang uncovered six settlements that the authorities claimed represented the Hsia period, including the capital of the dynasty, located at the confluence of the Yi and Lo rivers. Reconstructed models of the buildings of the palace together with excavated artifacts fill one room in the Historical Museum of Loyang. The model of the palace building said to date from the Hsia dynasty shows the same structure as that used in Shang time, which continued in all later Chinese architecture. Wooden pillars, whose foundations have been excavated, apparently held wooden beams on which the roofs rested, with walls as fill in, not as structural support. (See Plate 2.) The artifacts included pottery and bronze weapons, tools, and vessels, less perfect in their artistic form and technique than those of Shang times, as well as oracle bones—but uninscribed! With this discovery, legend and archaeology have become meshed in tracing Chinese history to the beginning of the dynastic system in the third millennium B.C.[3]

Aside from verifying some legends, archaeology has traced human life in China very far back. In 1927, paleontologists of the geological survey of China under the direction of J. G. Andersson[4] found skeletal remains of early man in a cave called Chou-k'ou-tien, thirty miles southwest of Peking. The find became known as "Peking Man," who is thought to have lived 500,000 years ago. In 1967 another discovery of human remains, "Lantien Man," at Lantien in Kansu province, could be dated earlier, about 600,000 years ago. These finds demonstrate that in China human life existed in Paleolithic time. These discoveries have fundamentally changed an earlier Western theory that held that Chinese culture originally came from Central Asia.

So far no link has been found between the early Paleolithic discoveries and the much later Neolithic finds. There is therefore no direct proof that China was inhabited continually by humans through the interval of several hundred thousand years between the earliest Paleolithic and later Neolithic ages. But a link between this earliest past and the latter time up to the present has indeed been construed. The Paleolithic human fossils as well as Neolithic human remains show some specific characteristics, such as a "peculiar thickening of the jaw bones," that indicate "direct genetic relations between Sinanthropus and the Mongolian group of recent mankind."[5] They also show the existence of the so-called shovel-shaped incisor tooth that has been found to appear in the same formation and variety in modern Chinese jaws. A direct relation between these earliest and later human finds on Chinese soil and modern Chinese man has therefore been assumed by leading historians of Chinese antiquity.[6]

In the rich Neolithic findings in China there have been uncovered two basically different types of pottery, one linked to pottery finds in Central Asia and the other of clearly indigenous Chinese origin.[7] The former, chiefly found in Kansu and Honan, but also in other sites in Western China, has great similarity with Neolithic pottery of Central Asia. From the name of a locality in northwestern Honan where it was first found and excavated in the early 1920s, it is called Yangshao culture. Also known as "painted pottery," its chief characteristic is red pottery painted with fascinating black decorative designs. The other, originating in today's Shantung province and known as the Lungshan culture, is uniquely Chinese. It is the overlapping and fusion of the two that mark the beginning of Chinese civilization. (See Plates 3a and 3b.)

In the northeastern region of China Proper a particular shape of vessel has been unearthed that has no parallel in the Northwest or as for that matter in Central Asia or elsewhere. It is a unique type of tripod, in Chinese called *li*. The form resembles a triple female breast. The Swedish archaeologist Andersson has suggested that this tripod originated from leaning together over a fire three pots with pointed bottoms, leading to the idea of fusing the three into one piece. This unusual tripod, first in pottery and later in bronze, remained a specifically Chinese type of vessel. (See Plate 4.)

Lungshan pottery, found in 1930–1931 in the East in Shantung province at Ch'eng-tzu-yai, east of Tsinan, by the National Research Institute, is named from the place of its discovery, Lungshan, but also is known as black pottery. However, it is the glossiness and the delicacy of this ware, sometimes less than a millimeter in thickness, that is characteristic of this pottery, rather than the color.

The two types of pottery appear to indicate two sources of culture, one indigenous, the other in contact at least with Central Asia, but which both contributed to the formation of Chinese life. Where the two met in the same territory, as for instance at Anyang, the black pottery culture has been found to overlay the painted pottery, implying a predominance[8] of the indigenous Chinese factor in the merger of prehistoric cultures.

Both painted and black pottery culture developed, however, a similarly organized way of life. In Shantung the black pottery people built a town, surrounded by a mile of walls of pounded earth, more than ten feet high and thirty feet wide at the base, the remains of which still exist today. The people of this age hunted and cultivated crops of millet; they domesticated dogs and pigs for food, and also oxen and horses, whose bones have been found at the sites. And, as in the following period of the Hsia and Shang dynasties, divination was practiced by roasting animal bones until cracks appeared, which were then, so we believe, interpreted by priests or scribes. It was a culture that must be assumed to have preceded directly that of the Hsia and Shang periods, from which historical reference, archaeological findings, and the documentation of the oracle bones provide us with greater detail of the lives and times of the beginnings of Chinese civilization.

Three

THE AGE OF MAGIC:

The Shang Dynasty

THE CULTURAL HISTORY of China truly begins with the period of the Shang Dynasty (ca. 1765–1123 B.C.). Two major cultural attainments characterize this stage in the course of Chinese development. One is a well-established form of writing, which provides an extensive record of the life of the time, and the other an extraordinarily brilliant and never-surpassed mastery of the art of bronze casting. The oracle bones and the Shang bronzes have bestowed upon this period a special fame in human history.

When we speak of the Shang Dynasty, we focus more often than not on Anyang, the location of a Shang capital and of the most important archaeological finds of Shang time. Actually, Anyang was only one of a number of successive capitals of the Shang Dynasty. The Shang Dynasty had already moved five times before locating its seat at this favorable location under the rule of King P'an-keng (ca. 1401–1374 B.C.). It was a well-chosen site: situated on a promontory of the Huan River in today's Honan province, easily defensible against surprise attacks, surrounded by fertile loess soil beneficial for agriculture, and close to mountainous forestland well suited for timber cutting and hunting. The town of Anyang was never captured but was eventually destroyed by flooding, one possible reason for the repeated translocation of Shang capitals.

Shang society flourished at a time when, as we know from recent archaeological finds and records, the climate and the flora and fauna differed substantially from later centuries. In Shang time the region was a subtropical area with marshes and forested mountains, sheltering an abundant animal population that included elephants, rhinoceroses, tigers, leopards, wild boars, buffalo, and large varieties of deer, all of which were hunted by the Shang rulers. Recorded lists from these hunts enumerate hundreds of deer as well as many other animals.

From the oracle bones we have learned that certain principles of Chinese writing, which possibly date back earlier, were established by Shang time. These have been retained until modern times. The characters that appear were at first pictographs and ideographs to which phonetic symbols were added to distinguish words of related meanings but different sounds. From indications on oracle bones we presume that the Shang had "books" but these were destroyed by decay.

What was Shang society like? Oracle bone writings and later records indicate evolution from a tribal into a more stratified society, an evolution that may have begun as early as the Lungshan period but appears clearly advanced by the time of the Hsia Dynasty. Obviously, much of this early history remains uncertain and its interpretation speculative. By Shang time though, the social stratification had clearly become reality. There was, as some historians have called it, a dichotomy between towns and rural settlements or villages. Like the Neolithic town of the Lungshan period, the Hsia and Shang towns were walled, indicating the connection between Lungshan, Hsia, and Shang. But the Hsia and Shang towns were comparatively small, indeed smaller than the town of the Lungshan period. They were dominated by the palace at the center, as indicated by the finds at Anyang and the newly excavated capital associated with the Hsia. In the capital town lived the ruler, his family, his servants, the aristocracy, the diviners or scribes and other officials, the artisans, their families, and other members of the court. In the surrounding villages lived the farming population that belonged to the ruler or the aristocratic lords. The farmers cultivated the fields, provided services, and were drafted into the armies of the ruler and the lords.

Political control, extending from the capital Anyang, was limited and indirect, except for the immediate surrounding area. Shang settlements have been found on both sides of the Yellow River, from today's Peking in the North to the Huai River area and beyond in the South, and from the Wei River valley in the West to the coast of the Yellow Sea in the East, and more may eventually be uncovered. Each settlement presumably had its own aristocratic leadership with control over nearby areas in a system that may best be described (in the terminology of Western historical interpretation) as protofeudal. The local power of government was left in the hands of these local lords who were expected to be loyal to the Shang ruler but could and indeed did challenge his authority in military campaigns, as was the case in other feudal systems. Warfare was waged against the ruler as well as among the vassal units and against the surrounding, less-advanced people. In fact, the overthrow of the Shang Dynasty was achieved by a former vassal state, the Chou, whose leader's name was mentioned in the oracle bones of Anyang as a vassal lord who had at one time served at the Shang court.

For these campaigns several thousand men on each occasion were raised from the farming population, a service that appears to have been dreaded. Armies were led by the aristocracy riding in three-man chariots, each drawn by two horses. Several dozen chariots took part in each campaign.

Warfare could lead to the overthrow of a rival feudal lord and expansion of territory, but more often the aim appears to have been simple looting and the capture of prisoners. Ten or twenty or more prisoners at a time were taken to be enslaved and used for household service, as soldiers, and sometimes as victims in human sacrifices. These human sacrifices are confirmed by the record of oracle bones and the skeletons of slaughtered people found in Shang tomb excavations. Such human sacrifices at burials were meant to provide service to the deceased king or lord in the netherworld; they appear to have included in early times both wives and officials of the deceased. This practice was, it seems, abandoned during the period of the Chou Dynasty. As a replacement, human and animal clay figurines were entombed with the dead, together with such objects as mini-models of buildings, utensils, furniture, ceramics, and the like, all to serve the dead. The high art of these tomb offerings has given us graphic testimony of the life-styles during different periods of Chinese cultural history and exquisite examples of the art of each period, in many cases more safely and better preserved than the objects above ground, exposed as they were to weather, nature, and the vicissitudes of historical events.

Contrary to Marxist-Leninist unilinear interpretation of all human history, which regards slavery as the first stage of class society anywhere and thus insists on finding slavery as a social stage also in early China, there is no indication at all that Shang was a "slave society." When slaves were incorporated into the captor's army as soldiers, they were obviously not treated as slaves in the Western sense, though their loyalty may have been somewhat uncertain. Agricultural labor was not carried on by slaves; there were no latifundia. The farming people were bound to the land and were granted and taken with it, not bought and sold like slaves. Thus Western analogy to this early period of Chinese history would have to use the terminology of serfdom rather than slavery, and Shang society might be described as protofeudal, preceding the more formal feudalism that developed under the Chou Dynasty.

Under Shang, human sacrifices were only part of a complex religious system that included belief in a spirit world and practice of many kinds of magic, either to assuage or to call forth spirits and forces in nature to prevent harm or to give support to human life. This religious system had rituals such as divination, sacrifices, shamanistic practices, ritualistic and orgiastic dances, drinking bouts, and fertility festivals. Deities to be assuaged were spirits both of nature and of departed human souls. Those dwelling in nature lived in mountains, rivers, forests, trees, and rocks, while human spirits dwelled in a netherworld.

For the latter, the Chinese developed a concept, believed to relate back to earliest prehistoric times, of the existence of two souls in each human being. These two souls were an animal soul (p'o), which remained with the body after death as a shadowy component, and a spiritual soul (hun), which departed into the netherworld. Both had to be cared for and nourished by sacrifices. The descendants within each clan had the obligation to carry on these ancestral sacrifices. Since earliest times the fear was that untended spirits became "hungry ghosts," intent on harming those who failed in their care as well as others. And the mollification and appeasement of untended spirits became a matter of actions as well as the subject of countless tales. Those spirits who were properly cared for would, however, be of benefit and support to their living descendants.

From this beginning has grown the Chinese ancestor cult, the most important quasi-religious tradition in Chinese culture. Male descendants were essential to carry on the ancestor cult, and therefore the continuity of the larger family, the clan, as an important social entity persisted from prehistoric into modern time. Burial sites, particularly of clan founders and important members, were to be maintained in perpetuity and became the location for the communal meal, the sharing of food between the spirits of the past and the living on the occasion of the Ch'ing Ming—the sweeping of the tombs—the Chinese All Souls festival.

In Shang time, the ancestors of the ruling clan leaders, both male and female, were worshipped, offered sacrifices, and were the objects of divination. The highest of these spirits was Shang-ti (the Lord-on-High), a personified deity in Heaven, regarded as the supreme ancestor of the Shang clan. Only the ruler himself could worship Shang-ti and enlist his help for the clan and his realm, and it was this religious function that elevated the ruler to the exalted position that sanctioned his authority.

Under Heaven was Earth, Ti. Heaven, the male principle, Yang, and Earth, the female principle, Yin, depicted in their interrelationship as Yin and Yang, the Chinese monad, were believed to provide the balance of nature that had to be retained by magic. Human welfare depended therefore on the sacrifices to Heaven and Earth; these sacrifices were continued by the Chinese emperors until modern times. On earth there were gods of the localities, of rivers, and of mountains that were revered and sacrificed to by local leaders and communities, such as Hou-tu, the god of the soil, who was to protect the harvests, and Hou-chi, the god of grain who was deified by the founder of the Shang Dynasty.

The importance these sacrifices bore to people living in an age of magic and of beliefs in spiritual forces are all the more understandable when one considers the precarious natural balance upon which successful harvests, indeed survival, depended. One has only to remember the frequent relocation of the capitals of the Shang Dynasty, resulting at least partly from natural calamities—floods and perhaps exhaustion of the adjoining soil—to understand the human fear of the unknown and dependence on the favors of nature. The always-present uncertainty of the water level and fear of the next change of course of the Yellow River was obviously of major concern. Among the river gods to be pacified, one stood out: Ho-p'o, the count of the river. Ho, meaning Huang Ho, the Yellow River, was simply "the River" par excellence. It appears that in earliest time sacrifices to the River may have included human victims, and up to modern time the common people's belief was that to deprive the River of its victims by saving those who drowned might invite greater disaster.

Aside from flood, there was drought, if the early summer rains were deficient or if they failed altogether. Rainmaking was therefore one of the major functions of the shamans who served the village communities. These shamans (Wu) could be either male or female, acted as mediums, and were believed to possess psychic powers that were brought forth in trances created by wild ritual dances to the sound of drums. At the central level of the whole polity, the ruler himself carried out such ritual dances. A primary question that appeared regularly on the oracle bones was whether enough rain would fall, and the advent of rain was carefully noted by the diviners.

For a society so dependent on agricultural success, an understanding of the seasonal cycle was of earliest importance. The Shang divided time into ten-day periods, consulting the oracle for the weather and coming events of the ten-day period ahead. The days were named in a sixty-day cycle by combining the symbols of ten "heavenly stems" with the twelve double hours of the day. The year was divided into twelve lunar months, with extra months inserted at regular intervals, based on a knowledge of astronomy, as indicated by the naming of stars and the accounts of eclipses of the sun and the moon appearing on the oracle bones.

As in other early stages of human societies, fertility rites seem to have been the occasion of yearly festivities. An echo of such fertility cults can be found in the account of festivals organized by the last ruler of the Shang house, during which naked maidens and young men pursued each other through gardens where viands and libations were suspended on trees. For later Confucian historians these orgiastic festivals were abhorrent examples of degeneration that led to the loss of the Mandate of Heaven and the downfall of the Shang Dynasty. There have been other indications that procreation, both in human propagation and in agricultural production, was the aim of religious rites. The ancestor cult itself had as one of its goals the continuous fertility of the clan. This was indicated by the symbol for ancestor depicted on the oracle bones, a symbol believed to have been derived from the sign of a phallus,[1] and the character for the god of the soil, likewise believed to have been derived from a phallic image. The magic of relating the forces of nature to human existence and survival was thus expressed in this direct and natural way. The magic was enhanced not only by the trances and the ritual dances of shamanistic practices but also by the heavy use of alcoholic beverages for which the Shang became famous—one of the sins that in Confucian belief led to the Shang's downfall.

Shang was thus a wild age of magic with a freer attitude towards human relations and to sex than was to exist later under the constraints of Confucian society. Even as late as the *Book of Poetry*, whose earlier poems reflect the life of the first half of the Chou Dynasty (before Confucius), one can still find poems in which women express their love for their men and the fulfillment of their desires. This free expression of emotions later Confucian scholars tried to interpret as allegorical metaphors for more worthy philosophical concepts.

The references to ancestor worship indicate also that the concept and institution of the family existed, but it appears that there was a distinction between the ruling class, where marriages were formal unions between families, and the common people, where sexual union preceded marriage, which resulted when the woman was with child. Divination on behalf of women of the upper class including queens indicates a degree of equality between the sexes. The oracle bones also tell us of one king who had three wives, and two who had two wives each, but of twenty-six who had only one each. As one modern Western historian explained: "Polygamy was probably practiced but with moderation."

Shang bronzes were long known in China and exhibited in the museums of the West before systematic excavations ended the looting of the tombs and established a more scientific archaeological method in unearthing the revealing evidence of the past. Today's great collections like that of the National Palace Museum in Taiwan or the Freer Gallery in Washington, D.C., have treated the period and its treasures in their display in scholarly and artistic array. Recent new findings of the 1970s and 1980s have greatly enriched the collections in the People's Republic.

Shang bronze art was clearly related to Shang belief and practice in magic. It is a highly stylized form of art. A variety of vessels, known by their Chinese names, most of which have been transmitted from earliest times, were employed chiefly for rituals and sacrifices.

The largest number are drinking vessels, used for alcoholic beverages during ceremonies, but also for consumption of alcohol by the leadership. Even after the Shang leaders were overthrown, but permitted to continue as feudal lords in one of the fiefs of the Chou system, they were taken to task again for their heavy drinking. (See Plate 5.)

A common and most graceful drinking vessel was a tall slender vase with a wide mouth called *ku*. Other types which appeared in several varieties of shapes were the *tsun*, a tall, broad, and often zoomorphic vase; the *yu*, a round vessel sometimes found in the shape of an animal; the *lei*, a thickset, curved vase often covered with a lid; the *chia* or *chüeh*, a three-legged vessel with two knobs at the top, and a variety of other forms. There were several types of food containers, aside from the previously mentioned *li*, the *ting*, a normally three-legged but sometimes four-legged large vat, the *p'an*, a large flat bowl, and numerous others. The types and names, established under the Shang, remained the same under the Chou and in later time, though several types disappeared and others came into use. Bronze bells, used by the Shang in ancestor worship ceremonies, were carefully tuned in groups and richly decorated. Recent excavations have brought to light many new examples of other forms of art, such as decorative pieces made of jade, stone sculpture, and glazed pottery, showing the high and sophisticated level of this early civilization. Still, it is primarily the art of bronze that attests to the high level of Shang culture.

Bronze was also used in weapons, in swords, daggers, and spearheads, dagger-axes and halberds, and it was this use and the power derived from it that elevated the Shang and to a lesser degree before them the Hsia to their powerful role, enabling them to unify the scattered tribal groups of North China. The metal was also used for chariot fittings and horses' bits found buried with the skeletons of horses and their drivers in tomb excavations at Anyang. To some archaeologists it appears significant that no farming tools made of bronze were found. Agricultural cultivation was done with a wooden plow. Bronze remained the stuff of military power and ritualized magic on which Shang rule rested.

How socially and politically important the rituals of the bronze vessels must have been was clearly indicated by the extraordinary craftsmanship devoted to the objects that have survived and by their sheer beauty. Their decorative art appears to express concepts and beliefs in the powerful magic that they served and that we can only speculatively surmise. It is an abstract art based on a technique of casting that has never been surpassed. The decorations are a com-bination of geometric designs combined with zoomorphic forms that are in themselves more or less stylized. One type of linear design is believed to have been derived from the depictment of a cicada, often in constantly repeated pattern of design. But there are other frequently recognizable though symbolized shapes of animal heads and bodies marvelously merged with the forms of the vessels, or in the patterns of the design. Figures like an owl with a large head and human-type ears, deep-set eyes, and feathers are fantastic creatures that appear to be symbolized representatives of animals connected with some magic. Special qualities of the animal often seem to be exag-gerated, such as jagged teeth or the oversized fangs of tigers.

The most frequent of these designs is the *t'ao t'ieh* mask, an ogrelike face with large, somber, gazing eyes, horns, or ears and claws, which has been explained as the symbolic image of a dragon, although it may be a symbol all its own. In Chinese mythology the dragon played a somewhat different role from that known in the West. It was mostly a beneficial animal and a propitious symbol, the provider of rain and, as a symbol of water, the protector against fire, and still later, the symbol of the emperor. Whether the *t'ao t'ieh* or dragon mask was connected with this concept or not we do not know. But it was clearly part of the sympathetic magic that was at the heart of the Shang society and that has provided us with the magnificent art of this powerful magical society with its great but somewhat stark and dark beauty. (See Plates 6a and 6b.)

Four

THE AGE OF REASON:

The Chou Dynasty

THE FALL OF the Shang and the establishment of the Chou Dynasty (ca. 1123–221 B.C.) was more than a dynastic change; it was the end of an era. The age of magic, with its wild dances, shamanism, divination, human sacrifices, fertility rites, and great drinking bouts was over. The belief in Shang-ti, the Lord-on-High, the ruler of the spirits and the ancestor of the Shang, was overturned. Shang-ti became merely one spirit among many others. In its place the Chou established a rational explanation of a moral universe. T'ien, Heaven, was the moral force that dominated the world and human existence.

The Chinese symbol for Heaven, *t'ien* (reaching the utmost), cannot be found in the Shang oracle bones; it was a new concept that was to dominate the ethical firmament of society and state for imperial China henceforth. Nor did the Shang oracles know the concept or character for *teh*, human morality, man's proper conduct in harmony with the moral principles of the universe, now instituted by the Chou. Man's relation to the surrounding world was no longer a matter of mastering magic but of accepting and conforming with an abstract universal ethical code, not deified by personification. Indeed, the introduction of these concepts of Heaven and human morality appears to be the most remarkable contribution made by the new Chou rulers, an intellectual foundation that became a cornerstone for the imperial Chinese system and its social order.

One can argue that for the new Chou rulers this break with the ideological past was a political necessity. The Chou had attacked the Shang capital from their western territory in the Wei valley,

27

while the main Shang forces were battling rebels in the East. The Chou had won the battle[1] and killed the Shang ruler but had yet to unify the realm and establish their claim to leadership. For this they could not make use of the clan divinity of their Shang rivals, Shang-ti. The revered Shang-ti was a dangerous antagonist and potential rallying point for the Shang opposition and had to be removed.

The Chou clan had no deity of equal power. The best they could do for themselves was to claim descent from Hou-chi, the grain god, thus strengthening their claim to promote good crops for their people. But this descent from a lesser god who had been deified only recently by the founder of the Shang Dynasty was hardly enough to compete with the sanction provided for the Shang by their supreme ancestor. Thus the Chou proclaimed that the new morality they had discovered was a universal force: Heaven sat in judgment over the leader of mankind and had granted the Mandate of Heaven to the ruler of mankind, making the ruler the intermediary between Heaven's command and human fate. For this responsibility the ruler and his successors had to have the moral power, the virtue, *teh*, that alone entitled them to assume authority over the realm. Reconstructing past history, the founders of the Chou Dynasty claimed that their predecessors—and they mentioned the Hsia Dynasty as well as the Shang—had bestowed upon them the heavenly mandate and held on to it over the ruling period of their many kings until, at the end, an unworthy ruler had gambled away his dynasty's precious heritage, had lost the mandate and, at Heaven's will, had been replaced by a new worthy ruling clan, the Hsia by the Shang, and now the Shang by the Chou.

An expedient explanation of their conquest, one might call this theory of the Chou, but it was clearly much more, a noble concept of government and a concept that proved its worth throughout Chinese imperial history. That it was meant to be not only a contemporary sanction of the Chou conquest, but indeed a standard for their own rule by which they should be measured, can be seen from the state documents of the founders that have come down to later dynasties and to us.

Three early founders of Chou power have remained famous throughout Chinese history: Wen Wang, Wu Wang and the Duke of Chou. *Wang* means king and all the early rulers of China held this title. The title *ti*, emperor, during this period was reserved for the lengendary Huang-ti, the Yellow Emperor, and the Shang-ti, the Lord-on-High, the spiritual ancestor and highest deity of the Shang clan. The Shang rulers themselves, much like their Hsia predecessors, had been wang, kings, not *ti*, emperors, and the Chou did not change this system, only challenging the Shang rule by assuming for themselves the title *wang*. King Wen, who organized the Chou polity, before he became king had been a high official at the Shang court, entrusted with the defense of the western border in the Wei valley, whence the Chou clan originated. Great qualities as a planner and organizer have been attributed to him; he framed the clan state structure, gained the support of neighboring tribes, and prepared the thrust against the Shang, laying the groundwork for the conquest of the realm. His son, King Wu, who first assumed claim to the Mandate of Heaven, marched against the Shang with the support of many allied tribal leaders who had previously given allegiance to his father. Wu Wang died in 1115 B.C., seven years after the conquest of power in 1122 B.C. and before the new Chou system was completed and entrenched.

According to the rule of succession of the Chou clan, derived from the tradition of their partially steppe origin, rule was to be transmitted to the next generation, to Ch'eng Wang, the son of Wu Wang, then still a youngster. Actual power fell into the hands of Wu Wang's younger brother, the Duke of Chou, the third of the illustrious founders and one of the greatest statesmen in Chinese history. It was he who first clearly formulated the theory of the Mandate of Heaven. Indeed, because his is the earliest detailed application of the new concept to the past, the present, and the future, one may wonder whether it was not the Duke of Chou who first conceived the idea of the Mandate of Heaven as a new and broader foundation of government and suggested it to his older brother, King Wu, at the time of the conquest of the state. The Duke of Chou later led the armies that crushed a Shang rebellion, thus finally establishing Chou rule; he is also credited with devising the Chou feudal system that provided a stable government for several hundred years. A man of his stature may well have been the creator of what has been called "the most distinctive aspect of Chou thought, and a point of fundamental difference from that of the Shang."[2]

Fortunately, we have a number of important documents—that leading scholars consider authentic—containing speeches by the Duke of Chou in which he enunciated and defined the concept of the Mandate of Heaven. These speeches were addressed to the young king and to the captured Shang people whose rebellion he had suppressed and whom he removed from their homes and set to work building a new secondary capital for the Chou at Loyang. The most memorable of these speeches is worth quoting here.

Now that the King has received the mandate, unbounded is the grace but also unbounded is the solicitude. Oh, how can he be but careful! Heaven has removed and made an end to the great state Yin's mandate. There are many former wise kings of Yin in Heaven, and the later kings and people here managed their mandate. But in the end (under the last king) wise and good men lived in misery so that, leading their wives and carrying their children, wailing and calling to Heaven, they went to where no one could come and seize them. Oh, Heaven had pity on the people of the four quarters, and looking with affection and giving its Mandate, it employed the zealous ones (the leaders of Chou). May the king now pay urgently careful attention to his virtue. Look at the ancient predecessors, the Lords of Hsia; Heaven indulged them and cherished and protected them. They strove to comprehend the obedience to Heaven; but in these times they have lost their mandate. . . . May the king come and take the work of the Lord-on-High and himself manage the government in the center of the land. . . . We should not fail to mirror ourselves in the lords of Hsia; we likewise should not fail to mirror ourselves in the lords of Yin. We do not presume and say that the lords of Hsia undertook Heaven's Mandate so as to have it for so-and-so many years; we do not presume to know and say that it could not have been prolonged. It was that they did not reverently attend to their virtue and so they prematurely renounced their mandate. We do not presume to know and say that the lords of Yin received Heaven's Mandate for so-and-so many years, we do not know and say it could not have been prolonged. It was that they did not reverently attend to their virtue and so they prematurely threw away their mandate. Now the king has succeeded to and received their mandate. . . . Being king,

his position will be that of a leader in virtue; the little people
will then imitate him in all the world. May those above and
below (the king and the people) labor and be anxiously
careful; may they say: We have received Heaven's Mandate,
may it grandly equal the span of years of the lords of Hsia
and not miss the span of years of the lords of Yin.[3]

In this and several other chronicled speeches the Duke of Chou
went far beyond the simple claim of a higher justification for Chou
rule. The Mandate of Heaven took on a special authority of its own,
an authority to which the Chou were as subject as were formerly
the Hsia and the Shang and that would remain the sanction and
set the standard for all future rulers. Each mandate was finite and
conditional and would last only so long as the Chou kings' "virtue"
was maintained—as long as the rule of the preceding dynasties, it
was hoped.

What was this "virtue" on which the authority and eventually
the continuation of the dynastic rule depended? It was above all
concern for the welfare of the people. It had been the suffering of
the people that ended the mandate for the Shang. And from the
outset Chou rulers stressed their concern for the people's happiness.
Many quotations of that time tell of the Chou rulers' attention to
the feeling of the people and to their well-being. King Wu went as
far as to order his officials to "attend to the helpless and solitary,
attend even to pregnant women" paralleling similar notions of
compassion in Western tradition. The Duke of Chou summed it up
when he said, "I am concerned only with Heaven and the people."[4]

The "virtue" of the rulers thus had a concrete content. It is,
of course, true that in this as in any other political system claim
and reality remained disparate, but the very acceptance of the principle
and the constant reference to it by all later dynasties gave the imperial
system a strength and vitality that goes far to explain its long
endurance. These are the very precepts that some six hundred years
later Confucius and later the Confucian school chose as their priorities
for the political and social order they espoused: the conditional and
temporal bestowal of the Mandate of Heaven, contingent on the
moral qualification of the ruler and the ruling house, and concern
for the well-being of the people as the first obligation of government.

These two precepts remained the basic foundation of government throughout imperial times.

Implied in this earliest stated political philosophy of imperial China by the Duke of Chou was yet another consideration—the transmission of authority from a supernatural source to that of rational government. The sentence: "May the king come and take over the work of the Lord-on-High and himself manage the government in the center of the land" denoted that the king's government on earth was to replace the concept of spiritual guidance and take over the responsibility and the work of government from the Lord-on-High. Decision making was to be by the rulers and his ministers, not by oracles. The sacrifices were to continue and were indeed essential to gain and maintain the favor of the spirits who were now to include the departed great rulers of the Chou; but politically the spirits have been demoted; a rational, responsible form of government has been instituted. Responsibility has shifted to the ruler and the ruling house; they are responsible to Heaven—not to the people, but it was believed to be the voice of the people through which Heaven spoke.

It appears that this new doctrine was indeed persuasive and widely accepted at the time. A poem in the *Book of Poetry*—one of several—dating from this period and written we are told by a member of the Shang clan confirms this belief in and support of the new theory:

> The charge is not easy to keep;
> may it not end in your persons.
> Display and make bright your good fame.
> and consider what Yin had received from Heaven.
> The doings of High Heaven
> have no sound no smell.
> Make King Wen your pattern
> and all the states will trust you.[5]

The question has been raised why this new concept of government was so easily accepted throughout Chou territory and was so successful in forming the basis for a realm that territorially outgrew the Shang domain.

Writing on this period, Herrlee Creel, a leading historian of China, points to two elements of Chou policy that ensured their power. First, the Chou were militarily far superior to the Shang or any other contemporary contender and proved it in battle. Survivors of the Shang clan had been given a fief to carry on their ancestral sacrifices. When they rebelled again, they were rapidly and decisively crushed militarily by the Duke of Chou. To prevent further such regional rebellions the Duke applied a second major strategem, the dispersal of Shang survivors.

This policy of dispersal and other forced migrations may be compared with other massive removals and transportation of large groups of peoples not only in ancient but also in modern times, and not only in Asia but in the Western world as well. Presumably this policy had a great deal to do with the success in breaking the cohesion and resistance of the Shang people, inducing Shang survivors to accept control by a group that must have appeared to them as a lesser culture of country oafs. It was to these survivors that the Duke of Chou addressed his most momentous speeches, with the obvious intent of breaking up the old cultural cohesion and creating a larger unity under the new ideological order. Final acceptance of Chou rule would depend on the success of its institutions and policy.

The new Chou order has often been called a feudal system. The king's brothers, some cousins, and a few allied leaders were installed as feudal lords over a number of fiefs into which the territory controlled by the Chou was divided, while the king retained his own domain. As known from the history of feudalism in Europe and Japan, feudal lords, though bound to the ruler by the oath of fealty, were a pretty independent lot, constantly at war with each other and at times with the ruler, whose authority they did not hesitate to challenge when they felt strong enough.

What distinguished the early Chou feudalism from European and Japanese models was the absence of recorded internal warfare. Once the rebellion of Shang was suppressed and a full feudal order instituted, peace appeared to have reigned within the realm for at least two-and-a-half centuries, except for some infrequent campaigns against outside "barbarians."

How then did Chou maintain the peace in a naturally unstable feudal order? It appears that the main factor was the Chou's success in superimposing over the presumably autonomous feudal territories a centralized control system, backed, as Creel has pointed out, by a much stronger royal military force than heretofore believed, consisting of fourteen armies rather than the six of traditional historical accounts. Perhaps even more decisive than this control by military superiority was the introduction of a dual administrative system of government, by which the autonomy of the feudal lords was contained within a complex royal administrative structure that extended to a considerable degree into the feudal domains. The existence of this royal government can be inferred from the large number of royal officials whose names and, occasionally, titles appear on the documents and bronzes of the time.

No administrative chart of that government structure exists; a systematic description, the *Chou-li*, ascribed to the Duke of Chou, is now known to have been a much later invention. Titles listed on contemporary sources are totally unsystematic and constantly changing; it appears that in this early system confidence in individuals who were also close relatives of the king was more important than any classification of ranks or functions. But these many officials clearly had authority and functions that both affected and curtailed the power of the local lords' administration.

What distinguished this order from a full-fledged bureaucracy was not only its feudal foundation but also the fact that the officials were themselves feudal lords, i.e., compensated by the grants of feudal estates rather than other forms of emolument such as salaries in money or kind. They held dual positions of lords in their own territories and officials at the court. In the latter capacity they might serve in different functions at different times; they were political appointees rather than professionals in the modern sense. All officials were thus feudal lords, but most lords were not officials. And although most of them were close relatives of the ruler, they were, as examples show, ruthlessly punished by death or banishment for any disobedience or resistance to royal orders. This organization may be called feudal but was also "protobureaucratic," a crucial factor in the later emergence of a bureaucratic society and state in imperial China.

However much the creation of an official bureaucratic superstructure may have enhanced central control, basically the Chou system remained feudal not only in the remuneration of its administrators, but also in the administration of its territory. Enfeoffment was given of land and people; and the people were "serfs" of their respective lords, and under the lords' jurisdiction.

To maintain peace and order was the king's primary responsibility. There were general laws for the kingdom, and, as indicated in proclamations of King Wu and others, some penal law of the Shang rulers appears to have been preserved and applied by the Chou. Quarrels among the lords and major vassals were adjudicated by the king, instead of through feudal warfare. It was this authority of the king, enforced by his military power and adjudicated by his court officials, which preserved the internal peace during the first two-and-a-half centuries of Chou rule.

Chou rule exerted control over most of the Northwest and the North China plain, the modern provinces of Shensi, part of Kansu, Shansi, Honan, Hopei, and Shantung and beyond that, an area that has been estimated as more than 282,000 square miles.[6] Its influence may have reached even further into the Yangtze valley, creating a unity in the Chinese core area that found expression in a sense of cultural identity carried over through history into modern times and extending its influence over neighboring cultures and peoples. To be part of this tradition of a moral human order under Heaven gave the Chinese a cultural pride in their great civilizing role, somewhat akin to the concepts of the Jews as the "chosen people," the French as "La grande nation," or the Germans calling themselves "Das Salz der Erde." It was the beginning of a great cultural tradition that shaped attitudes, actions, and the way of life throughout imperial time.

It has often been noted that these profound changes generated under the Chou did not lead to an abrupt break with the tradition of Shang art. Great craftsmanship in the casting of bronze vessels survived under early Chou, and a label of "late Shang or Western Chou" can often be found on museum bronzes whose place of origin remains unknown. Obviously the traditions of bronze craftsmen were taken over by the Chou, and some of the Shang bronze styles survived for about a century. Then the form of vessels began to be modified by a new style; some types disappeared altogether (the *ku*, *chüeh*, *kuang*, *yu*, and *fang i*), and some of the surface designs and patterns, such as the *t'ao t'ieh* mask and cicada motif, vanished from the Chou bronzes. Many Chou bronzes lost the ferocity that had characterized a good number of Shang pieces.

This change in form indicated more than a change in taste; it expressed differences in ideology as well as in usage of bronze vessels during the two periods. Shang bronzes had served Shang religious magic. Chou bronzes became documentary evidence of a new political order. Bronzes were cast on occasions of enfeoffment or to mark other memorable events; inscriptions recorded on the vessels were verification of legal actions or events, providing documentary evidence of the history of the time. With a change in usage came a change in style, transforming the purpose of a vessel from magic power to impressive decor, a development that eventually led to baroque overloading and disintegration of the former unity of form and design.

The same holds true for other famous Shang art forms, notably in jade and pottery. Some of the pottery pieces found to date are imitations of bronze vessels, an affectation that indicates how much the original meaning had been forgotten. Jade, by that time used chiefly for adornment rather than magic ritual, still retained some of its magic meaning. At burials, jade symbols were placed above, below, and at the four directions of the body to protect it from evil influences, and jade plugs were used to close the seven body orifices— a practice that led by Han time to the use of jade burial suits for deceased royalty.

What was lost in the great art derived from magic was gained in recorded history. The piecemeal and incidental record of the oracle bones came to an end when decision making by oracle discontinued. In its place came the beginning of recorded history. Many of the documents of the *Shu ching* (the *Book of Documents*) are now known to date from this period of the twelfth century B.C. and some of the poems of the *Shih-ching* (the *Book of Poetry*) dealt with topics of this time, as does the *I-ching* (the *Book of Changes*, or *Classic of Oracles*) that described a method of divination to take the place of political oracles of the Shang. Though often sparse, these records mark the beginning of that rich historical literature for which China has become so famous.

In retrospect, this period has been called the Western Chou, because the capital and political center of the rule was at Hao, near the present city of Sian in the Northwest, although the realm extended to the ocean, to the northern limits of the North China plain and to the Huai River and beyond toward the Yangtze in the South.

Eventually this period came to an end with the decline of Chou dynastic government. The unity under central control crumbled as a result of the growth of power of the feudal lords whose succession was no longer contingent upon the king's confirmation and who enlarged their territories and authority through conquest and incorporation of weaker neighbors. Out of the multitude of smaller feudal domains and some more distant territories emerged a few paramount states.

A court intrigue caused the final end of Western Chou. Legend has it that the last ruler, King Yu, was infatuated with a beautiful concubine and deposed the crown prince, borne by his queen, in order to designate the concubine's son as his successor. The queen's father, a powerful lord, gained the support of a nomadic tribe to attack and sack the capital and killed King Yu in 770 B.C. The legitimate crown prince was thereupon installed as ruler by the feudal lords, but the capital was moved eastward to Lo, farther away from the danger of the steppe people. Built under the Duke of Chou, Lo was formerly the secondary capital city, and now became the new center of Eastern Chou.

The period that followed is known as the "Ch'un Ch'iu" ("Spring and Autumn") period after the name of the Spring and Autumn Annals, a historical work covering the years from 722 to 481 B.C. in the first chronological account of Chinese history. This extremely sparse record has been extended by an important commentary, the Tso Chuan, a voluminous work that adds a great deal of detail to the history of this time and extends the account on to 464 B.C., the date that is now commonly used as end point of the Spring and Autumn period.

During the early part of this period, Chinese territory was divided among fifteen major feudal states interspersed with a large number of smaller fiefs about whose history very little is recorded. Of the larger feudal states, those on the periphery of the Chou realm were ruled by Chinese families who claimed kinship ties to the house of Chou but whose population was intermingled with non-Chinese people. These larger states were Ch'in, in today's Shensi province, Ch'u, in the middle Yangtze region, Wu, in the Yangtze delta and Yueh on the southeast coast. By now feudalism had overcome the protobureaucratic control of early (Western) Chou, and this led to a time of warfare, shifting alignments and conflicts. Only the prestige of the concept of the Mandate of Heaven enabled late Chou rulers to continue to reign from their shrinking central territory, under the protection of the hegemony alternately held by the more powerful feudal states.

These states were still in part separated by sparsely inhabited marshlands or mountain country peopled by pre-Chinese "barbarians." But with the steady growth of population, many tribal groups disappeared or were amalgamated and the stronger feudal states came into more direct contact and conflict. Their inner structure changed and the character of warfare changed with it. The feudal code of combat, under which the aristocratic leaders had treated each other with chivalry, had given way to wars of mutual annihilation, in which the weaker states were conquered and incorporated into the larger and stronger ones, until only seven states survived; these became engaged in a struggle for final victory in which the winner eliminated all others and unified the whole realm. These last centuries of a war of elimination have been called the period of the Warring States, lasting from 464 to the year 221 B.C., the year when the ruler of the state of Ch'in conquered and unified the whole country and assumed the title of emperor, Ch'in Shih Huang-ti, "first emperor of the state of Ch'in," China, as it became known to the outside world. Thirty-five years earlier, in 256 B.C., the king of Chou had made one of the last efforts to stop the advance of Ch'in but was routed and handed over his small domain to the victor. A last attempt by another Chou prince to continue resistance was similarly defeated in 249 B.C., when the Chou Dynasty came formally to an end.

By this time the society, the economy, the political structure, and the intellectual tradition itself had undergone radical changes. It was a revolutionary transformation, affecting every aspect of the social, economic, and political order—in short, the end of feudalism. Feudalism had come to its full flourishing during the Spring and Autumn era, when the weakening of Chou authority had undermined all central control and had permitted many feudal lords to gain their own independent power. Now, during the Warring States epoch, the feudal system was destroyed from within.

The change started in several peripheral large states of the realm, those bordering on non-Chinese tribal people, whom they absorbed. The traditional Chinese feudal structure was not suited for administering these tribal conquests. No fiefs were created in the tribal world. Instead new administrative districts, *hsien*, were set up under appointed state officials, and this new administrative structure was eventually introduced into the older feudal states in the center of the Chinese cultural world. A bureaucracy took the place of feudal aristocracy. The Chinese population itself rapidly expanded and filled the lands between the states, eliminating geographical separation and making conquest of close neighbors more inviting.

The drive to extend agricultural cultivation into new lands led in turn to the need for more damming of rivers, more drainage, and more irrigation. This was the time of extensive water works construction in today's Hopei, Szech'wan, and the Northwest by great hydraulic engineers whose names have remained famous throughout Chinese history. Such projects could not be undertaken by small feudatories; the construction required large-scale public works and the organization of large groups of laborers by an efficient professional state administration. The labor came from the peasants, the vast majority of the population who had been freed from serfdom and now owned the land that was nominally the king's. Private land-ownership and the free sale and purchase of land caused new problems, but basically it signified a new class of peasants free to move, to own their land, to pay taxes, and to perform corvée labor for the state.

Peasants also supplied the manpower of the new armies. Feudal warfare had been fought by the aristocracy from chariots, up to several hundred chariots surrounded by groups of footmen; a code of chivalry had been applied to a point that prevented the extinction of feudal families. In the battles of the Warring States large mass armies of infantry fought battles of annihilation. The slaughter of more than one hundred thousand men in a single battle is claimed in the records for some of these decisive military campaigns.[7] Even with the strictest discipline, the peasant soldier had to have a stake in the success of his country. That stake can only have been his new role as a freeholder.

However, the fact that land could be owned, inherited, bought, and sold introduced another form of economic dependence; that of landlordism and tenancy, and from this time landlordism and tenancy became a major issue in Chinese history, an issue that acerbated economic and political crises at various periods of imperial history. But the overemphasis placed on this issue in modern times, particularly under the influence of Marxist doctrine, has often resulted in a one-sided picture. The basic agricultural condition of most periods was the prevalance of the small peasant-owner, whose worry was tax, not rent, and who in this sophisticated, irrigated agricultural system had to possess knowledge and skills on which any increase in production substantially depended. Without this landowning peasantry the success of statism in the Warring States era cannot be understood or accounted for. Nor can the new type of warfare be explained without considering the role of the peasant-soldier.

This new type of warfare and a major increase in agricultural production were interlinked with momentous technical innovations. The Bronze Age made way for the Iron Age. Shortly after the introduction of iron in the late sixth century B.C., iron tools and weapons were produced on a mass scale. They were cast, a technique learned from bronze casting but improved by the invention of the use of bellows to create the high heat needed—in contrast to Europe where for some time iron was forged, a much slower process of production. In China, the rapid widespread use of the iron hoe and especially the iron plow made possible deep plowing, increasing production countrywide. In warfare, the iron sword became a new mass weapon. In addition, the invention of the crossbow with an iron cocking and triggering mechanism greatly increased firepower and accuracy in targeting.

An altogether new type of military force was introduced about the fourth century B.C. by the steppe nomads. Organizing units of mounted warriors on horseback, the steppe tribes became a formidable military threat. To counter this threat, Chinese frontier states instituted large-scale horsebreeding and formed their own cavalry units to meet the raiders in the field. Simultaneously, they constructed imposing defensive walls along the Inner Asian frontier to keep the nomads out of the settled land.

These efforts could only be undertaken by centralized organizations of bureaucratic states. The new economy and mass organization required expanded transportation and distribution of basic consumer goods. The self-sufficient small peasant economy with local contribution to the domain was being replaced by large villages, townships, and cities, generating trade and industry. Together with an enlarged state organization, there emerged a sizable merchant class.

In feudal times, craftsmen, living at the courts of the royal household and of the aristocracy, had produced luxury goods, and merchants had traded them. Now quantities of ordinary consumer commodities, cloth, salt, and grain, had to be bought, sold, and transported to serve the growing populations of the states and to provide for the logistics of military campaigns and massive development projects. Mining and manufacturing enterprises and commercial houses grew wealthy. Merchants financed state affairs. Towns and capital cities grew ever more, becoming commercial and industrial centers with large populations of merchants and craftsmen.

This was also the time of elegant living; art objects were acquired not only by the ruling families and their hangers-on, but also by the new wealthy upper-middle class; and, as had been the case since earliest times with the rulers and the aristocracy, members of this class were now also buried with many of the treasures and valuable household goods they had come to possess. Excavations of tombs of the times have brought to light richly decorated bronze vessels, inlaid with gold and silver patterns or figures of extraordinarily fine craftsmanship, rich finds of beautiful lacquerware and pottery decorated with an olive green glaze, the predecessor of porcelain and celadon. Jade carving reached a high perfection, and jade was widely used for personal ornaments, such as pendants, hairpins, garment hooks decorated with human figures, animals, or scenes of life and nature. Bronze mirrors must have been made in great abundance. They not only served to reflect a person's image, but also had symbolic value, reflecting personality and the meaning of thoughts and events. Blank on the mirror side, they were richly decorated on the back with magnificent designs. Many bronze bells have been uncovered, some from as early as Shang time, and impressive sets of bronze bells from late Chou tombs have preserved for us the tonal scales of Chou time.

The political divisions of the time were reflected in the diversity of art and life-styles between the northern and southern halves of the country. In the Northwest and the northern plain, the surviving Shang and the Chou traditions set the tone, but the necessity of dealing with the constant danger from across the frontier brought on a harsh military system of rule in the frontier state of Ch'in, retaining past traditions, but less favorably inclined toward the appreciation of aesthetic gratification than the more easygoing South.

In the southern region of the Yangtze valley, a more liberal culture flourished under the state of Ch'u. In this region pottery and lacquerware, recently found in newly excavated tombs, reached their most delicate beauty, and it is here that the earliest surviving brush paintings on silk have been found. In the same area poetry and music flourished as a rich cultural tradition that, though submerged under military defeat when the state of Ch'u was conquered in 223 B.C., was to retain a considerable and long-lasting influence on the arts and intellectual tradition of later centuries.

This refined cultural tradition was centered in the burgeoning new towns and cities. In contrast to European history at the end of the Middle Ages, these Chinese towns were not founded in opposition to a feudal aristocracy by a new class of burghers who gained political power along with their economic role. The Chinese towns were not built outside the political power system and in competition to it. They were the seat of the new officialdom, whether capital city or district towns. Neither in the countryside nor in the towns was there any movement for overthrowing a ruling aristocracy and seizing power from below. It was the ruler and the state that organized the revolutionary transformation and determined its character to the end of imperial time.

To achieve all this the ruler needed a new group of men, qualified to organize, direct, and plan the practice of power he had assumed. He needed officials, civil and military bureaucrats, educated people to fill the many positions of authority and administration that were essential to manage the vast administrative tasks. The warrior trained to excel in battle, who had typified the elite under feudalism, was now out of date, to be replaced by educated men who could keep records, calculate, plan, organize, and think in terms of the new social and political order. The term *shih*, which originally stood for the lower aristocracy, sons of nobility, the "knights" of the feudal system, changed its meaning and came to designate a man of letters, a man who gained his position not by inheritance, but by study and examination.

The new profession of administrators was formed by stages. The various rulers of the states gathered advisers as ministers at their courts, to plan and organize military strategy, political maneuvers, and economic policy. These men in turn assembled their own retinue of counselors, assistants, and followers to discuss and plan policy.

Men of skill and experience were sought after and thus could offer their services to the highest bidder or the most promising state. In a time of shifting alliances, of constant warfare, and devious tactics, motives and actions were no longer dictated by standards of loyalty as they had been in the feudal past, and officials moved easily from one state to another. It was an age of trickery and Machiavellianism, which brought victories but no stable order.

What was needed was a philosophical foundation for the new social and political order not only for political decision making, but also for sustaining a viable system of beliefs, values, and loyalties, a system that would be accepted by the new leaders as well as by society as a whole, a common code of ethics that could only be provided by a commonly accepted school of thought.

Five

INTELLECTUAL REVOLUTION:

A Hundred Schools of Thought

THIS NEW POLITICAL philosophy, needed for the new bureau-cratic state, emerged from a contention of competing schools of thought that vied with each other for acceptance at the courts. This was the period of the Hundred Schools of Thought, the period in which founders of philosophical schools gathered groups of students to teach them the particular schools' concepts of human order and government and, at the same time, sought to impress rulers with theoretical answers as well as practical programs for the problems of society and state. It was an age of intellectual ferment, providing a great wealth of new concepts, an age that coincided with other global intellectual stirrings: the birth of Buddhism in India and the foundation of Greek philosophy in the West. About this coincidence of concomitant human intellectual upheavals in various cultures in different parts of the globe one may but wonder.

The term *A Hundred Schools of Thought*, a slogan to indicate the large number of such rivaling schools, was not an actual count of those schools known to contemporaries or posterity. However counted, the actual number of schools was clearly much smaller than a hundred, and they were of uneven influence and significance, both then and later. By far the most important among them was the school of Confucius, whose tenets eventually became the accepted standard of morality for the social and political order of the Chinese empire down to the twentieth century.

K'ung Fu-tzu, or Master K'ung, known in the West under his latinized name Confucius, given to him at a later date by Jesuit missionaries, lived from 551 to 479 B.C., at a time when the great political disorder of the early Warring States period had begun to undermine the order and loyalties of the past. Coming from a family of the lower aristocracy, Confucius, like other philosophical teachers of his time, sought to enter state service and succeeded for a short time in gaining employment under the prince of his home state of Lu. He soon had to resign from this position, however, and his later attempts to enter an official career were not successful. For his followers and admirers this failure was explained later by the legend that blamed the loss of Confucius's employment on an intrigue by the neighboring ruler who, fearful of Confucius's influence and success in his state, distracted the prince of Lu from his administrative duties by gifts of beautiful maidens and magnificent horses until Confucius lost his influence and resigned in dismay. (See Plate 7.)

What Confucius wanted to provide for the new leadership of his time was not merely training in the practical art of government, but an education in a new set of moral values to suit the newly emerging polity and social structure. He saw the problems of the moral order of society as a whole and was especially concerned with providing moral standards for the *chün-tzu*, the noble men, the new bureaucrats, whom he saw as assuming the responsibility for leadership in society and state. Confucius sought to create a model for what one may call the "ideal bureaucrat."

Any bureaucracy, to function properly, must be based on common standards and concepts of ethics, held in accord by its members and instilled into them by uniform teaching. The system of educating the bureaucracy must be based on inherent, even if sometimes understated, values and beliefs, essential as the underlying foundation of any social order. It was such a code of ethics that Confucius advocated at a time of general amorality and ethical anarchy. The new bureaucrats' primary need was not so much to acquire knowledge of adminstrative skill, military strategy, or economic management, but rather to gain moral qualification and integrity. The same was even more true for the ruler himself. The "virtue" of the Mandate of Heaven, proclaimed by the founders of the Chou Dynasty, was now to be given its substantive content.

Among the fundamental precepts of this moral code the most intrinsic were the principles of *jen*, a moral feeling toward humanity, sometimes rendered as "humanism" or "humanity," and *i*, "integrity," a sense of one's own ethically right behavior. These qualities were to be developed in each person through character education in these and other Confucian precepts.

Confucius, in his own words, was a transmitter, not an innovator. The sages of an idealized past, Yao, Shun, and Yu, and the founders of the Chou Dynasty, especially the Duke of Chou, were the alleged models for his perfect social order. As for the present, the only human relationships that had retained their validity in a time of social and political chaos were the loyalties within the family, and these Confucius stressed and expanded to fashion the new social and political loyalties that he sought to introduce. He defined five such human relationships, three within the family, one social, and one political. The foremost of these was filial piety, the loyalty of son to father and of children to their parents. The other relationships were wife to husband, younger brother to older brother, friend to friend, and, finally, subject to ruler. All these relationships, with the possible exception of those between friends, were between an inferior and a superior and demanded loyalty and obedience on the one side and care and responsibility on the other. Through the practice of these loyalties and responsibilities in the family, society, and the state, peace and harmony would be reestablished and maintained.

What Confucius taught was an ethical code of human behavior, not a religion; he was not concerned with the issue of life after death and said so. However, his principle of filial piety was extended to include respect for the spirits of deceased ancestors and of sacrifice to them—such sacrifices to express the attitude of the living in upholding family continuity, leaving open all questions regarding the existence of spirits of the dead to whom the sacrifice was to be made "as if they were present."[1]

The acceptance of this moral code was to depend on the example of those who excelled through their knowledge and practice of it: the new educated elite, who owed their role in society and state not to any aristocratic right of birth, but to their education in these Confucian tenets. In his sayings, Confucius prescribed rules of behavior for this "noble man," the *chün-tzu*, asserting what the *chün-tzu* would and should do and what not, and contrasting his manner of action with that of the low person, acting from base instincts. For Confucius held that man, good by nature, needed education to bring out these moral qualities, and the *chün-tzu*, both by example and teaching, would lead society and state to moral harmony.

As "Confucius said: The noble man understands what is right; the inferior man understands what is profitable" and "the noble man makes demands on himself; the inferior man makes demands on others." And finally, "The resolute scholar and humane person will under no circumstances seek life at the expense of their humanity; on occasion they will sacrifice their lives to preserve their humanity."

This revolutionary doctrine abolished the status distinctions of a feudal society and replaced them with a new classification by educational level because education was assumed to raise man to a higher moral status. Confucius stated: "By nature men are pretty much alike; it is learning and practice that set them apart," and in his most revolutionary formulation, "In education there are no class distinctions."

These and many other principles were contained in discourses with princely rulers and with his students and collected by the latter to come down to later generations as the *Lun Yü*, the *Confucian Analects*, the most reliable source of Confucian teachings. Aside from this direct source, Confucius was believed to have had a hand in collecting or editing other classical sources of the time, the Spring and Autumn Annals, the *Book of Documents*, the *Book of Poetry*, the *Book of Changes*, and the *Book of Rites*, which, because they were ascribed to Confucius, became the core of the teaching of the *ju chia*, the Confucian school of literati.

One of the means emphasized by Confucius to stress the proper standards of behavior was the "rectification of names." It was the unwillingness of people to admit to the wrongness of actions that had characterized and corrupted the moral climate; to describe actions in proper terms, to call a spade a spade, was a most direct means to establish moral principles. In choosing the right name for characterizing a deed, distinguishing between murder and legitimate execution, between usurpation and legitimate power, was to clarify the moral principles behind all actions. The rectification of names remained an important literary tool of the Confucian tradition.

Although Confucius was not politically successful during his lifetime, his school eventually prevailed, providing the primary foundation for China's social and political order. The legacy of his teaching was carried on through an increasing number of faithful students. In centuries to come, these followers expanded his tenets and defended them against opposing schools. Almost two hundred years later the most brilliant of these Confucianists, Meng-tzu (372–289 B.C.), known in the West by his latinized name Mencius, restated and advanced the master's ideas and upheld them in contention with rival and, at the time, politically more successful schools.

Like Confucius, Mencius unsuccessfully attempted to offer his advice and services to the princes of the larger and more concentrated states of his time. The princes, involved in a battle of survival, were more interested in military strategems, matters of state, and economic organization than in value systems and the ethical foundation of their rule. As with Confucius, the time may not have been ripe for a new moral sanction of government—the battle for unification was still the primary concern—and Mencius too became famous only as a teacher and expounder of the Confucian tenets. His sayings and dialogues with his students and with rivals have been collected in the book *Meng-tzu* or *Mencius,* one of the Four Books that together with the Five Classics formed the basic stock of learning for the Confucian literati.

Mencius believed and stressed that man was by nature good, and education was the means to bring out this inherent quality of goodness in man; to accomplish this purpose, education must contain the moral principles laid down by Confucius as he had derived them from the wisdom of the ancient sages. In the scheme of his Confucian moral order Mencius placed special emphasis on the importance of the well-being of the people. It was the will of Heaven alone that gave the mandate to the ruler. But Heaven "did not speak," and it was the people's acceptance that confirmed or challenged the ruler's mandate. For "Heaven sees as the people see, Heaven hears as the people hear." And in the order of importance in the affairs of the world, "the people rank the highest, the spirits of land and grain come next, and the ruler counts the least."[2] It was this concept that gave the imperial system its durability.

The rationalism and moral absolutism of the Confucian school found its counterpart in a penchant toward mysticism and intuition, revealed in the writings of what has become known as the Taoist school of philosophy. In its disregard for the conventional, in its retreat from action into a world of questioning, in its tendency to escape from reality into a world of metaphysics and mysticism, Taoism complemented the Confucian moral order and provided a world of imagination, of aesthetics and of art without which the Confucian system would have become moralistic, dreary, and intolerable.

Taoist philosophy provided its own answers to the problems of life; the name is taken from the concept of Tao, "the Way," a cosmic principle that in this philosophy was much more broadly conceived than in Confucianism, where the same term was used to express the basic moral order. The Tao of the Taoists was not the moral force of the Confucians, but an amoral force that pervaded all; the Taoist political philosophy was not to apply the moral code to specific relations and situations, but to establish harmony through passive acceptance of the workings of this universal principle, the Tao. The basic precept of the Taoists was *wu-wei*, nonaction, yielding to the universal forces that assert themselves, swimming with the stream, a state free from strife and desire, of quietude, which would lead to a deeper intuitive understanding of the mysteries of life.

The classical book of Taoism is the *Tao-Teh-Ching*, the *Classic of the Way and Its Virtue*, which was ascribed to a philosopher called Lao-tzu, a legendary figure who, according to tradition, lived before the time of Confucius (supposedly about 590 B.C.). Lao-tzu is no longer believed to have been a historical person. The book ascribed to him may date about the third century B.C., though its mystical content is most likely of much earlier origin. Some of its magical practices, such as *yang sheng*, to "nourish the vital principle," may be traced back to the shamanism of the earliest times. Eventually these magical practices were to lead Taoist adherents to beliefs in supernatural powers of movement free from gravity and to experiments in alchemy.

Yet, the *Tao-Teh-Ching* is much more than a book of magic practices derived from past customs. It framed its own philosophical stand from the contention of ideas of the time. Negating the principles of morality, rituals, and political organizations, which it regarded as counterproductive, Taoism believed in simplicity, passivity, and ac-quiescence in the course of events:

> Tao invariably does nothing (*wu-wei*)
> and yet there is nothing that is not done.

If kings and barons can preserve it,
All things will go through their own transformations.
When they are transformed and desire to stir,
We would restrain them with the nameless primitivity.

Nameless primitivity will result in the absence of desires,

Absence of desires will lead to quietude;
The world will, of itself, find its equilibrium.[3]

As a philosophical foundation Taoism challenges all attempts at rational explanation of the universe. The mystery of the universe cannot be fathomed; and there has to be a distinction between primary cause and the appearance of things:

The Tao [Way] that can be told of
Is not the eternal Tao;
The name that can be named
Is not the eternal name.
Nameless, it is the origin of Heaven and earth;
Nameable, it is the mother of all things.

Always nonexistent,
That we may apprehend its inner secret;
Always existent,
That we may discern its outer manifestations.
These two are the same;
Only as they manifest themselves they receive different names.

That they are the same is the mystery.
Mystery of all mysteries!
The door to all subtleties![4]

This philosophy was clearly not meant as an answer to the problems of the social order of the time, nor was it a doctrine that had a practical application for large numbers of the common people. Rather it was a retreat from the miseries of the world to a simple natural state, a retreat based on solitude, indifference to ambitions and goals, and was a striving for an intuitive grasp of the mysteries of the Tao, which the philosopher alone could obtain. It represented a quasi-religious approach to an individual aspiration to accept the riddle of existence. As such it remained a potent force in Chinese thought, relating to later religious movements and, most of all, having a deep impact on Chinese art and poetry as an appreciation of nature in a contemplative state. In such a state man becomes an observer rather than center and master of his surroundings.

The greatest representative of the Taoist school, Chuang-tzu (369–286 B.C.?), dealt with this concept of Tao as presenting a supreme principle, and the grasp of its mysteries would free man from the confines of a self-centered outlook. Chuang-tzu doubted the capability of the human mind to rationalize and loved to demonstrate in paradoxes and satires the weaknesses of human rational thinking and the relativity of things. Some of his often repeated stories in the book of his sayings play on the enigma of reality and subconsciousness, the question of dreams and reality.

The best known is the allegory of Chuang-tzu and the butterfly:

> Once upon a time Chuang Chou (i.e., Chuang-tzu) dreamed
> that he was a butterfly, a butterfly fluttering about, enjoying
> himself. It did not know that it was Chuang Chou. Suddenly
> he woke with a start and he was Chuang Chou again. But he
> did not know whether he was Chuang Chou who had
> dreamed that he was a butterfly, or whether he was a
> butterfly dreaming that he was Chuang Chou. Between
> Chuang Chou and the butterfly there must be some
> distinction. This is what is called the transformation of
> things.[5]

The Taoist philosophers made no attempt to compete in the contest for official positions and for political gain. That would have been contrary to their disdain for the struggle of political life. Nonaction led to withdrawal and the life of a recluse, cultivated throughout Chinese history, especially in times of disorder and decline. Beyond this flight from bitter realities Taoist philosophy came to play a large part in Chinese thought. It remained an antidote to the constraints of Confucian moralizing, an escape not only from despair in periods of anarchy, but also a safety valve against the pressures of the social as well as the political system, adding a sense of detachment and of fantasy to the orderly world of emerging bureaucracy.

The two philosophical schools that gained acceptance in the disorderly age of the Warring States, the Mohists and the Legalists, did not concern themselves with questions of moral standards for society and the new bureaucracy or intuitive insight into the workings of the universe. They concentrated their thought and efforts on the practical questions of economics and of law and order.

The most popular teaching of the period of the Hundred Schools of Thought was that founded by Mo-tzu (470–391 B.C.?), also known as Mo-ti. The Mohist school became the main rival of the Confucianists and the main target of attack by Mencius; the school taught an outspoken utilitarianism. All human effort should be concentrated on providing the material needs of human life, food, clothing, and shelter; and all other human interests, including the rituals of formal etiquette and the arts were extravagant and should be abolished. Most extravagant of all was war, and Mo-tzu preached a militant pacifism, but he recognized the necessity for defense and military preparedness in this age of constant warfare; therefore he and his followers gave support and military advice to states attacked by their neighbors.

Like Confucius, Mo-tzu was revolutionary in his repudiation of the feudal order, but he went beyond the Confucian goal of creating a new elite of educated men. In contrast to the Confucian system in which authority was in the hands of an elite, although no longer a hereditary but rather a scholar-elite, Mo-tzu stressed the equality of all men—at least in principle. The Confucian concept of *jen*, charity or love in human relations, was graded and regulated through a system of human relations in which a leading partner had authority and responsibility, whereas Mo-tzu believed in the practice of universal human love without such regulating distinctions. In theory he preached a complete egalitarianism, but in practice this equality of all men and material comfort for all people were best achieved through a unity of purpose. This unity was maintained by a leader whom the people had to obey completely and who himself followed the will of Heaven as interpreted by Mo-tzu and his followers. As Mo-tzu stated, the princes must realize that: "Exaltation of the worthy is the foundation of government. . . . When the honorable and wise govern the ignorant and humble, there is order. But when the ignorant and humble govern the honorable and wise, there is disorder. Therefore we know that exaltation of the worthy is the foundation of government."[6] Successful in a time of political decline and intellectual uncertainty, the Mohist school disappeared without leaving a trace on Chinese cultural tradition once unity and a new moral order had been established.

Far more important in the process of unification and in its contribution to the institutions of the emerging Chinese imperial system was the school known as the Legalists. Although this school became a main antagonist of Confucianism (ridiculing its ethical concepts and the pretentious "cavaliers" who professed them), the school of Legalists traced its teaching in part to a man who was regarded as a student of Confuciansim. Hsün-tzu (fl. 298–238 B.C.) introduced a pessimistic view in his essays. In contrast to Mencius, Hsün-tzu held that man was by nature evil and had not only to be reformed by teaching, but also to be restrained by laws that were essential for maintaining order and for preventing a return to a state of barbarism. The school of Legalists had two brilliant representatives, both of whom were believed to have been students of Hsün-tzu. Han Fei-tzu (d. 233 B.C.) was a most outstanding scholar whose writings have been preserved and form our major source for Legalist thinking, and Li Ssu (d. 208 B.C.) was Ch'in's most important statesman and the chief intellect behind its state organization, victorious strategy, and ruthless policy of centralization and unification.

According to tradition, Legalist theory was first applied as policy in the state of Ch'in by an earlier minister, Kung-sun Yang, known by his title as Shang Yang, Lord Shang, (d. 330 B.C.?). A book ascribed to him, though believed to be the work of several authors and of much later origin, contains some of the definitions of the concept of law that is equal for all, protected by very careful specific precautions against any tampering with its rules, and is "clear, easy to know, and strictly applied." In this and in the more authentic book of Han Fei-tzu, the Legalist principles were clearly defined. They contain the most important concepts of law known also in the Western legal tradition.

Legalism was the most revolutionary of the contending schools at this time. Its chief goal was an all-powerful absolutist state, based on laws promulgated by the king, who alone held all authority but was himself bound by his own laws. All feudal authority was erased and replaced by appointed officials who, however, served at the pleasure of the king and who in turn had to obey and carry out

the laws. The objectivity of the law would guarantee orderly government even if the ruler were weak and the officials were only of
mediocre talent; in fact, it was better if they had no ideas of their
own but simply carried out the law.

Some followers of this school stressed the importance of the
power and authority of the king, some emphasized the art of statecraft,
but all focused on the concepts of law itself (*fa*). These laws dealt
with rewards and punishment for prescribed actions that were to
be measured by objective standards, not by intent. In practice these
rewards and punishments could be cruel: rewards according to the
number of heads of enemies slaughtered in battle, punishment as
the result of a killing, regardless of intent, or even accidental death.
In the words of Han Fei-tzu, "Rewards should be rich and certain
so that the people will be attracted by them; punishments should
be severe and definite so that people will fear them; and laws should
be uniform and steadfast so that people will be familiar with them."[7]

In their emphasis on objective laws, on the authority to enforce
them, and on reward and punishment as a method of maintaining
an orderly system, the Legalists were directly opposed to the school
of the Confucian literati, which stressed virtue, a moral code, rule
by persuasion and teaching, and the example of a scholar-elite and
of the king himself. Indeed, the Legalists were contemptuous of what
they regarded as the idle talk of scholars, who only sought an easy
life for themselves and misled others to respect a virtue that was
mostly pretense. The Legalists claimed to possess a more realistic
view of human nature and the needs of society and state. In time,
they were successful in implanting their system on the state of Ch'in,
and when Ch'in succeeded in a military unification of China, on
the whole newly unified empire in the first stage of its development.
It was Li Ssu, prime minister of Ch'in, who advised the ruler of
that state to accept policies that led to the conquest of the empire.
Li Ssu, who was responsible for the death of his rival, Han Fei-tzu,
advised the emperor against reintroducing feudal authority or nobility
after he had conquered and unified the whole country. Historically,
Li Ssu has become infamous for his "Memorial on the Burning of
Books," in which he recommended that the emperor eliminate all
scholarly opposition and criticism of imperial policy by burning all
their books in the imperial archives or in the hands of scholars and
executing those who resisted.

Although this Legalist order did not survive the Ch'in Dynasty, which collapsed shortly after the death of its first ruler, Ch'in Shih Huang-ti, Legalist concepts continued to play an important role within the imperial polity, when the state was reorganized into a Confucian system. Dynastic codes originating in the Han Dynasty continued to be issued by each successive dynasty to provide the necessary legal safeguards for the Confucian state and moral order.

Six

THE UNIFIED EMPIRE

THE CULTURAL LEGACY of over two millennia of early history provided the foundation on which the first Chinese empire was built. Its establishment was the proud attainment of two dynasties and brought about a complete transformation of China's political, social, economic, and ideological order from a declining feudal to a new bureaucratic society. The military unification and subsequent political and social reordering were accomplished by the first emperor of China, Ch'in Shih Huang-ti and his short-lived Ch'in Dynasty. He used draconic measures in the creation of a unified and enlarged Chinese polity that reverberated through East Asia and beyond and gave his country its name, China, the country of Ch'in. The succeeding Han Dynasty lasted for more than four centuries and gave the empire its intellectual and institutional cohesion. Under Han, Chinese power was expanded into Central, South, and Northeast Asia, and from Han the Chinese received their ethnic designation, *Han-tzu*, the sons of Han, proudly proclaimed by them to this day.

The newly created Ch'in and Han empire was a consummation of all the changes in the Chinese social, political, and intellectual tradition that had preceded it. The concept of the state and of dynastic rule under the Mandate of Heaven assumed by the Chou and the rich intellectual heritage of the Hundred Schools of Thought found a new expression, as China evolved from the Bronze to the Iron Age, from domains to private landownership, from small feudal units to large populous states, from aristocratic warfare to large battles by massed infantry and cavalry, from hereditary aristocratic leadership to appointed officialdom, and the people moved from serfdom to state subjects. The ritual masterpieces of the bronzes had long given way to elegant decorative and commemorative bronze vessels and to refined and beautiful ceramics and lacquerware; the tombs no longer contained human sacrifices, but figurines and paintings.

This Chinese cultural transformation now led to its political conclusion: the centralized empire. Henceforth China's rulers were no longer known as *wang*, "kings," a title that by now had been assumed by the heads of states and was therefore depreciated: They became *huang-ti*, emperors, transposing the title of the deified royal ancestors in Heaven to the living holders of the Mandate of Heaven on earth.

In the battles of the last centuries the armies of defeated enemies were often indiscriminately slaughtered. Ch'in, the victor, was a frontier state less hidebound by tradition than had been its competitors. Its population is believed to have been made up partly of non-Chinese Turkic ethnic groups that were not only farmers, but also cattle and horse breeders. From the fourth century B.C., cavalry had become an important factor in frontier warfare. Units of horsemen became a formidable mobile force. The first emperor of Ch'in was known to have been a horse fancier, whose favorite horses with names like "catcher of the wind" or "tracker of shadows" have become famous in historical writings. And in the tombs of the Han Dynasty we have found the terra cotta figures of large numbers of mounted soldiers and exquisite portrayals of galloping horses that demonstrate the artistic fascination of the time with the beauty of this animal.

The frontier location and loose tribal origin and organization may have given the state of Ch'in a still more important advantage. It did not have the entrenched feudal aristocracy that was the foundation of the ruling structure in the central Chinese states. And it was therefore easier to introduce in Ch'in bureaucratic rule by appointed military and political officials.

This fundamental reform was first carried out in Ch'in in the fourth century B.C. allegedly by the Legalist statesman, Kung-sun Yang, entitled Lord Shang, and known as Shang Yang. Shang Yang's reforms were first introduced in the state of Ch'in in 359 B.C. In essence they recognized the peasant, now a combatant in his own right, as a direct subject of the state and freed him from the control of aristocratic clans. He was given access to the new officialdom that was to replace hereditary noble positions. The villagers were organized into groups of five and ten families under their own leadership with a hierarchy of ranks granted according to services rendered. The state was divided into commanderies and districts and the capital was moved to Hsien-yang, close to the center of China. The organization was quasi-military and served a military purpose but also led to the opening and cultivation of new land, an increase of state income, population, and military power. All this was done under a system of law, the law promoted by the Legalist school.

In the *Book of Shang Yang*, which, if of somewhat later date, expresses the ideas of his time, the author takes great care to define the duties of the law officers who should give information on the law and ascertain that nobody tamper with it. "Thus there shall be no one among the government officials and people of the empire who does not know the law" so that the officials "dare not treat the people contrary to the law, nor do the people dare infringe the law."[1] Furthermore, the law bound the ruler himself who could not use arbitary power, but rather was the lawgiver and final guarantor. The law once given was to be an objective force, superior to all men, and not open to interpretations.

Aside from the Legalist advisers and officials, the men who came to power during these times of economic transition from feudalism to a money economy were primarily rich merchants who had managed to accumulate large fortunes and vast numbers of servants and employees and were therefore able to assist and finance the rulers, in some cases becoming ministers and advisers.

The intent of these merchant-politicians was clearly the expansion of their own states, the removal of frontiers, the abrogation of the feudal aristocracy, and the transfer of feudal power to the centralized authority of the rulers. For a short time this type of powerful merchant came to ministerial positions in several of the surviving larger states. In the state of Ch'in, the ruler's son named Chuang-hsiang had been sent as hostage to the neighboring state of Chao, a common practice, and was there befriended and supported by a rich merchant, Lü Pu-wei. Lü Pu-wei even gave Chuang-hsiang one of his own concubines as wife, who, gossip had it, had already become pregnant by Lü. When, after the death of his father, the prince Chuang-hsiang returned to Ch'in as the new king, he immediately appointed his benefactor, Lü, as prime minister for his government.

For twelve years, 249 to 237 B.C., Lü Pu-wei ably managed the politics of Ch'in, first under Chuang-hsiang and following Chuang-Hsiang's early death, as regent for his successor, Cheng-wang, the son of Lü Pu-Wei's former concubine.

Lü Pu-wei's administration was characterized by the building of canals and other public works and by his methods of attracting politicians and scholars from different schools of thought from all parts of the country. His diplomatic and military strategy prepared the ground that led eventually to Ch'in's final victory over the rival states. In 256, under Lü Pu-wei's direction, the remnants of the Chou Dynasty's territory was taken, the ruler executed, and the long Chou rule brought to a formal end. The way was open for a new candidate for the Mandate of Heaven. Alarmed by Ch'in's growing power, the other states, by now seven, concluded a south-north axis alignment to hold Ch'in at bay and defeat it. Lü Pu-wei's strategy, which eventually prevailed, divided the allies and defeated them individually.

Lü Pu-Wei carefully prepared Ch'in's rise to supremacy not only militarily and politically but also ideologically. Under his direction the scholars with whom he had surrounded himself, numbering according to some accounts nearly three thousand, composed a philosophical work, known as the *Lü-shih Ch'un-ch'iu*, which combined, reconciled, and integrated the chief philosophical schools of his time into a unified conceptional whole that, Lü hoped, would become the guiding philosophical foundation for the emerging empire. Following the Taoist concept of *wu-wei*—quiescence—the ruler should maintain order by calmly reposing in harmony with the course of the universe, the Tao, and affect human affairs by his example. State affairs would be handled by the officials. The state was to be administered as a bureaucracy; "The Empire was not the empire of the 'One Man,' it was the Empire of the whole community." This extraordinary document might be called an intended constituent charter of the coming united empire.[2]

The ritual through which the coming emperor was to manifest his function of holder of the mandate, a go-between for the universe, Heaven, and mankind, was prescribed in detail; Lü's book contained the rules for the emperor's sacrifice to Heaven. It is the only part of this document that, preserved in the work by the famous historian

Ssu-ma Ch'ien about a hundred years later, became in part the actual practice of the emperors down to our century.

Lü Pu-wei was not to see the realization of his plans. When the young ruler, Cheng-wang, came of age in 237 B.C., he banished Lü to his estates, and when Lü's supporters continued to hope for his return to power, Cheng-wang purged them and ordered Lü to commit suicide in 235 B.C. Cheng-wang intended to be his own master. With the help of his new Legalist advisor, Li Ssu, he continued the same strategy of divide and conquer that had been initiated under Lü's stewardship. One by one the other kingdoms fell; Han in 230 B.C., Chao in 228 B.C., Wei in 225 B.C., Ch'u in 223 B.C., Yen, in the north, in 222 B.C., and finally Ch'i in 221 B.C. Ch'in had unified China through military conquest. Cheng-wang became China's first emperor.

Ch'in Shih Huang-ti, the first emperor of Ch'in, is known in Chinese history as the great unifier who forced a new order on the Chinese land, politically, socially, economically, and intellectually, but he is even more perceived as an infamous tyrant and oppressor, a destroyer of old cultural values who burned the books, killed the scholars, and afflicted the people with forced labor for his massive public works. We have a personal description of the emperor that shows the disdain in which he was held by historians and scholars who prevailed after the fall of the Ch'in rule. He was said to have had "protruding eyes like a wasp, an aquiline nose, the chest of a bird, the high, hoarse, cruel voice of a wolf, and the heart of a tiger."[3] It is this latter image of the great tyrant that prevailed in Chinese history.

Ch'in Shih Huang-ti started his rule successfully on the basis of the military, administrative, and economic strength of the state. Obviously his state was the most advanced and best organized among the Chinese states of the time. Ch'in represented the emerging new social forces, the peasants freed from serfdom, the merchants eager for new wealth and opportunities within the unified realm and in the political arena, and the new breed of military officers and administrators eagerly viewing a field of unlimited scope for work and success in the unified empire. This advanced system was now to be applied to the whole empire. The borders between the states vanished, and customs barriers were abolished. Feudal estates, insofar as they still existed, were dissolved, and the land distributed among the farmers. All feudal authority was ended and the bureaucratic administration established under Ch'in was extended over the whole empire.

The memorials of the Legalist prime minister Li Ssu preserved by the historian Ssu-ma Ch'ien clearly express the argument of the time: "Now, with the might of Ch'in and the virtues of your Highness, at one stroke, like sweeping off the dust from a kitchen stove, the feudal lords can be annihilated, imperial rule can be established, and unification of the world can be brought about. This is the one moment in ten thousand ages."[4] And in answer to a suggestion of redistribution of the Ch'in territory through enfeoffment of the Ch'in princes and meritorious officials now proposed by some of the emperor's courtiers, Li Ssu warned of the example of the system of enfeoffment of the Chou clan members that was necessary then, but led eventually to estrangement and internal warfare. "Now owing to the divine intelligence of your Majesty, all the land within the seas is unified and it has been divided into commanderies and prefectures. The royal princes and the meritorious ministers have been granted titles and have been bountifully rewarded from the government treasury, and it has proved sufficient."[5] No need therefore for any enfeoffment that would disturb the peace. This coincided with the emperor's intent. All China was divided into thirty-six commanderies or provinces, soon increased to forty-eight with appointed governors paid by the imperial treasury and removable at the emperor's will.

To prevent organized resistance arising from former ruling houses and aristocracy, the emperor transferred 120,000 aristocratic families to the capital of Hsien-yang, thus removing them from their former feudal bases and bringing them under direct supervision. Frequent similar transferals of population groups, often applied under later emperors, went far to eliminate or reduce local particularism and to strengthen national cohesion.

Under this new political structure, the first emperor set to work to unify and fuse all essential aspects of social life. Equal weights and measures were adopted nationwide, many coins were systematized, and roads were built, and existing roads were connected to link the capital, Hsien-yang, with all parts of the empire. The size of the axles of carriages was standardized so that uniform tracks of wagons would facilitate nationwide transport. Most important for a unified administration, written characters were standardized in line with the tradition of Ch'in.

The danger of raids or invasions by mounted tribes of the steppe had earlier forced some of the Chinese frontier states to build walls along their frontiers to contain and repel nomad cavalry. Ch'in Shih Huang-ti linked these walls and extended them with his own massive fortification line into the "Great Wall," reaching from Kansu province to the sea at the northern part of the Liaotung Peninsula, a length of approximately 1,400 miles. The Great Wall became the first emperor's best known creation. Inside the country, however, walls and fortifications built as defense between the states were torn down and the population was disarmed by forbidding the possession of arms, collecting them, casting the metal into twelve giant statues, each allegedly weighing 240,000 Chinese pounds.

The problem of demobilizing the armies engaged in the final battles for supremacy was in part resolved by sending hundreds of thousands of discharged soldiers to work on the building of the Great Wall and other massive public works projects. Eventually corvée labor had to be supplied for these works, and the burden later became a major reason for the breakdown of Ch'in rule.

However, early in Ch'in, the land was at peace. A high priority of the central government was the promotion of agriculture so that, as the emperor proclaimed, "the blackhaired ones (the common people) are happy."[6] New land was brought under cultivation by resettlement of large groups of people from densely populated areas to virgin land; these settlers were exempted for a period of a dozen years from all corvée labor. With the end of warfare a new prosperity had arrived; by 216 B.C. as a result of surpluses in state tax income, the government was able to distribute to each village of the empire six hundred pounds of rice and two sheep. One of the richest agricultural areas incorporated into the realm of the first emperor in 211 B.C. was the Red Basin of Szech'wan, a great plain of a Yangtze tributary that caused much devastation through yearly floods and prevented stable development. A famous hydraulic engineer, Li Ping, sent by the imperial government, built a magnificently planned project consisting of a network of canals, flood dams, and locks, forming an artificial water system that covered the whole plain. This system has been maintained to modern time by dredging the canals and repairing the dams and locks each winter, converting the Red Basin of Szech'wan into one of the most fertile and densely populated areas of China.

In the Northwest major resettlement was undertaken along the frontier of the steppe to counter the threat posed by the cavalry of the Hsiung-nu (the Huns of European history), attracted by the prosperity of the Chinese development. Major irrigation canals were built to secure the land for Chinese agriculture and to prevent its use as pasture for invaders—canals that remain in use down to the present time. The region was divided into thirty-four new districts, with the settlers as peasant-soldiers providing the garrisons for defense. In 213 B.C. an expeditionary force of 100,000 men drove the Hsiung-nu out of the Ordos region. Other campaigns took Chinese armies into South China and Vietnam, resulting in the establishment of new commanderies at today's Canton, Kweilin, Foochow, and Hanoi. Thus Chinese control, even though tenuous for a long period of time, began to extend over much of China as it is known today and even further.

The tremendous power he had gained in such a short time and the rapid success of his revolutionary measures must have increased the emperor's inclination to believe in his own superhuman stature. He began to surround himself with an aura of mystery and with extraordinary pomp and luxury. At Hsien-yang he had built a gigantic palace, said to have been constructed by the labor of 700,000 corvée workers. Nearby he erected copies of the palaces of each of the rulers of the states he had conquered and had the palaces all interconnected by secret passages. All these palaces were provided with servants, beautiful women, and entertainers, so that the emperor could move constantly from one residence to another, keeping his whereabouts secret because he had once narrowly escaped assassination and feared attempts on his life. (See Plate 8.)

At the court the emperor was surrounded not only by Legalist scholars but also by Taoist magicians. The Taoist school of thought was linked philosophically with Legalism, thus forming a belief in an abstract order whose norms could be ascertained and applied to human life. Taoism had at the decline of the empire spread within the states of Ch'u, the home state of the Legalist Li Ssu, and in the northeastern frontier states of Yen and Ch'i and had turned strongly to magic practices, perhaps under the influence of Central Asian shamanism, seeking a way to make gold and to find a plant that would give the emperor immortality. To find this herb of life the emperor sent an expedition of one hundred young men and maidens of good families, together with artisans, across the sea to the "island of the gods" of which he had been told by a magician. The mission did not return, and it has been speculated that the voyagers landed in Japan and settled there. More ludicrous even were the emperor's puerile ideas of punishing a mountain that had hindered his ascent during a storm with high winds, by slashing the forests and painting the mountain red, and by personally shooting at a great fish that was believed to have obstructed his expedition to the island of the gods.

For his afterlife in imperial style Ch'in Shih Huang-ti provided himself with a grand and sumptuous underground palace of a tomb to reflect his life and power on earth. Seven hundred thousand convicts worked for ten years to build this subterranean mausoleum. Reportedly despoiled at the time of the downfall of the Ch'in rule, the tomb has not been excavated in modern times and all that is known about it comes from the account of the historian Ssu-ma Ch'ien. The main chamber, containing the sarcophagus, was built with a copper floor and lacquered walls as protection against dampness and decay. The interior was filled with a scale-model reproduction of the empire, including models of the palaces and administrative buildings and of the rivers and oceans, the latter formed by quicksilver. An artificial Heaven was studded with pearls and lit by lamps filled with slow-burning fish oil. The inner accesses were protected by crossbows, and in an effort to keep safe the secret entrance of the structure, some workers were said to have been walled in when the tomb was closed.

Whatever will be found when the tomb is finally opened by modern archaeologists, an indication of the magnificence of this funerary extravagance came to light in 1974 when workers excavating nearby for the foundation of a factory chanced accidentally on a caved-in underground hall in which life-sized terra cotta figures of soldiers and horses were uncovered. These figures turned out to be individual images—presumably portraits—of the bodyguard of the first emperor, some 7,000 of them, arrayed in formation to guard the emperor's tomb, located less than a mile away. (See Plate 9.) Later two magnificent ghost carriages of bronze, each with driver and four horses, were uncovered nearby, and one can only speculate as to what may still be found in the area of the tomb. The vast expanse of this grandiose funerary complex speaks for the splendor and scope of the creations of the first emperor, whose palaces have long ago been destroyed but whose tomb and the Great Wall, built under his orders, remain as his great historical monuments. (See Plate 10.)

The burden of corvée labor and taxes imposed for these monumental works created growing dissatisfaction throughout the country. At court, the opposition was led both by scholars of the Confucian and all other schools whose views had long been disregarded by the Legalist prime minister Li Ssu. To meet this growing opposition head-on, Li Ssu proposed that the emperor not only forbid all criticism of his measures but also that he destroy the literature of all rival schools of philosophy.

Li Ssu's "Memorial on the Burning of Books" is contained in Ssu-ma Chien's historical record. After complaining of the "independent schools, joining with each other, to criticize the codes of laws and instructions both at home and in the thoroughfare" and warning of the danger of their influence in "misleading the lowly multitude," Li Ssu suggested that

> all books in the imperial archives, save the memoirs of Ch'in, be burned. All persons in the empire, except members of the Academy of Learned Scholars (the Legalists and Taoists), in possession of the Book of Odes, the Book of History, and discourses of the hundred philosophers should take them to the local governors and have them indiscriminately burned. Those who dare to talk to each other about the Book of Odes and the Book of History should be executed and their bodies exposed on the market place. Anyone referring to the past to criticize the present should, together with all members of his family, be put to death. . . . Those who have not destroyed their books are to be branded and sent to build the Great Wall. Books not to be destroyed will be those on medicine and pharmacy, divination by the tortoise and milfoil, and agriculture and arboriculture.

Laconically the memorial ended, "People wishing to pursue learning should take the officials as their teachers."[7] The emperor approved;

in 213 B.C. the books were burned throughout the empire, and 460 scholars who protested were executed by being buried alive.

In a country with such a great record of historical and philosophical writing, the burning of the books remained an unforgivable crime. Though much was hidden away and reappeared later, many sources were destroyed forever. This calamity was irreparably worsened at the fall of the dynasty when the imperial library, holding the only copies of the proscribed books, went up in flames together with the rest of the palace. Politically, the emperor earned the undying hostility of the Confucian scholar class.

What did bring about the fall of empire, however, was not the alienation and hatred of the scholar class, nor the bitter enmity of the surviving remnants of the aristocracy, but the growing popular discontent and mounting outrage over the cruelty of the system of punishments and the intolerable burden of taxes and levies imposed for the massive public works that the emperor commanded. Crime increased as did the number of those condemned, tortured, mutilated, and exiled to labor gangs. As long as the emperor was alive, fear of his powerful and demoniacal personality held the empire together; after his death all the restraints broke, and the empire exploded in rebellion.

Ch'in Shih Huang-ti died in 211 B.C. during the last of many inspection journeys through his empire. The death of the emperor while away from the capital created a dangerous emergency for his counselors, the prime minister, Li Ssu, and the eunuch Chao Kao who were with him. They decided to return directly to the capital, keeping the death secret. To pretend that the emperor was still alive they held audiences behind the curtain of his carriage, but when, because of the summer heat, the odor of the emperor's body became clearly noticeable, they supposedly added a wagon of fish to the entourage to cover the evidence of death.

Earlier, the emperor's first son had been banished because of his disapproval of the harsh policies of the state and his sympathy with the Confucian scholars; however, the emperor, before his death, had wished for a reconciliation and called his first son back to have him succeed to the throne. Afraid for their own power and safety, Li Ssu and Chao Kao suppressed the emperor's letter and falsified another that ordered the crown prince to commit suicide. In his place they named the second youngest son, entirely controlled by them, as Erh Shih Huang-ti—second emperor. In 209, on a personal inspection journey, the young emperor became aware of the widespread discontent but was persuaded by Chao Kao to purge and execute numerous high- and middle-level officials and relatives and replace them with Chao Kao's followers. When widespread peasant risings occurred, Chao Kao turned on Li Ssu and had him assassinated, and when the young emperor finally turned against Chao, the intriguing eunuch murdered him in 207. A grandson of the first emperor, the son of his older son, now placed on the throne, in turn killed Chao Kao, but then in despair over the collapse of Ch'in power, committed suicide.

The Ch'in Dynasty thus ended in self-destruction. After the death of the first emperor, who by the end of his mandate ruled increasingly by terror, no accepted authority was left to provide the essential cohesion needed for a newly emerging order. The law of punishments and rewards did not suffice. No attempt had been made to provide an ethical foundation, a new value system for the new society. The elements for it had been conceived in the rich world of ideas of the Hundred Schools of Thought; Lü Pu-wei had tried to merge them into a compound system but had not succeeded. There would be still more warfare and disorder before a new dynasty would be able to rebuild Ch'in Shih Huang-ti's state and sustain it with an ideology that would last into modern time.

Seven

THE EMPIRE CONSOLIDATED:

The Han Dynasty

THE COLLAPSE OF the Ch'in Dynasty so soon after the death of its founder was not caused by the first emperor's revolutionary measures. The creation of a new centralized empire, the end of feudalism and of serfdom, the establishment of a bureaucratic administration, and the new role assumed by the peasants and merchants could not be reversed, even though an attempt was made for a short time to reestablish some kingdoms and aristocratic houses. A less powerful personality than Ch'in Shih Huang-ti might not have accomplished so much, so completely, in such a short time, but the coming of a new order had been clearly indicated by evolving social changes throughout all of China, long before the first emperor placed his stamp on the new scene.

The shortcomings of Ch'in—aside from self-destructive intrigues at the court—are most clearly observed not in the social and political revolutionary innovations but in the ruthlessness of the first emperor, the increasing oppressiveness of the burden of forced labor, and the cruelty of established punishments. Beyond that, moreover, a profound flaw appears in retrospect to have been instrumental in bringing about the abrupt end of the Ch'in Dynasty; this was the lack of an ideological foundation, of commonly accepted new values to provide essential cohesive strength to the new order. Lü Pu-wei's ideological ideas had been discarded, and rewards and punishments were not enough to serve as a new moral foundation of society.

This missing ideological element was provided by a new dynasty, the Han, which gained the throne after years of chaos and warfare.

Immediately following the first emperor's death, spontaneous uprisings led primarily by commoners occurred throughout the empire. The first of these were suppressed by still existing Ch'in armies. Later, better organized and much broader based rebellious movements brought about the end of Ch'in rule. Much has been made of the contrast between two leading figures of the anti-Ch'in rebellion. One, Hsiang Yü, was an aristocrat from the former state of Ch'u, fighting for the vague concept of restoring the old feudal order. He is described as a typical representative of the rapidly disappearing aristocratic class, tall, a trained warrior, also educated in literature and poetry, a refined and sophisticated though hot-tempered man, a reckless fighter who won his battles but lost his war. His victorious opponent, Liu Pang, born a peasant, was his opposite in temper and talent. A shrewd and cautious man of obviously remarkable ability both for scheming and organization, he had already moved up to a minor local administrative position under Ch'in rule. When the countryside exploded in rebellion, Liu organized his own force, then accepted a command under Hsiang Yü, only to split with him later and turn to become Hsiang Yü's chief rival for power. During the joint action against the Ch'in, Liu Pang was the first to reach the Ch'in capital, Hsien-yang, with his army. Instead of storming the capital city, a normal action, he negotiated a surrender, sparing both the Ch'in family and the inhabitants. When Hsiang Yü's forces arrived, Liu Pang withdrew, taking with him the imperial archives, which became so vital later for governing the country. Hsiang Yü occupied the city, executed the Ch'in child emperor and his family, slaughtered the entire male population, enslaved women and children, and put the city to the torch; it continued to burn for three months. Next Hsiang Yü appointed a child of the former Ch'u house as emperor, named himself generalissimo (*pa wang*), and installed many of his generals and lieutenants as kings over the various states. Returning later to Ch'u, he had the child emperor murdered and he himself assumed the title emperor.

Now Liu Pang, who had been named King of Shu in the lower Yangtze region, turned against Hsiang Yü. Five years of bitter warfare followed, during which so many of Hsiang Yü's generals defected to Liu Pang's side that Hsiang Yü's now inferior army was finally destroyed in a battle at the Huai River, where Hsiang Yü ended his own life. The drama of this struggle and the personalities of the contenders have been widely popularized by writers and poets and have become part of Chinese folklore.

Following his final victory, Liu Pang was formally named emperor by an assembly of generals, local rulers, and scholars. He assumed for his dynasty the title of Han, from the name of the river where he had first established his power.

The Han Dynasty (206 B.C.–A.D. 221) took over the government structure erected by the first emperor; basically the land was administered as heretofore by appointed officials in charge of commanderies and districts. However, as a conciliatory compromise, the emperor had at first to confirm the descendants of some old royal houses as well as newly created potentates in their positions as territorial lords in a quasi-feudal analogy with the previous order. But no subfiefs were permitted, and landownership remained private. The territories of the lords were mostly small enclaves, surrounded by commanderies directly administered by the central government. The lords were frequently transferred or deposed, and they were supervised by imperial commissioners so that their feudal status was more fiction than reality. Eventually the introduction of the principle of equal inheritance by all sons led to the end of all hereditary power. To assuage the widespread alienation caused by the cruelty of the Ch'in legal system, the Han emperor abrogated the harshest laws through edicts issued between 191 and 167 B.C. Finally mutilation as punishment was altogether abolished. In 196 B.C. the emperor issued an edict seeking out from all strata of the society able people who were to be brought to the capital in order to be trained for assuming official posts. The empire was to be administered by a growing bureaucracy, based on education and individual ability rather than on status, inheritance, military merits, connections, or family wealth—the latter especially important since the emergence of politically powerful land-rich families.

Private landownership, which had at the outset induced a commensurable distribution of land among small peasant-owners, led to large accumulations of land held by newly rich families of merchants, officials, and well-to-do peasants. Landlordism and the growing power of wealthy and entrenched families became a new problem in Chinese postfeudal society.

The problem of landlordism and tenancy has however been vastly exaggerated for all imperial history. This is partly due to the

Marxist-Leninist doctrinal interpretation of Chinese history, which followed the unilinear communist periodization of all human history as moving through similar stages of "primitive, slavery, feudal, and capitalist societies" before arriving at the socialist and communist millennium. In this doctrinal view, Chinese imperial history was "feudal," while the earlier, truly feudal period was classified as "slavery." Because in imperial time there were no enfeoffments, no feudal contracts, loyalties, or services, no lords, no knights, no serfs, and land could be bought and sold, the only feudalism that could be claimed by this doctrinal approach was "economic feudalism," based on landlordism and tenancy. This view not only confuses economic relationships with very precise legal and social-status concepts, but is even in its own assumptions factually untenable. Although land-lordism created its own problems, especially in early imperial time, there were always counterbalancing forces that kept it in line.

During most of Chinese imperial history the land was in the main held not by landlords but by small peasant-owners; and, except for short periods in earlier history, landed estates, as far as they existed, were rarely of large size. The absence of the principle of primogeniture in inheritance of property in Chinese law and custom resulted in constant redistribution of land even if large units had been accumulated by any one person; and occasional attempts to prevent this redistribution by consigning land to the clan proved to be failures. Class structure in imperial Chinese history was based not on landownership, all Marxist interpretations notwithstanding, but rather on professional distinctions.

Traditionally, Chinese scholars have distinguished four (some-times five) social classes in Chinese society: Scholars came first; farmers second; craftsmen third; merchants, even though wealthier, were counted fourth in general importance; and soldiers, when counted at all, last. This classification is often made light of as a self-serving statement on the part of the intellectual elite, used by the scholars to stress their own leading role and to keep in check the potential challenge of the merchants to the scholar-gentry's status of political and social power. And indeed that was its purpose, but it also characterized the actual ideological valuation and role of the differing groups in imperial society and state.

Traditional China became an open society with as much social mobility as there was to be found in any social order not based on hereditary status. Social mobility in the Chinese bureaucratic society was based on education and knowledge, not on wealth. The farmers, the largest population group, had access to the examinations and bureaucratic rank, as had the craftsmen, while the merchants had not only no special advantage, but were at times actually discriminated against in admission to the educational ladder.

The educated elite—the scholar-gentry—had the political and social power and prestige, and the merchant profession was officially disdained. In later time, scholars who happened to be also merchants often assumed different names for their double existence. The military per se did not have power either; indeed, the ordinary private soldier was scorned. A common saying was, "Good iron is not made into nails, good men are not made into soldiers." Officers, in contrast, were educated and theoretically made their careers on the basis of that qualification. Neither military men nor merchants were permitted to manage state and society; only the educated, the literati, the so-called scholar-gentry were to be entrusted with the leadership role; and it was this tradition inaugurated by the Han Dynasty that gave imperial China its special cultural character.

The fist Han emperor, Liu Pang, generally known under his posthumous name Kao-tsu, although a skilled administrator, was not an educated man and regarded scholars with suspicion. Nonetheless, he introduced the concept of training officials from all social strata and finally even accepted the Confucian tenet of professional service to the state, ceremonially sacrificing at the tomb of Confucius in 195 B.C. Later that same year the emperor died from a battle wound.

His successors continued to entrust the execution of their administration to a growing officialdom of educated men. At first their choice of candidates remained eclectic. The Legalists were discredited, but the Taoists were still accepted. Later Confucianists complained about the early Han emperors' predilection for Taoist advisers, whose claim to magical powers remained a special qualification in their favor until the emperors became more sophisticated about some of the most obvious deceptions.

The final stage in the creation of this scholar bureaucracy came under the famous Han emperor Wu-ti (140–87 B.C.), who not only appointed individual Confucian scholars to positions in government and administration, but also established in the capital in 124 B.C. an educational academy, a university, whose teachers and students were exclusively *ju chia*, Confucianists, and inaugurated for them a system of examinations that they had to pass to prove their qualifications for public service.

The term *scholar-gentry* for the educated Confucian upper class in China is unfortunate. It is a term first applied to this scholar-elite by British writers during the first modern contact between China and the Western world in the eighteenth century, when the British were the leading nation in the China trade and set the tone in policy and interpretation of the Chinese to the outside world. Naturally they compared the Chinese educated class that they encountered with the upper class they knew at home, where the landed gentry dominated the countryside and official careers, and thus the name "gentry" became general usage in English literature on China.

However, the two were clearly not alike. The British gentry inherited their positions under rules of primogeniture and drew their chief income from their landed estates. The position of the Chinese scholar-gentry was not based on inheritance but on individual educational qualification, certified by academic examination and degrees. Their income was not in the main derived from inherited land but from salary, emoluments, and social service. The Chinese group was generally more educated than its British namesakes and lived a totally different life-style. In contrast to the robust, foxhunting British, the Chinese prided themselves in later times on their scholarly frailty. Scholarly families did not, as a rule, hold their exalted positions through generations, but rose from commoner status and sank back to it, depending on the presence of academic members in their ranks. A popular Chinese saying claimed that "It takes three generations for a family to rise to the top and three generations to sink down again." Statistical studies made of eleventh-to-nineteenth-century Chinese gentry have determined a 30 percent social mobility, broadly agreeing with the popular wisdom. In contrast to the British gentry, the Chinese scholar-gentry was therefore a nonaristocratic, socially mobile group. Yet, the term *scholar-gentry* or simply *gentry* has found widespread acceptance and, if properly defined, will serve our purpose.[1]

The importance of the Han emperors' choice of Confucian scholars over all other schools for service to the state cannot easily be overstated. Confucian tenets postulated a moral universe whose precepts had to be followed by the emperor if he were to maintain the Mandate of Heaven; the scholars claimed the prerogative to interpret these tenets and thus exercise an authority independent of and even morally superior to that of the emperor. It was this dual system of authority by the emperor and the scholar-gentry that accounts for the durability of the Chinese imperial order of society and state.

The acceptance of Confucianism and with it of the Confucian concept of the emperor's rule by moral suasion limited in practice the authority of the state and restricted the number of officials, leaving management of social conflicts and of most of the economy largely to private professional leadership. The same scholar-gentry that held the monopoly on state offices was to assume also the role of arbiter of affairs in society. In the absence of a judicial system of civil law, the members of the gentry handled local conflicts through arbitration; they managed community enterprises such as the building of bridges, temples, or local dikes and other public works, collecting money, organizing, and supervising labor; they wrote the local histories and presented the problems of the locality to the officials; and, in time of crisis, organized protection against bandits or natural calamities. In this double function of officials and local leaders the scholar-gentry linked state and society while providing a counterpoint to the emperor's "omnipotent" rule.

In this new political and social monopoly position the scholar-gentry defended its status and the system on which it depended against two types of developments that could threaten the economic base of the system. One was the possibility already mentioned of the growth of large landed estates. Far from becoming a landed gentry, the group of Confucian scholars was the source of a strong opposition voiced from time to time against such accumulation of landed wealth at the expense of working farmer ownership. Another threat came from the state's policy of involvement in economic enterprises in mineral production or trade monopolies in order to expand state revenues. The scholar-gentry always turned against any such dilution of the order on which its ideological and practical role depended.

This Confucian role, gradually introduced by the first Han emperors, came to full fruition under emperor Wu-ti. The most important Confucian scholar of the time was Tung Chung-shu, who combined the political and ethical theories of Confucianism with cosmological concepts of the yin and yang and Five Agents schools, fashionable at the time. These concepts, taken from interpretations of the elements working throughout the universe, gave Confucianism a broader metaphysical foundation. Tung Chung-shu is therefore known for his cosmological theories and his stress on the importance of omens, an emphasis that remained characteristic of later Confucian theory.

Even more important for the characterization of the Confucian view now being introduced into the imperial order was Tung Chung-shu's position on land reform and on state control of commerce and industry, as expressed in his memorial to the emperor, submitted around 100 B.C.: "Ownership of land should be limited so that those who do not have enough may be relieved and the road to unlimited encroachment blocked. The rights to salt and iron should revert to the people."[2] This view, often expressed by leading Confucian scholars when economic crises occurred, helped to bring about policies of land redistribution and the limitation of state encroachment in the economy that punctuated the pages of imperial history.

The reign of Emperor Wu-ti, under whom these problems came to the fore, is regarded as the high point of Han rule. The administrative and political reorganization undertaken by the emperor and his predecessors brought internal peace and prosperity and strengthened the state, enabling the emperor to initiate a policy of expansion that extended the Han empire's military control over much of East and Central Asia almost to the borders of the Roman Empire. However, the expense of this foreign expansion in turn created economic problems that remained endemic in later imperial history.

The first colonizing efforts of the Han emperors were directed toward South China. Under the Ch'in emperor, Chinese control had been extended to Canton, at that time called the state of Nan Yueh. In 135 B.C. the state of Min Yueh, today's Fukien, was taken over and incorporated into the provincial system. In 112 B.C. a revolt in Nan Yueh was suppressed and the state divided into provincial administrations. When Korea, controlled during Ch'in Shih Huang-ti's empire, again became independent under a Chinese adventurer king, Wu-ti's armies broke the rebellion in 108 B.C. The Korean king was murdered by his own ministers and the northern third of modern Korea was placed under the Chinese commandery and district system of direct administration.

The chief advance of a new Chinese imperialism turned to Central Asia. What had started as a defense against a threat from the nomadic tribes of the Mongolian plateau, the Hsiung-nu, turned into a major Chinese thrust toward the heart of Asia, opening the way to a first contact with the Roman Empire through the intermediaries of Central Asian traders.

Parallel to the unification and centralization occurring in China, a corresponding unification occurred in the steppe. While the buildup for political union in China Proper was usually a lengthy elaborate military and administrative process, steppe empires could develop rapidly from small groups into large power conglomerations, based on the political attachment of a growing number of tribes to a strong leader. Such empires could equally rapidly fall apart if that attachment ended through internal conflict or outside manipulation. These mounted nomad warriors of the steppe, leading a life of herding and warfare and used to the harsh natural and political environment of their homeland, were always a potential threat to the sedentary people of China. The nomads' mobility and their swift attacks and raids, often over great distances, terrorized their neighbors. When united they became formidable, all the more so because their rapidly shifting political alignments were unpredictable. The danger was greatest when the tribal conglomeration occurred at the time of dynastic decline or disintegration in China, permitting the invaders to establish their own rule over China as conquest dynasties.

The Hsiung-nu had first become a threat at the time of the Warring States, when the Chinese frontier states had begun to build defense walls, linked by the first emperor into the Great Wall. After the fall of Ch'in, when these steppe nomads again threatened, the first Han emperor found it advisable to follow a policy of negotiations and appeasement, placating the barbarians with subventions of silk and grain and here and there the gift of a royal princess as bride for the tribal ruler. Under Emperor Wu-ti this changed. The Han emperor felt strong enough to confront the Hsiung-nu with military arms and diplomatic interference in their political system. Military colonies had already been established at the border and the Great Wall had been extended to enclose the region of today's Inner Mongolia.

The first military campaigns remained unsuccessful. But a diplomatic venture, starting in 138 B.C., awakened Chinese interest in

Central Asia. This venture opened all the political and commercial opportunities such contacts with the peoples of these regions could furnish. The emperor learned from a Hsiung-nu prisoner about a people called the Yueh-chih, living in the western part of the steppe empire. Those people had been subjugated by the Hsiung-nu but remained restless, and the emperor sent a diplomatic mission to the Yueh-chih to propose cooperation against the Hsiung-nu.

The mission was led by an official named Chang Ch'ien who has become famous for his extraordinary perseverance, resourcefulness, and good luck in carrying out what turned out to be one of the most adventurous journeys of exploration in all Chinese history. At the outset, the envoy was captured by the Hsiung-nu and remained ten years as a prisoner guarding animal herds. Finally he escaped, but rather than returning to China, valiantly traveled westward carrying out his original mission to find the Yueh-chih tribe, finally reaching them at the Oxus River in today's Soviet Central Asia. Chang Ch'ien stayed with the tribe for one year but failed to gain their support for military cooperation with China. On his return travels to China via the Tarim basin he was again captured by the Hsiung-nu and held for another year until he again escaped, finally, after twelve years of absence, making a triumphant return with his Hsiung-nu wife and only one of his original one hundred followers. The valuable information he had gained and now transmitted became the foundation of Chinese military and commercial advances into Central Asia, including a prolonged futile attempt to reach India via Southeast Asia.

A second mission undertaken by Chang Ch'ien in 115 B.C. resumed Chinese contacts with India, Parthia, and Bactria, and later extended military campaigns established Chinese power in Central Asia and opened trade routes to the borders of the Roman Empire. Known as the silk routes, to the north and south of the Tarim basin, these links between China and the West were protected by Chinese garrisons in the oasis settlements along the way. Throughout long periods of imperial history these caravan routes remained the political and commercial pivot of Chinese power in Inner Asia, providing indirect connections and exchange with the cultures of Central Asia and the West. China was thus established as the one great power and cultural center for all of East Asia.

Such imperialist expansion was costly: The caravan routes across Central Asia brought trade, but the profits went to the merchants and the textile manufacturers and not to the state that bore the expense of military campaigns, settlements, and administration. Soon the imperial government sought to tax the new trade and also ventured into government production and trade in the vital industries of iron and salt, and the fermentation of alcohol, by setting up government monopolies in these fields. In addition, a bureau of Equalization and Standardization established government marketing offices to collect taxes-in-kind and bought staple crops at a time of low prices to sell them when prices had risen. These measures were introduced under Emperor Wu-ti in 119 B.C., in the name of protecting people from usurers, but in practice at a profit for the government. At the time the government also began to experiment with currency manipulation, first by lowering the metal content of coins, and then by creating money from stamped pieces of deerskin, only to create inflation and destabilize the money system. Although the latter measures had to be given up, the government trading and manufacturing monopolies, especially the iron and salt monopolies, remained in force and were applied again under later dynasties.

To manage these monopolies, Han Wu-ti appointed wealthy merchants familiar with the trade to official positions. Thus Sang Hung-yang, a merchant, rose to become imperial secretary in charge of finance. This policy of appointing merchants to high office aroused the strong opposition of Confucian scholars as a violation of their monopoly of officeholding and of the principle of noninterference by the state into economic affairs. Under Wu-ti the opposition remained officially silent; but shortly after his death, in 81 B.C., his successor apparently found it expedient to arrange a debate at court between his officials, headed by Sang Hung-yang, and a group of Confucian scholars opposed to the policy. A record of this famous debate on "salt and iron" has been preserved, clearly articulating the opposing positions. The government rested its argument in the necessity of raising funds for the defense of the country against frequent incursions by the Hsiung-nu, which brought great suffering to the people. The protection of the trade routes to the West, moreover, brought many new goods to China and enriched the people's life, and control of grain marketing protected the people from private exploitation. The scholars maintained that government had no business in Central Asia, should make peace with the Hsiung-nu and avoid war. The new luxuries profited only the wealthy, and government monopolies led to corruption. These "outdated" attitudes and "empty talk" by the scholars earned them the sarcastic ridicule of Sang Hung-yang.

Like all such discussion this one remained inconclusive; but the topic of this debate—the limitation of the government's activities and interference in the realm of the national economy—continued to be one of the crucial issues of the imperial system. The major part of economic life was left outside of state control. Certain commodities, like salt production and distribution, remained, however, government monopolies, though they were not handled by an official bureaucracy but rather farmed out to groups of merchants who became very wealthy through their official monopoly.

The limitation on government management of the economy did not lead to the emergence of an independent and powerful merchant class. The scholar-gentry saw to that. This newly emerging class of privileged managers of social affairs was as concerned with keeping the merchant-competitor from power as it was anxious to keep the government out of the economy. The scholar-gentry used the power of its educational monopoly not only to demand exclusive access to government office, but also to dominate the control of economic affairs in the private realm of the economy. When the dust settled over this early contention for power between merchant and scholar, the latter emerged as the power broker, enabling members of the scholar-gentry to enter merchant activities—though often under assumed names—while making it advisable for merchants to obtain scholarly degrees for some member of their families for protection in their trade. It was not only the government that became bu-reaucratic, it was society as well that was to be managed by a degree-holding group of professionals—a bureaucratic social order that was to distinguish Chinese traditional society from that of the West as well as of Japan.

The problem of inadequate state revenues resulted in short-comings in government services: neglect of public works for protection from flood and drought, of defense against outside attack or banditry, and of welfare in times of distress. At the same time the monopoly position of the scholar-gentry promoted an unfair distribution of the tax burden—overloading the common farmers with surtaxes and corvée labor while favoring the influential scholar-gentry. Together these factors created recurring explosive situations that eventually led to uprisings and were among the chief causes for the cyclical fall of Chinese dynasties.

Simplified, the often recurring chain of events may be set forth as follows: A weakening government loses authority over its bureaucracy and over society; misuse of authority increases; corruption spreads; discontented and hardpressed farmers, despairing of improving their living conditions, band together to loot and raid; as order collapses, new leadership over rebellious forces establishes new government or outsiders from the steppe use the collapse to conquer China and set up their dynasties over the empire. The cycle has come full course. Yet, all new dynasties accepted the Confucian system; there was no social revolution.

Still another factor threatened each dynastic rule; it came from inside the court. The end of feudalism had removed the challenge to the emperor's clan from regional lords; instead, defiance could come from the families of the empresses or the concubines that the emperor raised to exalted status. Usurpation of power by imperial consorts or their families has led to disintegration, decline, or fall of several dynastic houses, Chinese as well as foreign.

During the Han Dynasty, in the last century B.C., empresses were selected from the Wang clan, whose leader became regent for infant emperors. In 22 B.C. Wang Mang, the most ambitious member of the Wang clan, became the real power behind the throne and used it to initiate a major reform attempt, aimed at ending the accumulation of landownership by a few powerful families and removing the problems of financial stringency that plagued the government. Declaring all land to be the property of the state, Wang Mang prohibited the sale and purchase of land, which should be distributed equally among all farmers, who had to contribute one-ninth of their product as state tax.

Wang Mang's professed goal was the reintroduction of the nine-field system, a theoretical scheme that allegedly had been practiced under the Chou Dyansty. He advocated a return to the golden age of antiquity by restoring this imaginary system of early Chou time, under which a central field, containing the well, would be worked for the benefit of the lord. Wang Mang saw himself in the role of the Duke of Chou and used as documentary support for his policy the classical text of the *Chou-li*, which idealized the early Chou order. His quite literal imitation of this system, utilizing Chou titles, costumes, and ceremonies, earned him the ridicule of later historians and apparently that of contemporaries as well. Believing in the magical powers of the Chou ritual that he derived from his ancient texts, he declared himself, in A.D. 1, emperor of a new dynasty, the Hsin, initiated with the proper ceremonies. This theatrical farce contributed to his rapid failure and downfall.

When his measures met powerful opposition, Wang Mang canceled the agrarian plans, creating in agriculture great confusion, intensified by his edicts issued to control markets and prices. The internal crisis was aggravated by unrest among the tribes of the Hsiung-nu, treated with condescension and humiliated by the decision to give their chieftains the lesser titles that had been used in Chou time. A military campaign against the Hsiung-nu failed, and this foreign defeat contributed to the internal collapse. A peasant uprising by a secret society, the "Red Eyebrows," swept through most of East China, finding allies among members of the deposed Han Dynasty. Wang Mang's remaining armies were defeated and his capital, Ch'ang-an captured. When rebels entered the palace, Wang Mang, in full imperial regalia, was found sitting on his throne praying to Heaven— by whom he still expected to be preserved. The rebels, at first stunned by the spectacle, quickly decapitated him.

The Han Dynasty was now restored, but moved its capital to Loyang. Thereafter known as the Eastern or Latter Han Dynasty (A.D. 23–220), it gained renewed vigor, partly by accepting some of Wang Mang's reforms such as the state trade monopolies, which provided additional income, and the salt monopoly, which remained in force until modern times. References to Chou era policies also continued, although the affected imitations of costumes and ranks were given up. Most of all, land redistribution was confirmed by the new Han emperors as planned by Wang Mang, but carried out in practice by the Red Eyebrows and other peasant groups during the years of rebellion. Inner conflicts among Hsiung-nu chiefs helped to preserve the security of the northwestern frontier. These conflicts were skillfully exploited by a policy of divide and rule. By the time the Hsiung-nu had recovered politically and militarily, the Western Han Dynasty had become strong enough to resume an aggressive Central Asian policy. General Pan Ch'ao, one of the greatest Chinese military commanders, marched into Turkestan in A.D. 73 with a large army, subjugated all the oasis states, and reestablished Chinese domination over the Central Asian corridor.

This conquest reopened the caravan routes to the West. It brought on contact and trade with the Roman Empire through Central Asian intermediaries. China's primary export was silk, *seres* in Latin, a name often applied to China itself. Other products, including iron, arrows, hides, and furs are also mentioned in Western sources, while China imported, among other goods, glass and glassware. The trade also served as a channel of information about Central Asia and the Western world for China. The most important long-range impact resulting from this caravan link with Central Asia occurred in the field of religion, the importation of Buddhism into China.

According to tradition, Buddhism was first introduced to China under the Han emperor Ming-ti (A.D. 58 to 75), who is said to have seen in a dream a golden statue and was told by his advisers that this was the Buddha, appearing as a sign that he was concerned with China. Ming-ti sent to India a mission, which returned with two Indian Buddhist monks, numerous sutras and images, carried, according to legend, on a white horse. The monks settled at a monastery near Loyang, appropriately named the White Horse Monastery, and set to translating their Sanskrit and Pali texts into Chinese. However, the general impact of Buddhism during Han time remained limited. Propagated chiefly by the two monks at White Horse Monastery and a few other foreign monks from India and Central Asia, it was of some interest to the court and to small foreign monastic communities, while the intellectual life continued to be dominated by Confucian scholars.

Even before the edict of the first emperor banning and burning the non-Legalist books was repealed in 191 B.C., Confucian scholars had begun to restore their literature. Concealed books were brought out of their hiding places and earlier memorized texts were now written down. Though much remained lost, more was recovered and restored, and the classical texts were treated with renewed reverence. Previous persecution and efforts to reclaim the literary heritage strengthened the already deep-rooted Chinese tradition of respect for the written word. The search for the records of the past resulted in a renaissance of careful scholarship that developed an extraordinary skill in text criticism and evaluation. In this sense Confucian scholarship may have profited from the period of adversity. A high point was reached under Emperor Wu-ti when the emperor's academy was opened and history began to be judged by Confucian interpretation.

The standard for the treatment of history was set at that time by the most famous of all Chinese historians, Ssu-ma Ch'ien (born about 136 B.C. and died about 85 B.C.). In his *Shih Chi* (*Historical Memoirs*), a work actually planned and begun by his father, Ssu-ma Ch'ien gave an elaborate account of the whole of Chinese history from the legendary period to his own time, copying faithfully all the accounts available to him at his time.

Ssu-ma Ch'ien was uniquely qualified to undertake this extraordinary work. Born of an aristocratic family, he had acquired the best education of his time, traveled widely, both during his youth and later, covering almost all parts of the empire, recording what he saw and learned and copying documents from the libraries that he visited. At the court of Wu-ti he held the not very demanding position of court astrologer, which gave him access to the holdings of the imperial archives. He thus had unique access to all the historical sources of his time, many of which he included in his history in the original form. To this he added his own accounts of the countries and people then known to China, such as the Hsiung-nu, the kingdoms of Central Asia, Korea, and South China. He had chapters on economic policy, on the hydraulic works of his time, on music, divination, and biographies of famous men from all spheres of life. His work is a rich mine of information on all aspects of Chinese civilization of his time.

The one omission in the work as it has come down to us is the chapter on Wu-ti, during whose reign Ssu-ma Ch'ien did most of his work and suffered his great personal tragedy. He had spoken in defense of a general who had surrendered to the Hsiung-nu after a valiant stand, and for this error Ssu-ma Ch'ien was accused of trying to deceive the emperor and condemned to castration. Unable to raise the money for the alternate payment of a fine and unwilling to take his own life before completing his historical work, he underwent the humiliating punishment. It is believed that the chapter on Wu-ti that has disappeared may have been colored by the author's bitterness. Ssu-ma Ch'ien's decision to carry on his book is known from his own words in a letter to a friend. His work has served as a model for later Chinese historians, in scope, organization, accuracy, and faithfulness to his sources.

Though the Confucian scholars maintained their intellectual authority throughout, politically they lost ground again to the ever-reappearing contenders, the political cliques at the court formed by the empresses or by favored ladies, their families, and the eunuchs, and the reestablished large landowning families. The reopening of the trade routes brought great profits to wealthy merchant families. They again accumulated large landed estates at the expense of the peasantry and used their influence for connections and positions at the court. During most of the final century of Han rule the emperors were minors, and court intrigue and favoritism determined appointments. The examination system lost importance, and the quality of the civil officials declined, as indicated by the complaints of the scholars. To counter the influence of the eunuchs, the scholars formed a political association, which at first had some success in expelling some of the worst offenders among the eunuchs and their following, but the scholars lost out when the eunuchs falsely accused them of conspiracy against the child emperor, and many were arrested and executed.

The declining cycle of Han rule resumed its downward course. Corruption at the court, especially the sale of offices, led to extortion and exactions in the countryside. Small peasant-owners, unable to bear their burden, abandoned the land, banded together in secret societies that accepted Taoist magical beliefs and rituals as their organizational bond, and began to challenge the government. In A.D. 184, such a secret society, called after their head dress the "Yellow Turbans," started an almost nationwide uprising that became the prototype of many such later risings throughout Chinese imperial history. Their leader, Chang Chueh, a Taoist magician who gained his renown at first by treating victims of epidemics with cures of drinking pure water, promised his followers invulnerability in battle through protective magic and medicinal potions—a system followed by many such secret societies, down to the Boxer Rebellion at the turn of the twentieth century.

The suppression of the Yellow Turbans' rebellion became a major military problem and forced the court to recruit and supply large armies and give their commanders absolute power. These efforts also provided new opportunities for corruption at the court, and in the crisis that ensued the military leaders clashed with the eunuchs and, in A.D. 189, provoked by the assassination of their leading general, took over the palace and slaughtered all the eunuchs they could find. In effect that episode signified the end of the Han Dynasty, though nominally imperial rule continued until A.D. 221. During these last years the emperors were in the hands of one or another of competing generals who established their own regional power. Eventually the generals themselves assumed the title of emperor without, however, being able to extend their authority over the whole country.

For a time China was divided into three kingdoms, a period (A.D. 221–280) of constant warfare, stratagems, and trickery that has been romanticized in the half-historical, half-legendary novel *San-kuo yen-i*, translated into English as *The Romance of the Three Kingdoms*. The concept of the unified empire was never given up, and official Chinese historiography regards the southern kingdom Shu Han as the legitimate dynasty of the time because of the emperor's relationship to the Liu family of the Han Dynasty. In practice though, China was to remain divided for several centuries between the South, where Chinese families succeeded each other as dynastic rulers, and the North, which eventually fell into the hands of conquest dynasties from the steppe, first the Hsiung-nu and then several Turkic tribes, among whom the T'o-pa, who established in North China the (T'o-pa) Wei Dynasty (A.D. 386–534), were the most successful in the adaptation of their political and social structure to the Chinese setting.

Taken together, the four centuries of Han rule were a time in which the intellectual and artistic trends that had emerged in the years of transformation, now stimulated by the contact with Central Asia, India, the Near East, and the West, reached a cultural height expressed in all forms of art, crafts, literature, and speculative thought. Much was destroyed in the centuries of disorder that followed, but what was preserved and has now been rediscovered testifies to the greatness and splendor of that period, in which imperial China was formed and flourished. Although the cities were burned and the libraries and art collections perished, much was saved by the belief that the spirits of the dead would still enjoy the comforts and aesthetic pleasure of life as it was on earth. Art went underground. Though often looted of valuables, the tombs have preserved the beauty of the past; many treasures have come to light in recent time, but much more undoubtedly remains in the vaults of the dead.

Funds for this flourishing of the arts and crafts came in part from the court, but even more from wealthy families that had established trading houses to profit from the opening of domestic and Central Asian trade routes. This trade was in private hands, organized into caravans that required substantial capital; some trade was carried on in the form of barter or large-scale gifts. In Chinese accounts we read of thousands and tens of thousands of bales of silk and of millions of pieces of craftware that were carried by these caravans from China to Central Asia, India, Persia, and Rome, directly or through intermediaries. The manufacture of these goods was largely undertaken by the same wealthy merchant families that established textile mills, constructed mines for iron and coal, steel foundries (first mentioned in the second century B.C.), and factories for lacquerware, enamel, and other craftware that were now produced in large numbers to satisfy a growing demand, both in China and abroad. This was a time of technical advancement and inventions. In North China the cart came into general use, facilitated by the axle-size standardization ordered by the first emperor; in the newly developing rice lands of Szech'wan, the Yangtze valley, and the South, the invention of the wheelbarrow greatly facilitated work and transport.

The growth in large-scale manufacturing required a sizable labor force, composed of uprooted peasants or craftsmen who became dependent or indebted and, to a lesser degree perhaps, of convicts. Some were serving in state mines or plants, but most became dependents of large wealthy merchant families, so-called k'o, literally "guests," a term often translated as slaves, although in practice entirely different from the slavery known in Western antiquity. They could not be bought and sold, and because they needed skills in their craft and work, they were more indispensable and therefore far better off than slaves of Western antiquity and probably even nineteenth century factory workers.

Their work remained largely anonymous, though sometimes the names of artists can be found on craftware. During the latter Han Dynasty a distinction appeared between the ordinary craftsmen who remained anonymous and the scholar-artists, whether painters or poets, whose names became famous in their time and for posterity.

All fields of art and crafts flourished. At the court, among the rich houses, in the scholar-gentry families, and among the common people, Han art, crafts, and thought displayed a vitality of cultural elements and a variety of forms that covered the whole range of cultural subject matter, styles, and expressions. Chinese art traditions, enriched by foreign trends from India, Persia, and Central Asia, expanded their role in the life of all classes. At the court as well as in the provinces special agencies assembled musicians, dancers or jugglers, and artisans for entertainment of the crowd, and craftsmen for the production of decorative robes, ritual vessels, textiles, lacquerware, pottery, and weapons, setting a trend that was taken up and expanded by wealthy families. In fact, the merchants did so well that their affluence and power aroused the concern of the scholar-officials, and from time to time, edicts set taxes on boats and carts, and the merchants were restricted in the number of courtyards and buildings they could live in, and occasionally were forbidden to wear silk, ride horses, or carry arms, attempts to reduce their image and prestige. Their wealth was primarily derived from trade and manufacturing, where the profits far outreached any return that could be obtained from land rent, so that landownership was used as a form of investment for safety rather than as a source of fortune.

This prosperous life-style found its most obvious expression in architecture. The first emperor had set the style of extravagant luxury in the many palaces he had built for his life and pleasure. The Han imitated this style. Their palaces in Ch'ang-an were larger than those built in Peking 1,600 years later by the Ming Dynasty, and the Loyang palace in the center of the city had a park with artificial lakes and hills and a dreamland landscape, duplicated in other parks, where strange and rare animals and birds were kept. The beauty of these palaces and parks and the hunts and spectacles performed there were the theme of a special kind of poetry, the *fu*, a flowery and excursive form of prose poem that became fashionable at the time.

The palaces were constructed of wood, in the architectural style that remained standard throughout Chinese history and within the cultural area of East Asia under the impact of the Chinese prototype. Wooden pillars carried crossbeams, supported by brackets on which the roof structure of horizontal and vertical beams rested, rising to the ridge and covered by slanting and curved tiling. The beauty of this architecture lay not only in the form and in the proportion of each building but especially in the relationship of the various buildings to each other, of the space, the angles, and in the symmetry of yards and structures that provided an impression of harmony. The beauty was accentuated by the colors of marble, paint, lacquer, and glaze, clearly set off in the dry air of the Northwest or North China.

Constructed of wood, these marvelous buildings were terribly vulnerable to destruction not only by natural causes but often by the fury of warfare that accompanied the fall of dynasties and the years of chaos in their wake. Again and again the capital cities went up in flames, and in the ashes of the palaces perished the treasures of art and the libraries so diligently collected by scholarly and artistically inclined rulers. From what little has survived and from poetry and descriptions of the time, we know of the great wall paintings in the palaces depicting the human world as well as that of the spirits. Again, however, some of this art has survived underground, and in some wall paintings of the tombs we have magnificent examples of human figures, of animals, and of the life of the time.

It is an art of lively naturalism that was produced to entertain the dead as much as it must have served the living. Art, no longer ritual or serving to display an authority of office, came to be art for art's sake, depicting life, telling stories, and stressing the aesthetic beauty of persons or animals in motion. Modeling in clay led to the use of clay molds for the casting of bronze figures and animals. If most of the paintings were destroyed, the stone reliefs surviving in the tombs provide other examples of the lively realism of the art of the time as does the extraordinary artistic perfection of some of the masterpieces that have been uncovered from the tombs, such as the gilt-bronze lamp held by a servant girl or the galloping horse poised on a swallow. (See Plates 11 and 12.) From these figurines, the ceramics, the lacquerware, the models of houses, watchtowers, and animals, and the group scenes in clay on top of some of the pottery vessels, one gains a vivid impression of the life of the time and of its common pleasures.

The excavation of the tombs of members of the royal house brought some additional surprises. Jade then as always was a highly valued precious stone, and with the introduction of iron-cutting drills, it became possible to produce delicate and beautiful art pieces of this always highly prized gemstone. But jade was also used for members of the dynastic family for burial suits made by sewing together with gold thread thousands of thin jade plates in an ostentatious display of pomp.

During the final decades of Han rule, when government disintegrated in the warfare of the generals, destruction and death ended the time of comparable well-being for all and brought despair and the search for escape from the grim realities. This was the time when Taoism became a refuge for many of the educated, who retreated to a reclusive life in the solitude of nature, and also for the common people, who found in Taoism the magical basis for a popular religion. Thenceforth Taoism in China became more a magic religion than a philosophy.

Yet Taoism, founded as a philosophical explanation of the universe and existence, did not appear to have fully satisfied the need for an abiding faith that only a religious path could provide. Buddhism engulfed China during this period of chaos and great suffering, which it promised to overcome by the realization of the unreality of conceived things and through the path of compassion.

Eight

THE COMING OF BUDDHISM

THE DISORDER FOLLOWING the fall of the Han Dynasty, the struggle among the Three Kingdoms, and the eventual division of China into a northern half ruled by alien invaders from the steppe and a southern half under tenuous Chinese rule, brought a prolonged period of strife and destruction. The suffering of the peasantry, the growing luxury of commercial life, rising prices, and currency depreciation led to a dangerous contrast between the extravagances of the newly rich and the impoverishment of the farming population. Insurrections and banditry disturbed the country, weakening resistance against increasing tribal invasions from the north. These invasions came from all sides of the northwestern frontier; from Mongolia, a proto-Mongol tribe; from Turkestan, the Hsiung-nu, and from Tibet, the Ch'iang. They fought each other in turn until most of the North was united under a semi-Turkish group called (T'o-pa) Wei (A.D. 336–534). In central China, the government was driven south of the Yangtze River, and here under military leaders a number of southern dynasties, established by great landed families, followed in succession, ruling one or another part of this large region. The invaders of the North never succeeded in crossing the Yangtze, perhaps partly because the terrain of the South was less suitable for cavalry. After a decisive defeat at the Huai River in A.D. 383 the northern invaders abandoned the effort, and China remained divided into north and south. The continuous warfare and the social and political decline led to a challenge to Confucianism, the tenets of which were based on the concept of a harmonious society and a central state. As heretofore Confucian scholars served various dynasties and kingdoms. But now they were on the defensive. For the common people, the campaigns and battles brought frequent destructions and great suffering. For the elite, the great expectations previously held for a unified empire were shattered, and Confucian precepts regarding the eventual triumph of virtuous government seemed absurd.

A critical text of the day ridicules the Confucian scholar and his myopic attitudes:

> Have you never seen a louse, living in a pair of trousers? He
> flees from a deep seam and hides in a break in the padding:
> he regards this as a good home. When he travels he dares
> not leave the seam, when he moves he dares not come out of
> the trousers. He feels that he has attained a well regulated
> life. When he is hungry he bites a man and regards this as
> an inexhaustible food supply. But flames overrun the hills, fire
> spreads, villages and towns are burned up. And all the lice
> will perish in the trousers, being unable to get out. As for
> your *chün-tzu*, living in a world of his own, how does he
> differ from a louse living in a pair of trousers?[1]

In this long period of despair, cynicism, and escapism, intellectual interest in Taoism revived and Buddhism, a foreign religion, gained a foothold for the first time both among the mass of the people and among the educated classes.

Yet the revival of Taoism and the powerful intrusion of a new religion did not signify a complete break with the past, for in spite of the failure to guarantee a workable order, Confucian ideals and basic principles were not abandoned. The ruling houses of both the North and the South upheld their claims to the heavenly mandate, and the concept of a united empire was never lost. Nor were the social ethics, the mainstay of the Confucian philosophy, challenged in principle. It was disillusionment with the practical failure of the system that led to escape from the troubles of the time in the promise of magic answers, philosophic acquiescence, and religious consolation.

Taoism was ideally suited to express the resignation of the educated class, arising from its failure to stem the tide of political decline. The idea of nonaction, of accepting the natural course of events, became a practical necessity. The Taoist saying, "What is difficult to acquire in the world is neither wealth nor glory but a sense of contentment," reflected the spirits of the times when the ambitions of the elite were so bitterly disappointed.

The educated developed a new transcendentalism in neo-Taoist thought, and a movement back to nature appeared among the sons of the wealthy. Some started a fashion of letting their hair grow long; there was heavy use of alcohol, and nudity became a vogue of the time.

This was the time when educated men retreated to places of natural solitude, as exemplified by the "Seven Sages of the Bamboo Grove," who met at a renowned place of nature north of the capital Loyang where "they all revered and exalted the Void and Non-action and disregarded the rites and law. They drank wine to excess and disdained the affairs of this world," according to their Confucian critics. The Seven Sages were all well-known statesmen and generals whose individual stories have remained famous in Chinese history. Many others joined *ch'ing t'an* or "pure conversation" groups for refined, witty, and philosophical free talk, engaged in poetry contests, and prided themselves on disregarding conventions.

The deflection of intellectual activity from the political scene to an enjoyment of nature's harmony led to a renewed flourishing of the arts, particularly the art of painting. When Chinese scholars from the North emigrated to the South to escape the barbarian conquest, they were deeply impressed by the scenic charm of the green mountains, the lakes, and the river valleys of a landscape so different from that of the plains and the barren, blue-violet loess mountains of the drier North. (See Plate 13.) Combined with the Taoist glorification of nature, this new interest led to an advancement of landscape painting from a secondary role as background for religious figures and portraits to a place of primary importance in Chinese painting.

Several texts of the time describe the painter's fascination with and enjoyment of nature and its meaning to him. Landscape painting, in Chinese, "mountains and water" painting, became much more than a matter of skillful representation of physical reality, rather a matter of sensing and representing the spirit believed to be manifested in nature. As one painter said of himself:

> and so I live in leisure and nourish my vital power. I drain
> clean the wine cup, play the lute, lay down the picture of

scenery, face it in silence, and, while seated, travel beyond the four borders of the land, never leaving the realm where nature exerts her influence, and alone responding to the call of wilderness. Here the cliffs and peaks seem to rise to soaring heights, and groves in the midst of clouds are dense and extend to the vanishing point. Sages and virtuous men of far antiquity come back to live in my imagination and all interesting things come together in my spirit and in my thoughts. What else need I do? I gratify my spirit, that is all. What is there that is so important than gratifying the spirit?[2]

Another painter of the time wrote:

Physical appearances are based upon physical forms, but the mind is changing and ever active. But spirit is invisible, and therefore what it enters into does not move. The eye is limited in scope, and therefore what it sees does not cover all. Thus by using one small brush, I draw the infinite vacuity (the universe in its undifferentiated state), and by employing the clear vision of my small pupils to the limit, I paint a large body. With a curved line I represent the Sung mountain ranges. With an interesting line I represent (the mythical mountain) Fang-chang. A swift stroke will be sufficient for the T'ai-hua Mountain, and some irregular dots will show a dragon's nose. (In the latter), the eyebrows, forehead, and cheeks all seem to be a serene smile, and (in the former), the lonely cliff is so luxuriant and sublime that it seems to emit clouds. With changes and variations in all directions, movement is created, and by applying proportions and measure, the spirit is revealed. After this, things like temples and shrines, and boats and carriages are grouped together according to kind, and creatures like dogs, horses, birds, and fish are distinguished according to their shape. This is the ultimate of painting.

Gazing upon the clouds of autumn, my spirit takes wings and soars. Facing the breeze of spring, my thoughts flow like great, powerful instruments and the treasure of priceless jade cannot match (the pleasure) of this. I unroll pictures and examine documents, I compare and distinguish the mountains and seas. The wind rises from the green forest, and foaming water rushes in the stream. Alas! Such paintings cannot be

achieved by the physical movements of the fingers and the
hand, but only by the spirit entering into them. This is the
nature of painting.[3]

Taoist philosophy had more to offer to these times of disarray
than philosophical escapism or stimulation to art. Its practitioners
claimed to have the answer to the problems of life that Confucianism
ignored. The mystical references to the Taoist texts, the *Tao-Teh
Ching* and *Chuang-tse*, were interpreted and extended by Taoist
magicians into claims that through mysterious and occult means they
could obtain immortality. At a lower level they would heal illness
and practice alchemy to make gold. Astrology, divination, and alchemy
became combined into a cult that served the religious need of the
ordinary people at a time when Confucianism, the statecraft of a
rational worldly order, disregarded all questions of life after death,
indeed any form of religious beliefs.

In the second century A.D. one such Taoist magician, Chang
Ling, famous for his magic and the mysterious content of his ideas,
became the founder of a Taoist religious organization. He was given
by his followers the title Heavenly Teacher, a title that became
hereditary and has been referred to colloquially as the Taoist "pope."
Off and on, imperial patronage gave support to this Taoist religion,
but it remained mostly a belief adhered to by the common uneducated
people and looked down upon by the educated elite. Some modern
scholars have referred to this dichotomy between the literary learning
of Confucianism and the Taoist experiments in alchemy, as well as
their study of medical plants and the internal alchemy of the body,
study that the Confucians disdained, as an explanation for the thwarted
development of modern science in China.

As a popular religion, however, Taoism had obvious limitations.
The Taoist refuge in nature and in magic provided no emotional
release, no true religion. Even though it copied extensively from
Buddhism in its monasticism and organization, it could not compete
with the far more profound and philosophically founded religious
faith that was entering China at this very time from its Indian
homeland.

Buddhism had reached China earlier during the latter Han
period through two Indian Buddhist scholars and their texts brought
to the White Horse Monastery in A.D. 67. During the Han Dynasty,

however, the new religion was of interest chiefly to certain Chinese scholars and emperors, and did not affect the thinking or feelings of large numbers of people, let alone enter statecraft. After the fall of Han, however, and under the chaotic conditions that followed, the Buddhist religion became a major intellectual and emotional force and a real challenge to Confucianism.

As noted, Buddhism entered China through two main routes; one through Central Asia and the other overland and by sea, from the south. It was mainly the Central Asian caravan route that gave us the many historical accounts and archeological findings. This route from Turkestan to Turfan, Tunhuang, and along the Kansu corridor penetrated deeper into the barbarian-ruled North than the culturally more Chinese South of the country. In the North, Buddhism served a double purpose, strengthening the emperor's ideological sanction as well as Chinese officials' authority, and moved in as a new source of magical power, a non-Chinese alternative; monks became useful officials, rulers became patrons and believers. For the impoverished North Chinese people, Buddhism became a refuge from despondency and a source of charity affecting the entire population, and thereby gaining a mass following. Throughout the land there was an orgy of temple building, and monastic life flourished. In the South, Buddhism remained at first chiefly an exercise of the elite in competition with, but not to the exclusion of, Confucianism. In fact Confucianism was strengthened and enriched by metaphysical and cosmological concepts borrowed from Buddhism, while in turn it added to the sinicization of Buddhist beliefs. Both in the North and the South Buddhism changed the social landscape. Eventually its all-Chinese pervasive impact contributed to reunification of the country. Later when Confucianism reasserted itself as the administrative foundation of a unified state, Buddhism remained as a cultural-religious factor, patronized by many rulers, flourishing in art and architecture.

This is not the place for a detailed treatment on Buddhism, but to show its impact on Chinese thought and culture, Buddhism's main tenets and schools will have to be traced. In many ways Buddhism was contrary to Confucianism, which was of this world and stressed family cohesion, while Buddhism was otherworldly and stressed the life of the monk and the nun. The Confucian concept of reason and of a moral order of human affairs as part of a moral universe was opposed to the mystical world of Buddhist religion, with its concept of void or emptiness and the unreality of the phenomenal world.

The essence of the teachings of Buddha is stated in the Four Noble Truths and the Eightfold Path. The Four Noble Truths are:

1. Life is inevitably sorrowful—birth, illness, age, and death are all unavoidable, and the quest is to find liberation from the suffering of this existence.
2. This sorrow arises from the sensual cravings and desires that bind man to this existence and to the chain of rebirth.
3. Liberation from this continued suffering through rebirth can be achieved through ending this craving.
4. Liberation can be obtained through proper moral conduct and enlightenment by following the Eightfold Path.[4]

The Buddhist explanation of existence and of liberation differs fundamentally from Jewish, Christian, or Islamic concepts of a unity of soul and of a deity. In Buddhism all things are composite and transient. The human craving for and clinging to samsara, the chain of existence, is due to a cosmic ignorance, including a delusion of selfhood. Everything perceived through the senses is impermanent. All beings and indeed all things, spiritual and material, have no self-entity, but they are a conglomeration that is composed of physical atomic particles and psychic unreducible moments, altogether "five aggregates"—*skanda*—that shape and reshape all temporary reality.[5] Liberation from the chain of rebirth and of suffering can be gained through enlightenment, a state of mind reached through moral conduct and meditation, which transcends the impermanence and unreality of the world of phenomena and leads to a larger essence, a supreme bliss, undefined and indescribable, the state of nirvana. The historical Buddha, his teachings, called Dharma, and the *sangha*, the "community of the faithful" are the Three Jewels of the Buddhist faith.

The Buddhism that was introduced to China had already gone through half a millennium of transformation since its genesis in India; its founder, the historical Gautama Buddha, lived in the sixth century B.C. (ca. 563–483 B.C.). During these intervening centuries

Buddhism had developed into several major schools and gained a rich philosophical and metaphysical tradition. The chief division in concept and organization is between Mahayana and Theravada Buddhism. Mahayana (Sanskrit) means the "larger vessel"; Theravada, the "teaching of the elders."[6] Theravada, the historically older school, moved to South and Southeast Asia, the countries of Ceylon (Sri Lanka) and Indochina. Mahayana Buddhism travelled along the Central Asian caravan routes to China, and from there eventually to Korea and Japan. At the beginning of the sixth century it also found a main sanctuary in Tibet.

These two main branches of the faith differ not in basic concepts but in the stress they place on the means toward gaining salvation. Theravada stresses learning and monastic discipline in applying the moral code. Mahayana claims a broader interpretation of the Buddhist tenets, which incorporates the monastic principles and practices of the older school but goes beyond them in stressing the importance of faith, prayer, emotional experience, and revelation through meditation in gaining enlightenment. Ontological Mahayana Buddhism follows the teachings of the great Indian philosopher Nagarjuna of the Madhyamika school—the school of the "middle-way"—who postulated that not only the empirical world is unreal, but so are dharma and samsara, which are all part of the cosmic flux. Beyond this empirical world is the void or emptiness that is the essence of all and incorporates everything. This doctrine of the emptiness or void is one of the two major tenets of the Mahayana school. It has been compared with the Taoist interpretation of Tao, and the parallel with Taoist philosophy undoubtedly facilitated the wide impact of Mahayana Buddhism in China.

Of equally great impact was the other major tenet of Mahayana Buddhism, the stress on the concept of bodhisattva. A bodhisattva—*bodhi* meaning "enlightenment" and *sattva* "being or essence," is an awakened being who, after having reached the state of enlightenment and ready to leave the suffering of continued existence and to enter nirvana, chooses voluntarily to be reborn out of compassion for all sentient beings in order to help in their liberation. This image of voluntary sacrifice for the liberation of all beings has had a tremendous appeal throughout East Asia and has become inseparably linked with Mahayana Buddhist religion. In Tibet it has become personified in the figures of living beings—the so-called Living Buddhas. (See Plate 14.)

A bodhisattva is believed to possess the two chief qualities, wisdom and compassion. Wisdom is the insight into the causality of all action as well as the deeper meaning behind the unreality of empirical experience. Compassion is the boundless feeling of charity for all sentient beings, of deepest and totally self-effacing concern for their lives and dignity and for their liberation from suffering. Those who trust in the bodhisattvas' guidance must share this selfless desire for the liberation of all sentient beings, desire that alone leads to one's own enlightenment and liberation. All sentient beings share the same path and there is the potential of Buddhahood in all of them.

Since in Buddha's teaching there is no selfhood, no individual soul, rebirth is explained in Mahayana Buddhism as a continuance of a stream of spiritual energy. The image is that of a river that continuously emits and collects water without changing its identity. It is also that of a flame that burns out when the wood is consumed but jumps over to a new life on a new base. In the case of the reincarnation of a bodhisattva, what moves on is the omniscience that results from wisdom and the compassion that is part of it. It is this energy that is part of the essence behind reality.

Over the course of time, under the influence of Mahayana Buddhism, there was created a whole pantheon of religious figures. Indian concepts of the ubiquitousness of the deity led to the idea of many Buddhas in many forms. Before the historical Buddha there were aeons of Buddhas, all beings who had moved into the state of bliss. There will be future Buddhas and there are many bodhisattvas, who assume the role of saintly beings, objects of prayers for help in gaining liberation. Buddhist legends and the emanations of emotional conditions and experiences also became transfixed and depicted in Buddhist art. One of the many Buddha figures in this tradition is Maitreya, the coming Buddha of the next cosmic age. Another is Vairocana, the primordial Buddha, and these two are frequently represented in Buddhist temples together with the historical Buddha as a triarchy of the paramount figures of the Buddha pantheon.

Buddhist influence on Chinese intellectual life and art is massive. It can be seen in the development of Chinese sculpture and landscape painting, and also in philosophy and in social concepts. As in other

great cultural adaptations, Buddhism became transformed and sinicized. In art perhaps the greatest infusion was Buddhist religious
sculpture and Buddhist influence on all sculptural tradition in China.
In this art form the transformation is of special interest as an
exceptionally demonstrable case of Eurasian connection.

Buddhism in India at first did not admit representation of the
Buddha or other holy figures. The first symbols of Buddhism were
the wheel, representing the wheel of law that the Buddha set in
motion, and the deer, from the deer park where the Buddha preached.
A willingness to represent the Buddha in human form developed
centuries after the death of Gautama.

It is not certain whether the first Buddha images developed in
India from Indian iconography or originated from outside models
brought to India through the Greek artists who followed Alexander
the Great's campaign to the borders of India. In the Northwest
Indian-Central Asian border region of Gandhara, early Buddha figures
show the transition from a Greek Apollo figure to that of an Oriental
Buddha in posture, clothing, and hair style, and the first Chinese
Buddha figures are stylistically linked to the Gandhara models. (See
Plate 15.) Those early images were succeeded by Buddha figures that
reflect the influence of Central Asian traditions. (See Plate 16.) The
stylistic features are most clearly expressed in the Buddhist cave
figures along the Central Asian silk route where both small and huge
Buddha sculptures were carved. They were made under the auspices
of pious patrons as objects of worship for travelers seeking protection
and solace on their long and dangerous journeys. These magnificent
and inspiring figures from Bamiyan in Afghanistan to Tunhuang,
Yünkang, or Lungmen, in China, are massive, pious, and impersonal.
They express an inner, otherwordly, and spiritual power, testifying
to the deep religious fervor of the time. (See Plate 17.)

This religious cave art in China, begun in the fourth century
A.D. and added to century by century until the time when China
was reunified under central dynastic rule, was the link that bound
the new religion in China to its Indian and Central Asian origin.
In China Proper, Buddhism changed the landscape. The temples and
monasteries—in Chinese architectural style—adorned the cities and
studded the rural scene. Pagodas, containing shrines for relics or
sacred texts, became almost symbolic of the Chinese landscape.

By the fourth century Buddhism had become a Chinese religion interpreted and spread by Chinese monks and scholars, who founded their own schools with explications of the transmitted teachings and scripts. The continual search for Buddhist scriptures and interpretations led back to India. A famous Chinese pilgrim of the time, Fa-hsien, traveled in A.D. 399 through Central Asia to India at a time when Buddhism was still thriving along the caravan route, though weakening in India, where the traveler stayed for several years. He returned to China via Ceylon and Java after fifteen years of absence and settled in Nanking to work on the translation of the many texts he had brought home.

All forms of Chinese art were profoundly affected by Buddhist influence. Buddhist statuary became a major impetus to the new flourishing of Chinese sculpture. The pious, impersonal, massive statues of Buddhas and disciples changed to elegant portrayals of religious figures and of portraits of monks, abbots, and secular personalities. The same transformation took place in the painting of human beings as well as of religious scenes. Buddhist landscape painting, originally used as a background to religious scenes, exerted a strong influence on the great Chinese landscape painting of these creative centuries. Along with it the rich tomb art of ceramic figures, both animal and human, is related to the great stimulation exerted by the foreign religion; and Buddhist sinicization and incorporation into Chinese culture was speeded by the fact that in India, the land of its origin, it had by this time practically disappeared as a major religion. When Confucianism reasserted itself as the administrative foundation for a unified state, Buddhism remained as a cultural factor, patronized by many rulers, flourishing in art and architecture.

The influence of Buddhism had some negative aspects as well. The monasteries, as protected establishments, became refuges for undesirable people. The wealth the monasteries acquired led to waste and corruption and eventually to political persecution that ended the Buddhist role in the polity. But Buddhism continued to serve an emotional need of the common people who sought their happiness and prosperity by praying to a new image of Maitreya Buddha, the popular form of the laughing plump Buddha, the Buddha of good fortune.

The many sects that emerged within Chinese Buddhism stressed chiefly faith, prayer, and emotional commitment as the way to salvation.

One sect in particular ultimately became dominant: the Amitabha cult, initiated in the early fifth century by two of the most renowned Buddhist monks in China, the Chinese monk Hui-yuan and Kumarajiva, an Indian monk from Central Asia. Amitabha, the Buddha of Shining Light, dwelt in the Pure Land or Western Paradise, a sphere without defilement where all those who believed in the Buddha were to be reborn. Hui-yuan established the Amitabha cult in A.D. 402 when, together with his followers, both monks and laymen, he called on the Buddha Amitabha and vowed to aspire to be reborn in his Western Paradise.

Kumarajiva (who included in his extensive translation work the Amida sutra) provided the textual foundation for the dominant school. Its essence was faith in the saving power of Buddha helping those who "with a believing heart rejoice for but a single moment of consciousness and with minds intent on being reborn in His land, shall be immediately able to go there and be reborn and stay there without return."[7] Only those who had committed the five cardinal sins of Buddhism or violated the Ten True Laws were to be excluded. The pure heart is gained by these believers through their great compassion for all sentient beings. This compassion leads to the desire of using their own merits and diverting them to all beings so that they may be reborn in that Pure Land. The Amitabha cult, introduced during the latter part of the north/south division, became the central creed of Chinese Buddhism during the following centuries. It was at the core of the strong religious movement that characterized this time and carried over into the period of the Sui and T'ang dynasties, enriching Chinese art, architecture, and intellectual tradition, and providing a religious faith that had been missing in the philosophies and local cults of the earlier Chinese civilization.

Nine

REUNIFICATION:

The Sui and T'ang Dynasties

THE DYNASTIES OF the period of division, both in the South and the North, were primarily military dictatorships, founded by generals or by the leading families of invading tribal groups. Such military conquests in the North were facilitated by the emergence of warrior families, basing their authority on the military ability to unite and lead tribal units in the nomadic steppe societies. Once assimilated to Chinese settled life in North China, these upper strata of the tribal world eventually formed a hereditary aristocracy of leading families, intermarried with Chinese and among each other, and accepted Chinese political and social concepts. They formed Chinese governments but were handicapped by the rivalry of their peers and the threat of the cousins from the steppe, ever covetous of a share of the Chinese spoils.

The Sui Dynasty (A.D. 589 to 618) was also founded as a military coup by General Yang Chien, a member of a northern reigning family who took first the northern capital Ch'ang-an, but went on to take Nanking in 589, removing the last of the southern dynasties and unifying the country again.

What distinguished the coup of Yang Chien, who assumed the ruling title of Sui Wen-ti, from other such military takeovers, was his ability to establish a state structure that went far beyond simple military control. By his successful administrative measures within and military action without, Emperor Wen-ti succeeded in overcoming both the threats from competition in the country and tribal aggressors on the borders. Internally he sought broader support by redistributing land to the peasants and reducing the land tax. He also modified the legal code, abolishing again the punishment of castration and limiting the application of capital punishment. More important still, he reestablished a civil bureaucracy. He and his successor reintroduced a system of examinations as the basis for a reinstituted civil service administration.

To stave off the dangers from across the steppe border, Emperor Wen-ti extended the Great Wall defense system by more than 200 miles toward the southwest. He chose Ch'ang-an as his primary capital, not only because it had been his home base but clearly also because of its strategic location for frontier defense, even though the center of Chinese development had in the meantime moved southward. Ch'ang-an was rebuilt in an imposing style, and there was a secondary capital at Loyang; thus both these historical capitals of previous dynasties were again to become the political focus of the empire.

However, the distance between these political centers and the new key economic area of the lower Yangtze area raised its own problems. By this time, the weight of population density and of economic production had shifted to the South. The North, impoverished by frequent warfare, had suffered population decline, irrigation works had been neglected, and what once had been the center of Chinese life came to depend on the economic support of the rich rice producing areas of the lower Yangtze.

The grave problem of the long distance between the political and the economic center of the country was solved by Emperor Wen-ti and his successor by the construction of a great canal to link Hangchow, south of the Yangtze, with the Yellow River and, through its tributaries, the Lo and Wei rivers, with the capitals of Sui. From there another canal dug across the North China plain linked the capitals with the region of the modern city Peking. This great canal system, the predecessor of the Grand or Imperial Canal built by the Mongol Dynasty seven centuries later, was the first of its kind in China and rightly added to the lasting fame of the Sui Dynasty. Along its course the emperors established relay posts and large granaries to facilitate the transport system. This canal made it possible not only for the Sui Dynasty but also for the succeeding T'ang Dynasty to maintain the political and cultural center at Ch'ang-an in the Wei Valley, although the economic hub of China and much of its cultural sophistication had moved southward to the Yangtze and beyond.

The Sui canal system, however, was never easy to operate. The canal itself, 130 feet wide, worked well enough; but on the last stretch of the route, upward on the Yellow River and the Wei River, the strong currents and shifting sandbars of high sediment made transport troublesome and expensive. The importance of Loyang as a secondary capital was attributable to the shorter distance for upriver transport of the rice, silk, and other commodities, necessities for the imperial court and the armies.

Wen-ti took a personal interest in the details of his administration and the working of his justice system and stressed frugality so that, by the time of his death, his son and successor Yang-ti received a well-filled treasury.

Yang-ti, the second Sui emperor (605–617), has been treated badly by Chinese historians. Because under his rule the Sui Dynasty collapsed, he had to bear the onus of the Confucian dictum that it was the emperor's lack of virtue that brought about the fall of a dynasty. Thus he has been characterized as a "megalomaniac" who, through his "excessive extravagance, unnecessary and unsuccessful wars with Korea and tyrannous misgovernment,"[1] destroyed the work of his prudent father and caused the downfall of the Sui. In fact, he appears to have been a refined, generous person who had a high regard for scholarship and literature and was responsible for many of the great accomplishments of Sui rule. Sui Yang-ti was the main architect of the great canal system, begun under his father. It was Yang-ti who reintroduced the examination system, reopened the university and provincial schools, invited renowned scholars to the court, and founded libraries and museums. He supported Central Asian trade, admitted large numbers of foreign merchants to his capitals, tolerated their religions, and received the traditional trade and tribute missions from more than two dozen states in Inner and Central Asia and even from Japan. He was a devotee of the arts, especially of music, and gathered native and foreign musicians, singers, and dancers at the capital, setting a trend that was copied by his officials and the merchants. New musical instruments, the lute, the harp, and the bamboo flute were introduced to China, and music of a new type was adopted at the court, soon becoming very popular with the emperor, his officials, and the rapidly growing urban population. A modern, sophisticated and artistic life-style was adopted and reached full fruition later under the T'ang Dynasty.

The Sui Dynasty came to an end when Yang-ti, hoping to increase his prestige, mounted against Korea two massive, expensive, and unsuccessful campaigns that brought forth a financial crisis. Increased tax burdens caused peasant unrest that provided the opportunity for another coup d'état, the end of Sui and the establishment of what became the most famous of all Chinese dynasties, the T'ang Dynasty.

The T'ang Dynasty (A.D. 618–907) was founded by Li Yüan, a general stationed at T'aiyuan and in charge of the defense of the Northwest border. The Li family, of partly Turkish origin, was the strongest of several military cliques contending in their aim of seizing the imperial throne at this time of general unrest. The real instigator of the coup and the spirit and directing force behind its success was Li Yüan's son Li Shih-min, who became Emperor T'ai-tsung and was responsible for the lasting renown of the T'ang Dynasty.

In his policies Emperor T'ang T'ai-tsung continued and brought to fruition what the Sui emperors had successfully begun; he instituted agrarian reform based on land distribution; reorganized the administration under a hierarchical civil service; reopened trade; introduced a legal order; promoted education and encouraged literature, art, and music. On this foundation the T'ang empire experienced its greatest expansion into Central, North, and Southeast Asia.

The land reform was basic. Again and again new dynasties had attempted to halt the accumulation of landownership by large landlord families and redistributed the land to the tiller not only to prevent peasant discontent and insurgencies but, more immediately, to preserve the tax base on which the imperial government depended. The method of equal distribution of land under the T'ang government in A.D. 624 permitted giving each peasant family enough land to feed itself and pay taxes. Land distribution was graded according to the number of adult males. Smaller units were allotted to the old, the ill, widows, and other noncultivators. About one-fifth of the land, houses and gardens, mulberry trees, and hemp fields were regarded as permanent possessions to be inherited within the family and could not be sold. From these land units property taxes were to be paid in silk or hemp. In times of bad harvests caused by weather or natural catastrophes the tax in kind was to be reduced or suspended.

But corvée labor, which maintained local waterworks or building of defense walls or other structures, was cancelled only in dire emergencies.

All the agricultural reform and tax system depended on an exact census and cadastral survey of people and land. In times of decline, when military families, eunuchs, and favorites at the court determined appointments and local rule, these elaborate measures were bound to fall into disarray; but any lasting rule depended on a return to a bureaucratic structure made up of professionals, the Confucian scholar-officials.

In their systematic reorganization the T'ang divided the country into ten provinces, later extended to eighteen. These were subdivided into prefectures and, at the local level, into districts (hsien), the smallest governmental unit in China and the point of contact between government and the people, the latter led by the local scholar-gentry. The number of court-appointed officials actually remained quite small; one magistrate at the local level handled a district of many thousands— later up to 200,000 people—but these officials cooperated with the scholar-gentry, their peers in local social leadership. The imperial officials at all levels were appointed; the secretarial staff of the district magistrates and of the higher officials were personally selected and paid by the officials in question. Drawing on previous dynasties' precedents, a strong bureaucratic structure was thus fully developed and perfected under the T'ang.

The T'ang functionally divided the central government into six ministries—civil affairs, finance, rites, army, justice, and public works— a system that lasted until modern times. A chancellery and a grand secretariat dealt with imperial decrees. A council of state met with the emperor for policy decisions.

Among several other offices, the court of censors—first introduced as far back as Ch'in—was the most important. It served as a supervisory agency over the administration but also over the emperor himself, and was charged with watching over governmental practices, investigating complaints, and checking on corruption, acting as guardian of the Confucian principles that the government had to uphold. The censors could, and sometimes did, accuse the emperor of violation of these higher principles, but the emperor in turn theoretically had the power to accuse the censor of false accusations, which could lead to the censor's execution. Such action would, however, be most damning to the emperor's reputation and would therefore not easily be taken. A precarious balance was thus maintained between the two powers of government, the emperor's actual supreme authority and the scholar-gentry's reference to the higher rules of Confucian ethics as represented in the person of the censors.

To rebuild this professional officialdom, and its source, the scholar-gentry, which also provided the leadership in the communities essential for the working of the system, T'ang emperor T'ai-tsung and his successors expanded and strengthened the examination system and enlarged the imperial college at the capital Ch'ang-an. Eight thousand scholars were enrolled in this institution, upon which the emperor frequently bestowed special favors. The emphasis on this Confucian system of government was all the more remarkable because it came at a time when Buddhism as a religion and philosophy reached its most flourishing period.

The ethics of the Confucian code, the *li*, or "rites," remained the moral basis of the political and social order. But as ever since the time of the first emperor, law, that is, criminal law, remained the last resort of government authority. The T'ang code, first proclaimed in 624, has been preserved in its entirety down to present time. It linked punishment to crime not only on the basis of the act committed but also in regard to the perpetrator's relation to the object of the crime. It provided models of crimes and permitted punishment by analogy. Punishments were harsh, consisting of strokes with a cane, strokes with a bamboo stick, forced labor, exile, strangulation, and decapitation. The number of death penalties, however, was reduced and the punishment of castration was once more abolished. Other legal regulations were issued as special laws, decrees, and promulgations at the local level by the district magistrates, who combined the functions of prosecutor and judge.

This political and social reorganization was paralleled by a restoration of China's military power. In contrast to the civil structure, which was based on Confucian professionals, the products of education for a civil service career, the military leadership continued to be drawn from military families of the Northwest and their troops who provided the best units of the armies. To these descendants of the tribal warriors of steppe warfare, the military art had remained a prime interest and professional choice. The early T'ang emperor was himself one of them, respected by all for his military prowess and ability. As long as the emperor was accepted by these military commanders as their superior, his power was safe despite the dualism of the political-military structure that he had to dominate. In later times, however, when the emperor was no longer a recognized military leader, the different background and independent power of the northwest generals remained a source of danger for the T'ang as well as later dynasties. Under T'ang T'ai-tsung it was this military leadership that made possible Chinese conquests of Central Asia, Korea, and the South, and through them a vast expansion of the Chinese empire.

The core of the T'ang army, its aggressive force, was cavalry. It was the horse that made the steppe people so dangerous to the settled Chinese, and it was the horse that enabled the Chinese to carry the war into the steppe. Foot soldiers could garrison the strong places, but the vast armies of hundreds of thousands that reconquered Central Asia were made up mostly of cavalry.

The use of cavalry in Chinese warfare was of course not new, but the number of horses mounted in previous campaigns had never been so great. This was the result of a program of horse breeding by the T'ang emperors that raised the number of horses available from a few thousand at the beginning of the dynasty to some seven hundred thousand, according to official count. They were bred on large studfarms in the provinces of the Northwest and in Szech'wan, where the main armies were organized. In later times, when these regions were again lost to tribal invasions, Chinese military defense against tribal invaders became precarious.

By this time the little Mongolian horse that had been the common type used by the steppe people had been crossbred with the taller animals from Central Asia and Arabia. From the descriptions and the art of the time we know something of the taste for beautiful horses that were used in war as well as in the daily life of the elite in the capital and in the provincial centers. Famous in art are the eight chargers of the emperor T'ai-tsung that have been immortalized in the bas reliefs from his funerary complex, as well as the magnificent pottery "T'ang horses" found in so many tombs of the period. (See Plate 18.) Not only men, but also women rode on horses, and the game of polo was popular among both sexes. Graceful figurines of the polo-playing court ladies have been found among the many funerary statuettes uncovered in our time. (See Plate 19.)

Once prepared, T'ai-tsung and his successors went on the offensive against the Turkish tribes and the kingdoms of Central Asia, against Manchuria and Korea, and against Annam in the South. By the end of the seventh century, China under the T'ang Dynasty had extended its control over Korea and Manchuria, North Vietnam, and all along the Central Asian corridor to Samarkand, Tashkent, and Bukhara as far as the Tigris, and into Northern India, establishing administrative districts or military protectorates to incorporate in one form or another this far-flung territory into the Chinese empire. The T'ang empire thus became the greatest power in Asia, and its cultural and political influence extended far beyond its military control.

The reopening of the caravan routes to the West, the sea route to India, and the expansion into Manchuria and Korea opened China to contacts with the civilizations of Asia and the Mediterranean and in turn brought Chinese cultural, philosophical, and political influence that would affect in differing degrees the history and culture of East and Central Asia. The T'ang capital of Ch'ang-an, then the largest metropolis anywhere on the globe, was the center of this cosmopolitan culture. As a trading center it became a city of great wealth, not only for the court, but also for a large and growing middle class. It attracted merchants, artists, religious leaders, refugees, and political missions from many lands.

Thousands of artists are said to have provided culture and entertainment at the capital. Female singers and dancers lived in special quarters and served not only the court but could be hired as well by wealthy families and visitors. A new music with a seven-tone scale and new musical instruments introduced from Central Asia and other foreign lands became popular among all circles. New dances and artistic performances became favorites at the homes of the wealthy. At popular festivities people wore masks and dressed up in fantastic costumes, and men and women mingled on freer terms than ever before or later in Confucian society. The emperor, orthodox Confucian in his reorganization and conduct of government, was tolerant of all religions and philosophies.

Buddhism was of course foremost among these religions. By now it had become thoroughly sinicized, leaving a lasting impact on Chinese popular beliefs as well as on Confucian philosophy itself. This was the age of the emergence of the great Buddhist sects that spread from China to Korea and Japan. In A.D. 629 the Chinese

Buddhist monk and great Sanskrit scholar Hsüan-tsang went on a pilgrimage to India, a prolonged dangerous and adventurous journey that has become the theme of popular tales and novels. Leaving despite an imperial order to remain in China, the monk traveled overland through Turkestan, spent two years in Kashmir, five years at the Buddhist center of Nalanda, toured the whole of India, and returned by sea after an absence of sixteen years, reaching Ch'ang-an in 645 with a vast number of religious texts. On his triumphal return, the emperor in person welcomed him outside the capital gates. Hsüan-tsang, who became the most illustrious of a number of Chinese pilgrims of the time, spent the rest of his years in organizing the translation of Sanskrit texts into Chinese. He was responsible for about a quarter of all such translations.

Though Buddhism was the dominant foreign religion in Ch'ang-an, other foreign beliefs were equally accepted and tolerated. In A.D. 635 Emperor T'ai-tsung received a Nestorian monk and decreed, after interviewing him, that his doctines were to be preached freely in the empire. Earlier, Manichaean religion had been introduced under the sponsorship of the Uighurs, and Manichaean churches were built in several Chinese towns. Zoroastrian religion was introduced by Persian merchants. From about the mid-eighth century, Muslim and Jewish traders practiced their faith at the capital and in the chief trading centers of the country. The art and life-style of the time reflected the influence of these many foreigners who lived amidst the Chinese people. Their appearance and personalities are preserved in paintings and tomb figurines, showing a Chinese sense of gentle amusement at the features and customs of these strangers.

The emperor T'ai-tsung died in 649 at the age of only forty-eight. He had succeeded in rebuilding the imperial order, and his rule initiated what has been called the "golden age," the time when Chinese civilization was most prosperous, cultured, and sophisticated, a center of cosmopolitan greatness in the arts, literature, in philosophy, and religion, and in its impact on Asia and beyond.

What Emperor T'ai-tsung had initiated was continued by two outstanding rulers who dominated T'ang politics during the end of the seventh and the first half of the eighth century and who became as famous in Chinese history as the great founder of the T'ang dynasty himself. One was Empress Wu (624-705), the only empress recognized as actual ruler by Chinese historians, and the other,

Emperor Hsüan-tsung (712–756), whose reign encompassed the apogee of T'ang greatness but who, at the end, brought about the decline and the beginning of the disintegration of T'ang rule.

Wu Chao, Empress Wu, had entered the palace in 637 at the age of twelve as concubine to T'ai-tsung. At the emperor's death she had entered a Buddhist convent with all other concubines, as prescribed by court rules. But when the young emperor Kao-tsung (649–683) paid a ceremonial visit to the convent, the beautiful and intelligent young woman won his affection and returned to the palace as the young emperor's concubine and eventually became his first consort and empress. Wu Chao was obviously a formidable woman, the daughter of a minister, skilled in literature and history, clever and witty, who soon managed affairs for the weak and indulgent emperor Kao-tsung. After the emperor's death in 683 she reigned as empress and a few years later, in 690, she placed a formal stamp on her rule by changing the name of the dynasty to Chou, assumed the name of Emperor Tse-t'ien, and introduced new titles for her officials and officers, taken from the classic Chou-li—which served not for the first time the political purpose of usurpers.

Actually, the empress Wu continued the policy of T'ai-tsung, restraining the great military aristocratic families and slowly replacing them with Confucian professional bureaucrats. Under her rule the examination system was fully organized as the basis for the selection of her officials, and she obviously had the ability to select able administrators. She was ruthless in eliminating the heads of the great families as well as a number of members of the imperial Li family, having hundreds of them executed when they resisted her policies. In her personal beliefs she was a strong adherent of Buddhism, and it appears likely that the support of Buddhist monks combined with that of Confucian scholar officialdom enabled her to augment her unorthodox authority and even to attempt to set up a new dynastic rule, perhaps acceptable, particularly since she did not attempt to bring members of her own family to power. Only in 705 at the end of her long life, when she was eighty years old and in declining health, was she finally forced to abdicate her powers in a move of reconciliation with the Li family. A few months later she died, and her monumental mountain tomb, near Sian, though deprived of its surface palaces, still testifies to the extraordinary role that this empress played at the height of Chinese imperial history. Her claim to a separate Chou Dynasty was simply ignored under later Chinese official dynastic accounting.

After a short interval in which an empress of the Wei family attempted to follow Empress Wu's example and gain power under a weak emperor, but succeeded only in creating massive corruption and infighting at the court, another long-lasting rule provided the foundation for what has been regarded as the most brilliant period in the history of the T'ang Dynasty. Li Lung-chi, known as Emperor Hsüan-tsung, began his reign with a restoration of the financial system and the reordering of a properly functioning administrative structure. He was the first emperor to order measures against the abuse of privileges by the Buddhist establishment, which had undermined the government's tax structure. The largesse to the monasteries was stopped; many Buddhist statues were melted down and the metal used for coins. More than 120,000 monks and nuns, suspected of having entered convents to escape taxation, were forced to return to civilian life and financial accountability. Moreover, palace expenses were also reduced, and some of the imperial manufacturers closed down.

One fatal measure of economy was military reform, the abolition of the militia system, leading to complete reliance on the powers and initiative of professional military leaders that T'ai-tsung and Empress Wu had successfully curbed. The formation of professional armies under frontier generals did not halt the Arab advance in Central Asia, yet Hsüan-tsung continued to favor the generals, and this misplaced partiality was in the end to endanger the government itself. In time, the emperor's favoritism reopened the conflict between officialdom and the military leadership, leading finally to rebellion and catastrophe.

For almost a century, the new reorganization brought about peace and prosperity, a period of great cultural refinement that has been compared to that of Florence under the Medici. During the seventh and eighth centuries Chinese prestige was at its height in all countries of East Asia; this was also the period of its greatest influence in Japan. T'ang China affected Japanese political and social institutions, Japanese language and literature, as well as philosophies and religion, and especially its art and architecture. In all phases of life Japan copied and greatly admired the Chinese model. Plans of the Japanese capitals of Nara and Kyoto were drawn after the prototype of the Chinese capital, Ch'ang-an; Buddhist temple architecture followed Chinese examples, the Taika reforms, an attempt at centralized administration, the legal code, the first histories written in Chinese characters, all this and the cultural and intellectual life in general were deeply affected by the greatly admired Chinese system. Commerce, pilgrimages, and embassies provided a constant link between the islands of Japan and the Chinese mainland. Indeed, when Ch'ang-an and other T'ang cities were destroyed in the chaos that followed the centuries of T'ang rule, it was in Japan that examples of the architecture and of T'ang traditions survived—even up to modern times.

Hsüan-tsung's rule provided the most glamorous period of T'ang. Ch'ang-an, the capital, became even greater than it had been under the earlier emperors, a world metropolis inhabited by large colonies of merchants from the East Indies, Ceylon, and India. Embassies were exchanged with Byzantium, and the emperor gave refuge for a time to a Persian ruler when that land was conquered by the Arabs. More than a hundred thousand foreign merchants and missionaries lived in the capital, and similar large communities existed in other cities of the realm, among them many Arabs but also adherents of all major beliefs of the time.

This cultural culmination, in which Chinese intellectual and artistic fashions, fused with Indian religious and artistic influences and with other elements of Central Asian and even some Western art and life-styles, reached a height of sophistication and brought forth an extraordinary era of human attainment, comparable to any civilization in global history. From surviving documents that list artists and describe their work, and from the few examples of copies that have survived, from the underground art of the tombs, recently uncovered, and from borrowed and transplanted samples of Korea and Japan, we have an inkling of the glory that was T'ang.

However, the illustrious rule of Hsüan-tsung was to end in tragedy. Late in life, in his sixties, the emperor fell in love with a great beauty, Yang Kuei-fei, became influenced by her whims and appointed her protégés and members of her family to high office. Among her favorites was An Lu-shan, a general of Central Asian origin, a vulgar, clownish, crude, and ambitious person, who was given command of the frontier armies. Reports that he was planning treason were not believed by the emperor until in A.D. 765, completely prepared, An Lu-shan led his armies in rebellion against the capital. Unable to defend the city, the emperor had to flee with his court and some loyal Szech'wan guard troops; but en route, at a small village, the guard mutinied, accusing Yang Kuei-fei and her relatives of being responsible for the disaster. They forced the emperor to sacrifice his favorite, who was strangled by the chief eunuch in the pagoda of the village. This story has been immortalized in Chinese poetry by a famous song, "The Everlasting Wrong," expressing the emperor's remorse.

General An Lu-shan was eventually defeated and died; the emperor abdicated in favor of the crown prince, and after years of fighting the capital was recovered with the help of Tibetan and Uighur allies, and another period of peace followed. Inner Asia, however, remained lost to the empire and the glory of the T'ang Dynasty came to an end.

The final period of the T'ang Dynasty brought some major changes. The Tibetans, unified by a strong king, became a threatening military power. They raided the western and northwestern border regions and in 763 looted the capital Ch'ang-an. With the loss of the central Asian lands went the loss of the profit on which the luxurious life of cities in the Northwest had been based. More serious still than this geographical retreat was the military decline that came in the wake of the An Lu-shan rebellion. The best central armies had been lost in crushing the rebellion, and those Chinese commanders that had participated in the suppression formed their own personally loyal armies. These commanders were no longer members of the earlier aristocratic military families of partly tribal origin, but rather regional upstarts who had risen through the ranks, often elevated to command by their subordinates on the basis of personal ability and leadership qualities. Central control over the armies was lost, and further disintegration of central authority eventually destroyed the dynasty.

Although the North and Northwest had suffered greatly from the campaigns, Central and South China had remained mostly unaffected and prosperous. As a result, Central and South China became the new key economic areas of the country while the Northwest, the cradle of Chinese civilization, declined. The T'ang was the last dynasty that had its capital in this historic region.

Henceforth a new center of China's cultural life grew in the South, creating new trends in art and literature.

Loss of central control over the North gravely affected the government's revenue. The policy of maintaining peasant family landownership as a tax base was breaking up, and landlordism by officials, generals, and wealthy merchants again increased as at other times of declining dynastic power. To make up for the loss, the government introduced in 780 a new revenue policy based not on farm families, but on land and crops; this tax system remained in force to the end of imperial time. In addition the government relied, as it had under Han rule, on state monopolies such as the salt tax as well as a tax on the trade in tea, which had become a widely accepted popular drink during T'ang time.

The economic shift from the Northwest to Central and South China was enhanced by a new agricultural technique. Central and South China was rice country and the technique of first planting seedlings in seedbeds and later transplanting them into fields manifestly increased the yield per unit of land and remained one of the most productive agricultural methods until modern time. It also required a skill and knowledge of the layout of the land that secured for the Chinese peasant, even as tenant farmer, a higher status than the peasant in other premodern agricultural societies. This principle that "the peasant knows best" has, even in modern China, somewhat stayed the hand of the planner.

It was the independence of the military that eventually brought the downfall of the dynasty. A northern army, sent south to fight the independent state of Nan-chao, in today's Yünnan, mutinied and traveled northward, pillaging and looting the cities, particularly seeking out for slaughter the communities of foreign merchants. The rebellion is known as the Huang Ch'ao rebellion from the name of its leader, a thwarted examination candidate, the type that often in Chinese history switched to rebel leadership. Canton was captured by these rebels in 879 and more than one hundred thousand foreign merchants are said to have been massacred. Ch'ang-an was captured in 881 and totally destroyed. Though the rebellion was put down in 884, it meant the practical end of the T'ang Dynasty, whose rulers fell into the hands of rival generals, until the last was forced to abdicate in 907.

Notwithstanding the eventual decline through rebellion and regional warfare, T'ang has remained in imperial history the greatest period of the arts—architecture, sculpture, painting, music, the crafts, and perhaps most of all, poetry. There is a listing of more than two thousand well-known poets of the time and much of their work, less vulnerable to the destruction of war and fire than other cultural assets, has survived. The greatest names are those of Tu Fu and Li Po, the latter better known also outside of China, because his poetry was less weighted with classical Chinese allusions than that of Tu Fu and could be more broadly appreciated.

Li Po (A.D. 705–762) was born in Szech'wan to a family of what we might call independent means. He traveled widely and joined for a time the group of the "six idlers of the Bamboo stream" in Shantung who drank together and held poetry competitions. In 742 Li Po went to the capital to become a court poet. For a while he seemed to adjust to court life, but then he incurred the animosity of Yang Kuei-fei, was banned, and traveled again during the dangerous time of the rebellion. He died, according to legend, under the influence of wine; while attempting to capture the reflection of the moon on the river from his boat, he fell overboard and drowned.

His poetry was written in the new style of the time, the so-called regulated verse consisting of rhymes with juxtaposed meaning and tone in parallel lines. The topics of his poetry were a combination of romanticism and realism, dealing with friendship among the educated, who knew each other from study, examinations, and office, with nature, love, and the pleasures of wine, but also with the political crisis of the time, the devastation, and the suffering of the people. Even in translation [the author's is used here], one of Li's poems gives some of the flavor of his great art:

> In front of the bed
> Bright moonlight
> Almost like frost on the ground
> I lift my head and look at the bright moon
> I lower my head and think of my old home.

In architecture, few of the great buildings of the time, save some pagodas, survived in China. What is left and what we know from the great examples in Japan demonstrate the strength and simplicity of the structures that follow the tradition of earlier history in their wooden construction, interlinked without nails, providing resilience against earthquakes—though unfortunately quite vulnerable to fire, which has destroyed most of this great architectural heritage of the past.

T'ang art was tremendously enriched by the increasing demands of Buddhism for religious representations that engaged most of the sculptors and painters of the time. None of the major T'ang bronze sculptures survived the persecution of 845, but the great cave sculptures in stone (the Vairocana Buddha in Lungmen near Loyang, or the Buddha statues in T'ien-lung-shan in Shansi) have survived and provide us with a display of inward-looking serenity and an artistic and spiritual excellence that has become the standard for all later Buddhist art in China and in the Chinese cultural orbit.

Contemporary writers have given us names and catalogues of famous works of T'ang painters, almost all of which perished during the rebellions, fires, and natural disasters that destroyed the temples and palaces containing the collections. A handful of originals and early copies survived, and we know at least the names of the greatest of the painters, such as Wu Tao-tzu, whose vigorous work has been described by eyewitnesses and whose figures have been used for reliefs, or Yen Li-pen, a court painter and minister to whom one surviving handscroll of Chinese emperors is ascribed, or Wang Wei, a scholar and poet, whose charming landscapes bear testimony to the poetic feeling of being attuned to nature.

One important survival of T'ang art are the wall paintings in the caves at Tunhuang, the Chinese starting point of the Central Asian silk road, where over the centuries the evolving style of landscape painting can be clearly followed. First used as background to religious figures and then as a setting for religious scenes, caravans, pilgrimages, and warfare, these frescoes were painted to edify the merchant and pilgrim travelers. The recent opening of newly dis-covered T'ang tombs, richly decorated with wall paintings, have added to the findings, but the most promising great T'ang tombs, such as that of Emperor Kao-tsung and Empress Wu Tse-t'ien, still await modern scholarly exploration.

During the T'ang period all the crafts reached a new perfection. Goldsmiths and silversmiths developed new designs, some of them under Near Eastern influence. Designs of animals and figures, flowers, birds, and hunting scenes were traced in metal. The few pieces that have survived the destruction of the times of rebellion and chaos demonstrate the extraordinary ability of the Chinese craftsmen to master foreign forms and to incorporate and fuse them with their own tradition. Perhaps the greatest accomplishment of the period was the perfection reached in the creation of ceramics, the new delicate shapes, the extraordinary colored glazes and a new, superb technique. This was the time when Chinese craftsmen finally succeeded in creating true porcelain, a translucent ware of great hardness and creamy whiteness or of delicate shades of color, such as the pale green celadon ware. Porcelain soon became popular in China and famous abroad, and the kilns multiplied wherever proper clay could be found. Much of this delicate ware perished over time, but those preserved pieces in museums and private collections still indicate the extraordinary beauty of the craftsmanship reached in this period. (See Plate 20.)

Tombs have of course been the chief preservers of the great art forms of the period, showing us the bowls, jars, vessels, and animals, especially the painted glazed pottery and figurines given to the dead for their enjoyment in the hereafter. These tomb figures provide for us something of the gaiety and worldliness of the urban and court life of the time, the fashions, and the entertainment. They are graceful, vibrant, intimate, and individual, becoming animated to the close observer. They are still the best witnesses to the time and tastes of the people of T'ang.

CHINESE ART

1. Oracle Bone rubbing.

2. Traditional architecture, 2nd millenium, B.C. Drawing from Pan-lung-ch'eng Huang-p'i, Hupei. Courtesy of the Freer Gallery of Art Library.

3. Lungshan and Yangshao pottery. a. Lungshan bowl. b. Yangshao urn. Courtesy of The Museum of Far Eastern Antiquities, Stockholm, Sweden.

4. Pottery tripod of type *kuei*, Late Neolithic period. Shantung province. Courtesy of the Freer Gallery of Art Library.

5. Bronze Owl, Shang dynasty. Courtesy of the Freer Gallery of Art Library.

6. a. Chinese bronze: Early Western Chou, late 11th–early 10th century, B.C. Ceremonian vessel, with cover (slightly damaged) type *fang i*. 35.1 × 24.1 cm over all. (13-13/16″) Depth: about 22.5 cm (8-7/8″). Courtesy of the Freer Gallery of Art Library. b. Chinese bronze: Middle Eastern Chou, ca. 500 B.C. Li-yu type; Late Spring & Autumn—early Warring States. H: 26.5 cm (10-1/2″) L: 20.0 cm (7-7/8″) W: 13.5 cm (5-5/16″). Courtesy of the Freer Gallery of Art Library.

7. Confucius, rubbing. Reproduced by Edouard Chavannes, *Mission archeologigue dans la Chine septentrionale*, Paris 1913.

8. Attempted assassination of Ch'in Shih Huang-ti, rubbing, Wu Liang-tzu family shrine, Shantung. Reproduced by Edouard Chavannes, *Mission archeologigue dans la Chine septentrionale*, Paris 1913.

9. Life-size pottery figures of soldiers found in the tomb of emperor Ch'in Shih Huang-ti.

10. The Great Wall, rebuilt in Ming time. Photograph by the author.

11. "The Flying Horse," a Han dynasty tomb figure, bronze, Kansu province. The horse had become important in military campaigns and in the arts.

12. Gilt bronze lamp with servant, from Han dynasty tomb at Man-ch'eng, Hopei province. Courtesy of the Freer Gallery of Art Library.

13. Landscape of the Li River near Kweilin. Photograph by the author.

14. "The Bodhisattva, Kuan-yin," Shansi province, 11th to early 12th century. Polychromed wood, H: 7'11"; W: 5'5". Courtesy of the Nelson-Atkins Museum of Art, Kansas City, Missouri (Nelson Fund).

15. Buddha figure from Gandhara, Kabul Museum. Photograph by the author.

16. Standing Buddha, Northern Wei dynasty, 5th Century A.D. 477. Gilt bronze. H: 55-1/4". Front view. Courtesy of The Metropolitan Museum of Art, Kennedy Fund, 1926.

17. Buddhist caves at Bamiyan, Afghanistan, on the Silk Road. Photograph by the author.

18. T'ang charger from tomb of T'ang T'ai-tsung with groom withdrawing arrow from forequarters of horse. Courtesy of The University Museum, University of Pennsylvania, Philadelphia, Pennsylvania.

19. "Four Ladies of the Court Playing Polo," late 7th, early 8th century A.D. Red pottery with traces of pigment, H: 10"; W: 5-1/2"; L: 13-1/2". Courtesy of the Nelson-Atkins Museum of Art, Kansas City, Missouri (Gift of Miss Katherine Harvey).

20. Ju ware vase, copper rimmed, Sung dynasty. H: 9-3/4" (25 cm). Courtesy of the Percival David Foundation of Chinese Art, University of London, England.

21. Bodhisattva from Hua-yen-ssu, Ta-t'ung, Shantung province. Courtesy of the Freer Gallery of Art Library.

22. Lohan, Sung dynasty, Hangchow rubbing. Courtesy of the Freer Gallery of Art Library.

23. "Li Po Chanting a Poem." Liang K'ai, Southern Sung. Courtesy of the Tokyo National Museum, Tokyo, Japan.

24. "A Solitary Temple Amid Clearing Peaks" by Li Ch'eng, hanging scroll, ink and slight color on silk (H: 111.8 cm; W: 56.0 cm). Courtesy of the Nelson-Atkins Museum of Art, Kansas City, Missouri (Nelson Fund).

25. "A Solitary Scholar Contemplating the Landscape," Southern Sung, ca. 1500. Mountainous landscape, rocks and trees; man and attendant approaching building. H: 134.0 × W: 74.0 cm (52-3/4 × 29-1/8″). Courtesy of the Freer Gallery of Art Library.

26. "Travelers Among Mountains and Streams," Fan K'uan, Southern Sung. Courtesy of National Palace Museum, Taipei, Taiwan, Republic of China.

27. Main hall in the Forbidden City, Peking. Photograph by the author.

28. Temple of Heaven, Peking. Photograph by the author.

29. Portrait of the K'ang-hsi emperor as a Confucian scholar. Courtesy of the Freer Gallery of Art Library.

30. "Ma-ch'ang Chasing the Enemy," Lang Shih-ning (Castiglione). Courtesy of National Palace Museum, Taipei, Taiwan, Republic of China.

31. Landscape by Liu Hao-su. Courtesy of the Freer Gallery of Art Library.

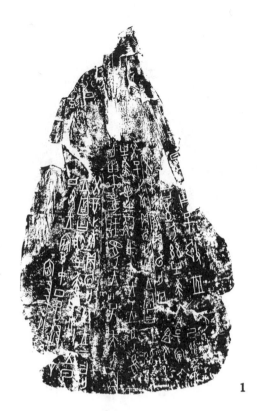

1

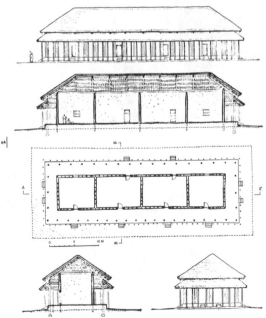

2

3a

3b

4

5

6b

6a

7

8

9

10

11

12

13

14

15

16

17

18

19

20

21

22

23

24

25

26

27

28

29

31

Ten

A CHINESE RENAISSANCE:

The Sung Dynasty

WHEN THE GLORY of T'ang ended in military collapse there followed half a century of dynastic usurpations: the Five Dynasties, in reality no more than military dictatorships that controlled only part of North China. When China was again united under one dynasty, the Sung Dynasty (A.D. 960–1279), it was a much smaller empire and a more inward-looking country that emerged from the tribulations and agonies of the decades of the last years of T'ang and the interregnum. By the time of unification under the Sung, not only was a great part of the empire lost to nomad invaders from the steppes of Central Asia and the forests of Manchuria, but even a part of China Proper south of the wall remained in the hands of these intruders. The remaining smaller empire was continuously threatened by invaders, and eventually the Mongols under Genghis Khan and his successors conquered it all.

It was under these external threats that Chinese culture turned inward, returning to a Chinese heritage in philosophy, literature, and political thought and in this contemplative process reached new heights in the field of art. It was a time of consummation of the Chinese tradition, a period called "the age of maturity," when artists and scholars produced works of enduring fame. The most famous Sung art was landscape painting, but also testifying to the advanced techniques and taste of the time was the perfection of form and exquisite simplicity of the white and greyish-green colored Sung porcelain. This cultural richness in art, literature, and the crafts had a parallel in the realm of philosophy and statesmanship where argument and practice explored the potentials of all dimensions of the Confucian world.

The ascent to power of the Chao family, founders of the Sung Dynasty, did not differ from that of preceding military rules. General Chao K'uang-yin, in charge of the army in the field against the Khitan in the North, was surprised one night in his tent by his officers, who woke him, wrapped around his shoulders a robe with the imperial colors, and proclaimed him emperor. Thus compromised, the general led his troops back to K'ai-feng, took the capital without a fight—removing the child emperor of the short-lived Later Chou Dynasty—and gave his new dynasty the name of Sung. What started out as but another military venture became, however, the least military civilian form of government of Chinese imperial history.

The change was not altogether without overture. The Later Chou had already attempted an agrarian reform policy that was to give land to the tiller and used corvée labor to repair the dikes and canals as a way of strengthening the financial base of the government. Before the military revolt, successful campaigns had extended Later Chou dynastic control over the Yangtze area, a new and culturally more sophisticated, rich agricultural area where much of the northern educated and artistic elite had taken refuge. It was therefore already a culturally Chinese realm that the Sung Dynasty took over.

Chao K'uang-yin, who became Emperor T'ai-tsu, emerged from a family that had long furnished civil officials and governors under the T'ang Dynasty. Though an able general, he appears to have realized from the outset the importance of restoring an effective civil administration. By giving the civilian officials a decisive role in government, he gained the support of the bureaucracy throughout the empire. This greatly facilitated the recovery of the Chinese states in the South that had remained outside the empire after the fall of T'ang. The states of Nan-p'ing (Hupei) and of Shu (Szech'wan) acceded without military resistance, and their rulers went to live honorably and in comfort at the capital K'ai-feng, where the family of the later Chou Dynasty also lived. The states of Nan Han (Kwangtung and Kwangsi) and of Nan T'ang (Anhwei and Kiangsi provinces) surrendered after short resistance. The concept of a unified empire and civil administration had by now been accepted throughout Chinese territory, especially by the educated elite, which provided the civil administration and social leadership. This mood can be adduced from the T'ai-tsu's remark to the king of Nan T'ang, when the king was pressed to accede to unification. The king offered to retain his domain as a feudal territory under the emperor, but was told by T'ai-tsu, "What crime has the land South of the river committed that it should be separated from the empire?"[1]

One event that occurred during the preceding period of the Five Dynasties helped to prepare the ground for renewed respect for civil administration. The wood-block printing of the Confucian classics, completed in 953, contributed decisively to the broadening of Confucian education and the strengthening of the scholar-elite's role in society and state.

The time had thus come for the Sung emperor to install full civil control over his government—but his method was unique for China at the time. He invited his military commanders, those who had conspired to choose him as their new emperor, to a feast, and when they had indulged in wine and food and were in a festive mood, the emperor made his move. He complained that he could not sleep at night, thinking that one of them would want to overthrow his rule and seize the throne. When the officers protested their loyalty, the emperor reminded them that he himself had no wish to rebel but was forced by their collusion to ascend the throne and found a new dynasty. When the commanders asked what the emperor wanted them to do to show their devotion, the emperor lectured them on the happiness of a peaceful life in great comfort and offered to pay them off in estates of their choosing in honorable retirement. The story is perhaps allegorical, but it could be regarded as an indication of the spirit of the time that they accepted.

T'ai-tsu was succeeded in turn by his brother who became Emperor T'ai-tsung (976–997). The choice of the brother instead of a child of the emperor was influenced by the emperor's mother, who is said to have reminded her first son that his own accession was not due to Heaven's intercession as much as to the fact that the late Chou emperor had been a young child easily removed and that the Sung might suffer the same fate if the position of the emperor was entrusted again to a minor son.

T'ai-tsung and his successors completed the work of the first Sung emperor. In addition a restored local administrative system, a reformed system of centralization, control, and information enabled the emperor and the newly important prime minister to exercise a more direct authority over the whole empire. The central government was simplified and became more functional. In this task, both T'ai-tsu and T'ai-tsung found an able helper and administrator in their first minister, Chao P'u, who, however, had not much classical education. T'ai-tsu, it is reported, advised his chief minister to study, and thereafter Chao P'u "was never seen without a book in his hands."[2] Confucian education soon regained its former prestige.

The same emphasis on Confucian education was placed on the selection and appointment of the civil officialdom. The examination system, leading back to Han and T'ang times, was reestablished and perfected. Examinations were held on three levels—in the prefectures, in the capital, and at the palace. These examinations were divided by subject matter. Most prestigious was the examination in general knowledge and literary ability, but the topics covered the spectrum of the academic knowledge of the time: the Confucian classics, law, calligraphy and history of writing, and mathematics, as well as military ability and military strength and arts. To avoid the temptation of cheating or collusion between candidates and examiners, special measures were introduced such as the rewriting of papers by scribes to prevent recognition of the candidate's handwriting. This rigid examination system was the foundation for the respect with which the scholar-elite, whether in office or not, was regarded by the public and by the emperor himself. It was the basis for both the authority and the prestige that enabled them to govern the country and manage society.

This revival of a Chinese Confucian administration was, however, accomplished at a price. The full removal of military leadership meant military weakness. The policy of the Sung emperors towards the tribal intruders in the North and West, who maintained their own dynastic rule over the territories they had conquered, was one of appeasement. When, occasionally, military campaigns were mounted, they ended mostly in disaster. With the loss of control over the "barbarians," the Sung lost the use of barbarian auxiliary forces that had been of such assistance during the T'ang reign over the empire. The Chinese adage "to fight barbarians with barbarians" depended on a policy of imperial expansion that the Sung were unable and unwilling to attempt. The Chinese troops, without cavalry units and deprived of the command of the warrior families of the North, declined rapidly in morale, discipline, and fighting value. In order not to interfere with agricultural production, recruits were drawn from the unsettled, landless, and shiftless rural elements; picked up by recruiting officers on scouting trips to the countryside; and taken from convicts released on condition they join the army. Their lack of discipline was accentuated by the lack of training in peacetime. The constant growth in numbers of these mercenary troops increased the government's financial burden but did nothing to augment the troops' fighting value.

Not even the policy of appeasement was consistently adhered to. After a disastrous campaign ending in defeat North of K'ai-feng, the third Sung emperor concluded in 1005 a peace treaty that left the Khitan-Liao in possession of Chinese territory south of the Great Wall and, in addition, promised the payment of a substantial annual "subsidy."

A similar relationship was instituted with the Hsi Hsia empire in the West, which was formed in Southern Mongolia, Kokonor, and the Chinese provinces of Shansi, Shensi, and Kansu by the Tangut, a Tibetan group. In 1044, the Sung concluded a peace treaty with this dangerous neighbor, paying an even larger subsidy without receiving any guarantee for safety from further attacks.

This three-power system in the North and Northwest was overturned when a new tribe from Manchuria, the Jurchen, founded a new dynasty, the Chin, and attacked the Khitan from the north. The Sung made common cause with the new aggressor against their common enemy, the Khitan-Liao, but when the Chin succeeded in taking over the Chinese territory south of the Great Wall, the Sung attempted to challenge them over the conquered region in North China. This policy led to disaster. Chin cavalry swept south across the North China plain, took the Sung capital of K'ai-feng and captured the emperor and the court.

The debacle was at first patched over. The emperor abdicated in favor of his son, and his prime minister Ts-ai Ching negotiated a settlement with the Chin, arranging for a large ransom to induce them to relinquish the court, the city, and the land they had overrun. Soon the prime minister, accused of betrayal, was forced into exile, and his successors persuaded the emperor to break the agreement and send an army after the retreating Chin. The Chin turned, vanquished the Chinese army, again captured the capital and the court (A.D. 1126), and this time took their prisoners to their Manchurian base. Again they swept south, briefly crossed the Yangtze River, capturing and looting the cities of Hangchow and Ningpo. Only slowly was resistance in Central China reorganized by Sung successors and administrators under a famous general, Yüeh Fei, who regained the territory south of the Huai River, the area of rice paddies where the Chin cavalry could not maneuver as freely as in the North China plain. But the North remained lost, and a new period began, the period of the Southern Sung with their capital at Hangchow. This Southern Sung Dynasty lasted until 1279 when the Mongols overran all of China.

Under these persistent military threats, the Chinese polity, both in Northern and Southern Sung time, reached a new height of Confucian civilization. For Central China, this was a period of prosperity, increasing population, and growing urban culture and commerce, extending to the southern seas.

However, prosperity brought with it domestic economic problems inherent within the system and recurring ever since the establishment of a bureaucratic centralized, but limited, state under the Han Dynasty. In time of peace, the scholar-elite, both as officials and as scholar-gentry leaders of society, were able to accumulate wealth that—in preindustrial time—could be invested in land, and by some, in money lending, pawnshops, and commerce. The scholar-gentry had seen to it that this investment did not, by itself, undermine the system. Merchant wealth and landlordism did not become a basis for political power in competition with educational qualification. Besides, accumulation of large landed estates was impeded by the absence of the right of primogeniture. Property was divided among male offspring, again and again reducing landownership by redistribution of land among male children for every new generation.

But the exemption from corvée labor and the avoidance of surtaxes by the families of those holding academic degrees shifted the tax burden to the large number of commoner farmers and exempted the land of the scholar-elite, even when the units of land held by this elite were small, adding to the tax of the farmer-owner. It was not so much landlordism that burdened the small farmers as the increase in the tax burden and the surtaxes that eventually began to make the farmers' lot intolerable. When the peasants had to borrow money in spring at high interest rates or pawn their winter clothing to be repaid at the time of harvest in the fall, they continually sank deeper into debt. The peasants grew poorer, the state lost tax income, and the weakened central power was rendered unable to control the profiteering of its own scholar-elite. Moreover, reduced tax income affected vital services, irrigation and diking declined, and drought or flood aggravated the misery of the peasant population. This was the time for banditry, unrest, and uprisings—the time of dynastic decline.

The Sung Dynasty proved to be no exception. In the middle of the eleventh century signs of economic crisis became apparent. Whereas at the end of T'ang and during the Five Dynasties the military struggles within the country had tended to blur an economic background of increasing difficulties, now a government of civilian officials brought the inherent economic problems into focus. The threat from outside made the question of inner stability all the more urgent.

This was the time when basic policy differences on these economic and military problems were argued out by opposing factions within the scholar-officialdom. Two parties, reformers and conservatives, debated policies heatedly and put into practice their policies when in power. The reformers aimed at strengthening the power of the state, both militarily in the face of the foreign threat, and domestically in curbing the growth of speculation and local usury. The conservatives resented state interference in the economy and opposed the replacement of mercenary armies by a national force recruited from militias. Both sides held power for some time, but the conservatives, who eventually won out, wrote the history of the time and in their writing condemned the reformers and favored those emperors who had listened to their conservative policies.

This confrontation occurred during the eleventh century, the Northern Sung period. The chief antagonists were Wang An-shih (1021-1086), the greatest reformer in Chinese imperial history, supported by a group of younger scholar-officials and sustained by Emperor Shen-tsung (1068-1085), and, on the conservative side, the great historian Ssu-ma Kuang (1019-1086), Wang An-shih's contemporary and chief opponent.

Wang An-shih was born into a poor official family. After passing his first examination he held a series of official positions that gave him experience and familiarity with the economic and social problems of the country. In his posts he had to deal with matters of hydraulic engineering, juridical and financial affairs, grain administration, and finally a combination of all these tasks as district magistrate. On the basis of his experience he memorialized the throne in 1058 in a lengthy document of "ten thousand words" on the need for reorganization of the civil service. He proposed that instead of being educated only in the ethical concepts of Confucian ideology and the abstract knowledge of the time, officials should be trained also in practical administration, with concentration upon fields of specialization. Instead of literary scholar-officials, he wanted experts who, being paid adequate salaries, should be rendered at least relatively immune to the temptations of graft, which had become a widespread problem. Army officers, taught specifically in military subjects, were to supplant uneducated mercenary leaders from the ranks and untrained scholars in defending the country.

The memorial, unacknowledged, must have had some impact, for at the age of forty-eight Wang An-shih became vice grand counselor under the new emperor Shen-tsung and was given full leeway to carry out much more formidable changes than he had originally proposed. Wang An-shih began by appointing a special financial counselor as a kind of "brain truster." Then he changed the current system of centralized taxation-in-kind. Instead of transporting the grain taken in taxes to the capital, creating a glut that reduced the price at sale there, he had it redistributed locally for the adjustment of scarcity and surplus. This led to a form of price control, elimination of private speculation and hoarding, and eventually a practical state trade monopoly. Connected with this procedure was a system of government loans. From the local government granaries, loans of grain were advanced to farmers at seed time at very low interest rates to be repaid after harvest. These measures were to end speculation by grain merchants and exploitation of farmers by moneylenders and pawnshops, which had become the chief burden of the peasant population.

To modify the inequalities created by corvée labor, borne by the peasants but not the scholar-gentry who served "not with their brawn but with their brain," Wang An-shih introduced the Public Services Act. Corvée was transformed into hired labor, and to pay for it, a tax was added to be paid by all on a prorated basis of five grades, according to landed income. The value of the land itself was reclassified periodically, and an equitable land tax measure was to shift the tax burden more to those who were better off.

These measures of domestic policy, designed to avert the traditional agrarian problem linked to the cyclical rise and fall of dynasties, were complemented by a military policy to prepare the state for the contest with the tribal empires of the North and West. Wang An-shih's intent was to dissolve the large and ineffective mercenary army by stages and replace it with a newly organized militia. His Militia Act introduced the *pao-chia* system, organizing the rural population in groups of ten families, which were militarily trained, supplied with arms, and led by their headmen. These in turn were combined in units of one hundred families and even larger groups as a recruiting ground for a regular military force that was first to be used for the protection of their own regions, but later organized into a conscript army for the defense of the country. The *pao-chia* system was also to be used as a police force, responsible for security and the suppression of crime in its home localities and liable for any act committed by members of the group. While building up this militia, Wang An-shih succeeded in reducing the strength of the mercenary army from its highest number of 1,200,000 to 600,000 men, at substantial savings for the government's treasury. He also introduced a horse breeding program in the northern provinces to equip both the militia and part of the army with enough horses to match the mounted enemy in the North.

To administer these new civil and military tasks the government needed a special type of civil and military official, so Wang An-shih founded government schools that taught practical administration. To provide textbooks, Wang himself wrote commentaries and additions to the standard Confucian works, which were still to remain the foundation of Wang's reforms. The value system of the social and political order was to continue to be based on the Confucian classics, which Wang An-shih quoted to justify his policies.

Yet taken as a whole, Wang's program differed fundamentally from the classical Confucian concept of the limited state and the autonomous society. By extending the power of the state militarily, in police matters, and in the control of the economy, Wang An-shih had changed the political power balance at the expense of social autonomy. In his scheme of things, the domestic and foreign threat to the dynasty would be lessened, the cyclical causes of the rise and fall of dynasties reduced, but at the expense of the autonomous social order and its ability to survive a political collapse. When the dynasty fell, the survival of the social order, much more intimately linked to the particular dynastic regime, might have been wagered in the process. The dualism of the system, which provided a guarantee for continuity, would have been weakened.

This may have been part of the consideration that caused such violent opposition by a majority of the scholar-elite against Wang An-shih's reforms. In addition, the strange combination of pacifism and belief in Chinese moral superiority as adequate defense that characterized the policy of the scholar-conservatives, combined with the concern about state control of local communities, provoked fierce opposition by the scholar-elite against the *pao-chia* system and the militia army. The immediate concern, though, was surely the self-interest of this scholar-elite whose privileges and sources of income were at stake. These conservatives claimed that the reforms were oppressive, causing suffering for the people, and when the emperor died and the opposition came to power under a regency, Ssu-ma Kuang, recalled to office, threw out the whole system of the new laws and returned to the traditional limitations of administrative action.

The effectiveness of Wang's reforms has remained a moot question. In the almost twenty years during which they were in force, they appear to have worked well. There is no record of peasant rebellions or serious disorder—only of the complaints of the scholars who opposed the reforms. One weakness to which these critics harked back was the shortage of properly trained loyal officials willing to carry out the policies. Apparently there was some sabotage and disregard of, and misuse of orders, which may have led to instances of corruption. Wang An-shih's personality was also an obvious irritant. He was known for his arrogant manner and lack of tolerance for different views, an attitude that alienated many and that appears to have been copied by the ambitious young men who surrounded him. Besides, Wang An-shih, unmindful of himself to the point of disregard for attire and appearance, was criticized for lack of personal neatness.

With the return of the conservative party to power, the orthodox ideas of the Confucian system were restored. For a time followers of the reformers' school alternated with conservatives in dominating court politics. The resulting policy vacillations weakened and disorganized the government at the very time when the danger from the growing Jurchen-Chin power required a consistent, unified strategy. The Confucian struggle was still continuing when the Chin captured the capital, and the court and both parties succumbed in a common ruin.

After the fall of the Northern Sung, no other attempts were made to modify the relationship between state and society. With the uncontrolled play of economic forces, there continued the cycle of crises that led, after a period of prosperity, to the fall of each succeeding dynasty, domestic or foreign.

If the Sung period did not bring about a restructuring of the political system of state and society, it provided a widely expanded, new philosophical background. Confucianism in the past had been a political and social system based on ethical grounds. The philosophers of Sung time added to it a metaphysical system that they conceived in contention with and under the influence of Buddhism and Taoism, a Taosim that had itself assumed new religious traits from its Buddhist competitor. The Confucianism that emerged from this infusion has been called Neo-Confucianism.

To the Confucian scholars of Sung time, Buddhists and Taoists were primarily competitors who had influenced the political and social order of the preceding centuries through their teachings. To the Confucianists, the Buddhist and Taoist monastic life was a violation of loyalty to the family and, indeed, to society and state for the selfish purpose of individual salvation. Beyond that, the Buddhist idea of the "Void," or the negation of the independent reality of things, was anathema to Confucian scholars, who emphatically disputed this mystical and negative philosophy. To counter such a concept, they sought for a basic philosophical starting point of their own and found it in the I'ching, the Book of Changes, the pre-Confucian divination manual, which they accepted as a classical Confucian text. There they found such a basic force in the concept of T'ai-chi, rendered as the "Great Ultimate," which though immaterial in itself engendered yang and yin, the active and passive principles. Through their interplay the yin and yang were believed to bring about the Five Agents or elements—earth, fire, wood, metal, and water—that in turn in harmonious interaction produced the world of phenomena. On such an interpretation and correlation of assumed forces in nature a number of Confucian philosophers construed a concept of natural order, regarded as the physical frame of Confucian morality. Their ideas were eventually brought into a complete system during the Southern Sung Dynasty by Chu Hsi (1130–1200), who provided a synthesis of the concepts worked out by his predecessors. The Confucian social doctrine became a cosmic system; the law of nature was to be identical with the moral law that should determine human conduct. The world of phenomena, created by *T'ai-chi* through yin and yang and the Five Elements, was permeated by the moral law that was to be followed by mankind through the practice of four chief Confucian virtues: humanism, integrity, reverence, and wisdom. The mind of man, itself containing this ultimate principle, *T'ai-chi*, was capable of being aware of it and of applying it to man's own conduct, thus gaining self-realization and full development of human potential (*jen*, or "humanism"), bringing man into harmony with the universe. This humanism was to be gained through learning and moral discipline.

During his lifetime Chu Hsi was attacked, persecuted, and driven from office by a rival school and political faction, as had been Confucius in his time. But after his death, Chu Hsi's interpretation of Confucianism became the accepted school of thought and the basis for the official examinations until the end of imperial history. Neo-Confucianism, as this school was named, became the official version of the Confucian tradition.

The philosophical bent and the scholarly tradition of the Sung period found expression in the art of the time. It was during the Sung Dynasty that the greatest of Chinese arts, landscape painting, reached its supreme classical height. It was the climax of a great tradition that had begun during the North-South division and flourished under the T'ang Dynasty.

In the North, under the alien rulers of the Liao and Chin Dynasties, Buddhist art continued to prosper, and the great accomplishments of T'ang art were continued and preserved. The richness and splendor of the Buddha and bodhisattva figures at Hua-yen-ssu in Shansi and at other great centers in North China attest to this evolution. The flowing garments and the free postures and poses converted the serenity of the early images and the elegance of T'ang sculpture into a baroque comeliness and grace designed to uplift the believer. (See Plate 21.) Buddhist art also turned to eccentric imagery. Because Buddhism had branched out into sects, the teachings affected religious portrayal in sculpture and especially in painting. The Ch'an sect, which discarded prolonged rational study and stressed intuition and spontaneity in religious experience, aiming at the spirit behind form, introduced radical new approaches to the presentation of religious figures and apparitions. Buddhist disciples, the *Lohan*, were depicted not only as grotesquely ugly but almost as caricatures of beings through deliberate distortions of faces, figures, and movements. The shock treatment as a means of religious instruction found its parallel in the depiction of ugliness as an eccentric form of art. (See Plate 22.)

More than that, a technique that was to inspire intuition had to be sparse in presenting its visions and ideas—to note essential elements, rather than spell out detail. This technique had to leave room for imagination and fantasy. A style of art developed that was self limiting to a minimum of form and color. The brush and monochrome ink, the tools of calligraphy, in a master's hand were most suited to provide this effect. Whether portraying Buddhist or Taoist figures, famous poets, scholars, or people in action, the artist expressed an intensity and immediacy of action for which Sung painting has been rightly famous and that has profoundly affected art in Japan and in other countries of East Asia. (See Plate 23.) The same has been true for Sung landscape painting. But here it was philosophy rather than religion that fused with the art of painting and gave it a unique character.

The Chinese name for landscape—*shan-shui,* "mountains and water"—describes the characteristic elements that for Chinese painters, poets, and writers designated the natural setting for human existence. (See Plate 24.) It is not nature by itself but the contemplation of nature by the philosophically minded spirit that is the theme of the Chinese landscape painter. A typical landscape painting includes a scholar or philosopher, not as the centerpiece but as a small figure at the side on an outcropping or under a pavilion or gazebo. This figure represents an observer and contemplator of a scene of pine trees, waterfalls, rock formations, and mountains that are to inspire him and, through him, the viewer. In its purest form this style aimed at a free expression of ideas and at a spontaneity that sought out what appeared essential to the painter. Even the empty space— containing the unexpressed part of the painter's and the viewer's vision—was integral in this impressionist style. (See Plate 25.)

To express this vision, the painter has to avoid a specific stand from which to measure the relationship to the vista before him. The traditional Chinese painter does not use the rules of perspective because they impose limits on a scene that is to be imagined in its totality. Instead, the so-called bird perspective permits the viewer to wander over the landscape in his imagination, to shift his stand at will, and to follow in his mind a path that leads a course wherever the lines and formations of nature and his own fantasy take him. In practice this concept found its most germane expression in the painting of scrolls of scenery that were meant to be unrolled and contemplated scene by scene as the viewer unfolded each section and wandered along a shifting scenery. The counterpoint to this free-flow of scenery and the sparsity of color is the carefully detailed representation of flowers, birds, and fish in faithful depiction of their forms, their colors, and their movements. They show the beautiful and charming products of that magic of nature of which all is a part.

This was the most honored art of the time, practiced, admired, and responded to by the educated, amateurs or professionals, and indeed by the court itself. Of the galaxy of famous painters—more than two thousand are known—the greatest names have become famous not only in Asia but in the West. Works by Ma Yuan, Hsia Kuei, Kuo Hsi, Fan Chung-cheng (Fan K'uan), Mi Fu, to mention but a few, are found in museums, galleries, and private collections worldwide. (See Plate 26.)

Their rise to fame in the society and era when they lived was furthered greatly by the court in which the emperors themselves became connoisseurs and benefactors. Hui-tsung (1101–1165), the next to last of the emperors of Northern Sung, who eventually was captured by the barbarians and lost his throne, was not only a patron of the arts but also an outstanding painter of birds and flowers. He was the moving spirit of a painting academy at the palace, and he himself announced the subject matter for painting competitions and gave prizes for the best response. Hui-tsung was also a great and zealous collector of paintings of the past and of his own time—unfortunately so—for when the capital was captured and his palace went up in flames, the greater part of the most famous works of the country were lost forever.

The refined taste of the scholar-elite and the court also led to the production and collection of an art form and craft for which China has become rightly famous: porcelain, first known in the West as chinaware or china. The beginnings of Chinese ingenuity in this form of pottery led back to Han times, and during the T'ang Dynasty real porcelain was manufactured. But the classical quality of material and purity of form reached in Sung time was the culminating height of an art form that has never been surpassed. The numerous kilns, first chiefly in the North and later near Hangchow, produced a great number and variety of wares, bowls, vases, vessels, cups, bottles, and porcelain pillows and figurines that found ready markets not only in China, but across the ocean as well in Japan—where they stimulated a Japanese industry—and in the Near East and the West. The creamy white glaze produced near Tingchow in Hopei is as well known worldwide as are some of the colors, glazes, and tinges from other well known kilns. The greenish-blue celadon, said to have received its foreign name from a green-clad shepherd in a French play of the early seventeenth century, was produced chiefly at kilns near Hangchow during the Southern Sung period. Also during that time a revolutionary technique of overglaze painting was used to decorate bowls and dishes with birds or flowers. This technique has been regarded as the genesis of enameling and was brought to perfection under the Ming Dynasty. The superb colors, shapes, and forms have remained one of the proudest cultural achievements of imperial China.

Concentrating on matters of philosophy and art and the aesthetics of their lifestyle, the Southern Sung at Hangchow, as had their predecessors in the North at K'ai-feng, paid scant attention to the threat of barbarian conquest that faced them throughout the land. After the South was secured against the cavalry armies of the Jurchen-Chin, no attempt was made to regain the lost northern provinces. The southern empire enjoyed one more half-century of peace, until another, vastly stronger invader from the steppe, the Mongol power, overran the whole of China and unified it again under barbarian rule.

Eleven

THE MONGOL EMPIRE

STEPPE SOCIETY WAS always mercurial. The nomad life of constant movement from summer to winter pastures and back again demanded capable leadership for organized migration by whole communities. Clashes over pasture rights were common. The nomads were armed people; the leader who could guarantee protection as well as conquest could rapidly increase his following; conversely, if he failed, his following would break up. This importance of leadership and its success in warfare can explain the rapidity with which steppe empires rose and fell apart.

The Mongol empire, the greatest of these steppe empires and the largest of all land empires in history, was forged by one leader in a few decades through the unification of all the steppe people in Central Asia under one clan. The empire was created in one generation; it broke apart two generations later, first splitting into four separate empires, each of which collapsed when its military cohesion ended.

These steppe empires depended on relationships to the settled agricultural world across their economic and political frontiers. Whether by trade or tribute, a regular exchange of animals and animal products in return for grain, textiles, and the work of craftsmen complemented the economies and life-styles of the nomadic and the sedentary societies in time of peace. When the steppe tribes were divided and the government of the sedentary world of China was strong, Chinese dynasties could reach out into the steppe and dominate the tribal groups. When the dynastic rule in China was weak or disintegrating, and steppe societies were united, nomad conquerors could invade China and set up their conquest dynasties over Chinese society.

Neither side could change the other's economy or polity: The steppe remained tribal; China, bureaucratic, though they affected and influenced each other.

The Northern Chinese empires of the Khitan-Liao, the Tangut-Hsi Hsia, and the Jurchen-Chin could be called "amphibious" empires. Half their states and indeed their roots were in their nomad steppe or forest origins and the other half in their acculturated Chinese civilization. They had moved into China not only by conquest, but also by administrative transformation. They had mastered Chinese government and administrative methods, had taken Chinese officials into their political structure, and had learned and come to profess Chinese political ideology. Even though these empires had embraced Buddhism, the Confucian concepts of sanction for authority of the ruler and the standards of officialdom had become a mainstay of their polity. The more Chinese they had become, the better the chance of their successful rule over Chinese people and their territory. The chief danger to their rule came from across the frontier, from new waves of tribal people who in their turn were attracted by the high rewards of conquest of Chinese territory.

The Mongol case was altogether different. The Mongols were steppe people par excellence; they detested agricultural labor for themselves and believed in the freer life of the steppe, of animal husbandry, and of the warrior. Their primary goal was the creation of a great steppe empire that would extend its conquests in all directions to neighboring countries.

This steppe empire was the creation of one man, one of the greatest and most brutal and fearful leaders of all time, Temuchin (1167-1227), who received the title Genghis Khan, the Great Khan of all steppe people. Like most of the rising steppe leaders, Temuchin started as a small tribal chieftain, a man skilled in tribal warfare who was challenged in his position, had to fight for survival and recognition, and moved on from success and conquest to more conquest until he had unified all the people of the steppe, who received under him the name of Mongols.

In his strategy Genghis Khan differed from the leaders of the Hsi Hsia, the Liao, and the Chin states who had all started at the Chinese frontier but had immediately turned into China to set up Chinese dynasties that were open to further attack from the tribal world of the steppe. Genghis Khan took Peking—from the Chin—

in 1215 but then returned to the steppe, attacking and uniting the peoples of Mongolia, Central Asia, and the tribes along China's western frontier, creating a base from which he could carry the Mongol advance in all directions: Russia, Europe, the Near East, Iran, and China. This rapid expansion introduced a centrifugal factor that eventually ended the Mongol unity based on control from the steppe.

Europe was saved from conquest when the successful Mongol armies, having heard of the death of Ogotai, son and successor of Genghis Khan, turned back in 1241 to Karakorum, the capital of the Mongol empire, to participate in the election of his successor. The conquest of Iran ended at the Persian Gulf with the establishment of the khanate of Il-Khan. Russia remained under the khanate of the "Golden Horde" until the fifteenth century, Central Asia under the khanate of Chagatai. But the final dilution of the centripetal cohesion of the Mongol polity, as established by Genghis Khan, came with the conquest of China, and the shift of the capital from Mongolia to Peking, then called Khambalik (Cambulac). China became the most important of the Mongols' domains, altering the character of the steppe empire, and accelerating its disintegration.

Genghis Khan's steppe empire was based on military organization. Through local wars, negotiated submission, and asserted authority, Temuchin joined together some fifty tribes and was elected by them as khan. Other tribes were attached to this core, and in 1206 Temuchin was elected Genghis Khan—Genghis meaning "limitless strength"—by a general assembly of all the tribes, the Great Kurultai.

The Great (Genghis) Khan's first task was to organize his tribal adherents into a unified "national" force. The various tribal groups of fighting men were formed into an imperial army in units of 10, 100, 1,000, and 10,000 men under appointed officers chosen from existing leaders. Genghis Khan's main instrument of power, which he founded at the same time, was an imperial guard, selected from the best fighters of each larger unit, as a privileged loyal force to control the army and the nation at large.

As administrators, Genghis Khan first took men from the Central Asian oasis towns of Turkestan where agriculture and waterworks had necessitated trained administrative authority. A Mongol script was invented, taken not from China but from a Syriac script as adapted by the Uighur Turks in Turkestan. The customary laws of the steppe were formulated into a written imperial code, the *Yasa*, which dealt chiefly with property issues, conflict situations, and crimes.

In contrast to founders of other tribal kingdoms, Genghis Khan did not borrow his governmental structure from the Chinese tradition but created his own out of the military order of the steppe. This difference in the basic concept and structure of the Mongol empire remained valid even after Kublai Khan, grandson of Genghis Khan, had moved his capital to Peking and his forces had conquered all of China. The Mongols remained in China an alien people of conquerors whose aim was to exploit and enjoy the products of the labor of the conquered population. To rule they employed mostly alien people, Central and Inner Asians, Persians, Arabs, and Europeans. Only at a lower level and especially in South China was it unavoidable to use Chinese officials, who in turn shared in the exploitation of their countrymen. When dissatisfaction exploded, the Chinese collaborators became as much the target of popular fury as did the Mongols and their foreign officials.

For the purpose of conquest, the military machine that Genghis Khan created was the most formidable of the time. The cavalry formations of mounted archers were the most mobile force known and were feared by all. The stirrup, which had come into use in the fourth century A.D., permitted greater control of the horse when massed columns of cavalry were maneuvered, a tactic fully developed by the Mongols. The powerful compound bow, made of horn and wooden pieces, could be used from the galloping horse in attack as well as in feint retreat—the so-called Parthian shot. In their blitzkrieg strategy the Mongols overran the more traditional armies of their enemies. But for the siege and capture of walled cities, the Mongols had to dismount and needed special new techniques of warfare, and these they obtained from the Chinese, from whom the Mongols learned the use of large catapults and explosive missiles. Their greatest weapon, however, was psychological: They spread before them fear of terror and slaughter. Their declared rule was that any town that resisted, if only shortly, would be totally destroyed, all inhabitants, men, women, and children massacred, and all structures leveled to the ground, so that a horse galloping over the ground at night would not stumble. It was sheer lust of conquest that fired the Mongols. Genghis Khan is known to have claimed that the greatest joy in life was to kill one's rivals, sleep with their wives and daughters, and ride their horses.

Self-sufficient within their steppe economy in the essentials of life, the Mongols depended on external input only for agricultural products and the ware of craftsmen. To obtain such wares the Mongols favored foreign traders and artisans who provided them with luxuries, as well as the goods they wanted or needed. In their own nomadic social system, no special merchant or artisan class was possible or permitted, but trade caravans, merchants, and artisans from foreign countries were supported, protected, and patronized. And because the steppe was the traveling route for the caravans that linked the West with East Asia, the Mongols, in command of the steppe, profited greatly from their monopoly control over the trade routes.

One other area of human aspiration in which this ruthless power proved to be most tolerant was religion. The Mongol's own early faith was shamanism, but since they sought for their administrative organization and conquests trained foreign experts, they had to accept the religions and educational systems of their many foreign functionaries. Among their officials and merchants were Muslims, Buddhists, Nestorians, Manichaeans, and European Christians, and as far as acceptance of foreign religious faiths was concerned, the Mongols were the most cosmopolitan and tolerant power of the time. Kublai Khan corresponded with the pope and had plans to invite several hundred Catholic priests to his country. Though this invitation was disregarded, several Franciscan and Dominican monks visited China during Mongol rule, and some left important records of their observations.

The Mongol conquest of China was accomplished at a tremendous cost both in lives and physical destruction. When Genghis Khan took Peking, he followed the rule of slaughtering the total population and laying waste to the city, as he did wherever he met with any defiance. Yet exceptions began to be made. It was a Khitan aristocrat, Yeh-lü Ch'u-ts'ai (1190–1244), formerly an official under the Chin Dynasty and captured by the Mongols, who advised the Great Khan that the slaughter of the whole population of cities would mean the loss to the Mongols of the skill of the craftsmen and artisans who lived there, and the destruction of the population of the rural areas would deprive them of tax income. The Mongol ideal of turning conquered territory into grazing land for their horses was impractical in China. China had to be governed by Chinese administrative methods. In the words of Yeh-lü Ch'u-ts'ai, "You can conquer China on horseback but you have to dismount to rule her." Yeh-lü Ch'u-ts'ai's advice saved the inhabitants of K'ai-feng after it had fallen and may have prevented wholesale slaughter in other Chinese cities, although the populations of some cities along the conquest route to Nanking and Hangchow were not spared by the conqueror.

Kublai Khan (1215–1294), Genghis Khan's grandson, who was elected Great Khan in the Mongol capital of Karakorum in 1260, moved his capital from there to Peking (Khambalik) in 1263, and in 1271 assumed the Chinese dynastic name of Yüan Dynasty after capturing most of North and Central China. The remainder of the Sung empire fell between 1272 and 1279, when the Mongol conquest of China was completed. Nominally Kublai Khan remained the head of the whole Mongol empire, but he had to fight wars against some of his brothers and cousins who led parts of it. Even the nominal unity ended after Kublai's death in 1295, when the three western khanates that had accepted Islam as their faith and ideology refused to recognize the authority of Kublai's successor in Peking. The latter favored Lamaist Buddhism and was in their eyes an infidel. The cohesion of the Mongol continental empire thus lasted less than ninety years and the Mongol Yüan Dynasty in China came to an end in 1368.

In China as in all their conquered countries, the Mongols remained an alien power, more successful in conquest than in establishing a lasting political system. Kublai Khan's government in China controlled a system of rude exploitation based on racial discrimination against the Chinese. The population was divided into four ethnic groups. Ranked first were the Mongols, who occupied all key governing posts, including most of the civil governorships of the administrative districts; they formed the Mongol army and, unlike the Chinese, were entitled to possess and carry arms. Next came those non-Mongol and non-Chinese foreigners who were not sinicized. They either served in Mongol officialdom or were merchants and professionals, favored by the Mongols. Third were the Chinese from North China, the populations of the former Liao and Chin states, including the sinicized tribal people. At the bottom of the scale came the Chinese from South China, the last to be conquered and lowest in status, who carried the heaviest burden in tax and corvée labor.

The well-known Venetian traveler Marco Polo, who came to Kublai Khan's court in 1275 as a young man accompanying his father and uncle on their trading journey, has left a famous account of his journeys and adventures.[1] Kublai Khan took an interest in the young man, offered him a position as government official, and entrusted him with several important missions in the course of which Marco Polo visited a number of cities and regions of Kublai's empire. Though he was clearly treated exceptionally during almost twenty years of service in China, Marco Polo's role did not differ basically from that of other foreigners taken into service by the Mongols. His descriptions characterize the Mongol system: the splendor of the Mongol court and the comforts of the Mongols' life, their interest in trade and manufacture, and their disregard for the Chinese people. Marco Polo, who claimed to know four Asian languages (presumably Mongol, Persian, Arabic, and Central Asian Turkic), despite all his years in China obviously did not know or have a need for the Chinese language. In his accounts he had very little to say about the indigenous Chinese population of the empire that he served, an indication how far apart the Mongols lived from the people whom they had subjugated and whose labor provided them with all their needs and luxuries. Conversely, Marco Polo was very impressed with the power of Kublai and the great splendor of his court. The emperor had 4 chief wives, each of whom had as many as 10,000 attendants, and his harem contained 500 women selected from all over his empire.

Under Kublai Khan, the official in charge of revenues was an Iranian Muslim, Ahmad, much hated for his corruption and his exploitative taxation and eventually assassinated in 1280. The Chinese who became officials at lower levels primarily in South China and collaborated with the conqueror were rewarded like their foreign colleagues with large landed estates. When the tables turned against the Mongols, these collaborators were swept away together with their foreign masters.

For the Chinese people the Mongol rule was a disaster. The warfare and the strategy of annihilation of urban populations, the heavy taxation, and the ruin of the waterworks, especially in Northwest China, reduced the population, which at Sung time had stood at more than 100 million taxpayers, to little more than half that number. The Northwest of China, originally the cradle of Chinese civilization, never fully recovered from the impoverishment and destruction resulting from Mongol conquest and Mongol rule. Although the reopening of the Central Asian trade routes brought in merchants from Arabian and Mediterranean countries and created in some of the cities what has been called a "gaudy sumptuousness" of life for the Mongols, the privileged foreigners, and some Chinese collaborators, this Mongol prosperity was paid for by a decline in agriculture, accentuated by the development of large landed estates with little consideration for the fate of the farmer. The chasm between the foreign rulers and the Chinese people widened. Chinese officials, who eventually did form a majority at the lower levels of the administration, had little influence in the policy-making high councils of the dynasty. At the court there was disunity and continuous conflict among the Mongol nobility over succession, political power, and privileges. With the weakening of imperial authority, corruption in the provinces increased.

The Chinese people, suffering under the burden of ever-increasing taxation and the general economic decline, which resulted in inflation aggravated by experiments with paper money, and hating the foreign officials and their Chinese collaborators, began from the turn of the fourteenth century on to organize rebellions led by secret societies. In the middle of the fourteenth century, the Red Turbans initiated large uprisings in the North China plain and the Yangtze area, uprisings that eventually led to the collapse of Mongol rule, the expulsion of the Mongols from China, and the establishment of a Chinese dynasty.

During Sung time, the Chinese scholarly elite had truly come into its own; scholars had debated and determined policies; they had firmly established their leadership in society and state and had integrated their philosophy and their art with the polity of the country. Whichever of their factions had the upper hand in the political contention dominated the life of the court, and the emperors themselves not only understood but also could participate in the cultural and artistic life as set by the scholar-elite.

Under the Mongols, this link was broken. The Mongols regarded themselves as masters over the Chinese, and Chinese scholars for the most part disdained the barbarian and his foreign functionaries and retreated into a self-contained elite group that, though powerless, felt its inherent superiority over the outsiders. The scholars were convinced that the refined culture that they possessed was far above the crudity of the Mongol power system. In fact, most Chinese scholar-literati sought escape from the affairs of government in the world of literature and art. And it was therefore under this alien rule that some of the best scholarly cultural tradition of Sung time was carried on.

This attitude of scholarly superiority and intellectual elitism, combined with the conviction that government service was less worthy than the free and independent life of the scholar, the true *chün-tzu*, never quite disappeared throughout the remainder of imperial history, even after the Mongols were driven out and the foreigners were gone from government, again replaced by the Confucian scholar-official. This elitism made the scholar-gentry a more independent group to deal with for both the Chinese Ming Dynasty and the Manchu Ch'ing Dynasty and carried over even into the special role that Chinese intellectuals assumed for themselves after the Revolution of 1911.

Under the Mongols, the Chinese scholar-gentry, excluded from official service by the rulers or by their own volition, made their living by teaching or unofficial community service. Those talented enough turned to writing, poetry, calligraphy, and especially to painting. The Sung tradition of landscape painting lived on in the art of the scholar-painters under the Yüan Dynasty, sometimes intimating in their subject matter ideas of protest against the alien rule.

The picture of a scholar contemplating scenes of nature would convey to the viewer the impression of thoughts of melancholy disapproval of the political reality. The painting of bamboo with its manifold symbolic meanings was especially popular. Bamboo stood for elastic strength and integrity under adverse wind and weather, the very qualities proclaimed by the proud and defiant scholar. It was also the ideal subject for the brush, monochrome ink, and an undefined object that could be singled out in a blank and empty setting.

A few painters, however, collaborated, were taken into the service of the court of Kublai Khan, and attached to the emperor's Han Lin Academy. Among them was Chao Meng-fu, famous as a calligrapher but also for his great art of painting horses, a subject that the Mongols obviously appreciated. His landscapes, combining "a direct spontaneous explosion of feeling with a deep reverence for the antique,"[2] had a strong impact on all subsequent scholar-painters.

One area of literary pursuit reached a special height during Yüan time, the theater. Like theater in the West, Chinese theater originated in religious performances. Chinese Buddhist monks presented stories and legends of the life of Buddha for the edification of the faithful. From this setting emerged a primitive form of verse drama, developed during the Sui and T'ang periods.

During that time another form of stage play became popular at the court. The role of the court jester was used to introduce comical performances in which certain types of characters became the butts of jocular ridicule. A stupid and dishonest official, represented by a painted face and poked fun at by a clown, was one of the standard performers at such entertainments. The use of painted faces to indicate types remained one of the characterizations of Chinese theater.

The thirteenth century, however, brought about dramatic changes and advances in the evolution of Chinese theater. Plays were written not merely for expression of religious devotion and for edification of believers, but to appeal to the sympathy of a larger audience and to evoke identification with the story. This was the period of prominent dramatists whose names became as famous as those of admired painters. Most of these dramatists came from North China, and thus we speak of the Northern School of Drama. Toward the end of Yüan, several southern schools of theater emerged, revising texts and music and introducing local dialects into the performances.

The subject material of these playwrights was drawn from historical themes, legend, and fiction, sources written by scholars who dealt with political history as well as with romantic tales of lovers, their emotions, their suffering, and separations. Like Western opera, the stories were presented in a combination of song and colloquy. Scenery and properties were extremely simple; gestures, well understood by the audience, replaced the setting. Language and music were more important than acting and background. As in some early Western theater, female parts were played by male actors because the low moral reputation of actors in general prevented the appearance of women on the stage. As a result, some great performers gained special fame for their impersonation of female roles.

It was in this form that the theater gained its popularity, providing a make-believe world for escape from the political and economic reality. The Mongols, who enjoyed colorful performances, approved, and their love for gymnastics was responsible for adding athletic spectacles to the performances.

It is from this Yüan drama that the so-called Peking opera emerged. This Chinese opera, sung in the high-pitched voices of the actors and accompanied by an orchestra of traditional Chinese instruments, became a special art form with its experts, connoisseurs, and devotees. More importantly, it was received with broad popular approbation and enthusiasm by large audiences who became familiar with the stories and the music. The performances with their falsetto singing, their clangorous orchestras, their sumptuous costumes, and their carefully choreographed movements remain spectacles that require experience for a full appreciation.

At the height of Mongol power, Kublai Khan attempted to extend his empire toward Japan and Southeast Asia. Two expeditions to Japan, in 1274 and 1281, failed completely when the Mongol fleets manned by Chinese sailors fell victims to storms and the survivors were destroyed by Japanese warriors. In Burma and Indochina the tropical heat and illness, more than the military resistance, defeated the horsemen from the steppe. Mongol power had passed its apogee, and the effects of the exploitative policy in China soon led to the internal upheavals that ended Mongol rule. The last Yüan emperors began to be concerned about the Chinese economic decline and made several efforts to reduce the land tax. They also showed an interest in Chinese literature and art. But these efforts came too late. The Mongol court was no longer able to check the encroachments of the Mongol nobility, the profits of the foreign merchants, and the exploitation by Mongol and Chinese estate owners and financiers. In the end, acute calamities caused by floods and failing harvests led to open rebellions throughout the country; and when a mismanaged attempt to regulate the Yellow River ended in a terrible catastrophe, a general Chinese uprising drove the Mongols out of the country.

Twelve

CHINESE RESTORATION:

The Ming Dynasty

THE YÜAN DYNASTY fell before an uprising of Chinese peasants. The rebellion was directed not only against the foreign conqueror but also against Chinese officials and landlords who had collaborated with the oppressive Mongol rule and had profited from it. Yet, like all such "peasant" rebellions in imperial time before the Western impact, its goal was not a social revolution, but rather the reestablishment of a Chinese dynasty and of the Confucian order of society and state, which the Mongols with their racial policy had violated.

The rebellion, however, was not one unified movement. Outbreaks occurred all over China wherever conditions had become intolerable. In the Yellow River area, where floods had caused massive destruction and famine, the uprising of the Red Turbans, a secret society with a messianic belief in the coming of the future Buddha Maitreya, was the most widespread of the insurrections. In the lower Yangtze region, salt-field workers who labored under wretched conditions and boat people who transported the salt revolted under their own leaders. And smaller outbreaks led to local insurrections in many provinces. At issue at the outset was the question of which movement and leaders would gain the upper hand and then would drive out the foreign rule, which was at the point of disintegrating from its own inner rivalries and decline.

The man who eventually won out in this struggle for supremacy among the rebels was a landless peasant, Chu Yüan-chang, born in Anhui province in 1328. When his parents and older brother died in a famine, he entered a monastery. As monasteries had property

145

and political influence, he gained some knowledge of the mechanism of management, although he had no share in authority. When his monastery was destroyed in local fighting he joined a force of peasant rebels and quickly rose to be their leader. He worked together with the Red Turbans, defeated some of his rivals, and enlarged his force until he became a local power. In 1356 he captured Nanking and made it his capital. It took Chu Yüan-chang more than ten years to destroy his rivals. Only then did he send his army north against Peking. Peking was taken in 1368, the year Chu made himself emperor and established in Nanking the Ming Dynasty (1368–1644). Military superiority had now passed to the Chinese armies, who pursued the Mongols into the steppe and burned their steppe capital Karakorum in 1372.

The emperor, who took the reign title Hung-wu[1] (1368–1398), though a man of little education, was not only an able military leader but clearly an extraordinarily capable organizer and administrator who managed in a short time to restore both the government and the economy. He reestablished regional and provincial administrations, dividing the country into fifteen provinces, which with later sub-divisions and additions constituted the core of the imperial, nationalist, and Communist provincial systems. By reviving and rebuilding the neglected and devastated irrigation works and restoring abandoned acreage to cultivation, he increased agricultural production and derived from it an income from land tax, which again became the main source of state revenue, replacing commercial dues.

This reorganization, however, went beyond a restoration of the traditional Chinese order. Imitating a Mongol system of social man-agement, Emperor Hung-wu divided the population into three status groups, peasants, soldiers, and artisans, each meant to be hereditary and each under the control of a department within the central government. The soldiers' families were given land as self-sufficient agricultural colonies in large or small garrison settlements called *wei* and *so*. These garrisons were concentrated not only near Nanking and later Peking, but stationed also in a defensive arc along the borders of settled Chinese territory, in the North in Manchuria, and along the northwestern border against the steppe and forest nomads, in the Southwest in Yunnan and Kweichow against non-Chinese tribal groups, and along the coast in Chekiang against the inroads of Japanese pirates. These garrison settlements, at first effective, soon declined. They were later used in the North as models for the Manchurian invaders, who copied them for the first stage of transformation to a form of Chinese administrative system. Militarily, the garrison settlements' combat strength decreased through large-scale desertions, so that in later Ming time mercenaries were again needed to fill the ranks of mobile armies. The concept of regional defense, however, remained a valid part of Chinese military thinking. It was later in Ming time reapplied by the formation of local armies under local commanders at the coast, against the increasing problem of Japanese raiders, and under the Manchu dynasty by the organization of provincial armies under provincial leaders against local rebellions. The attempt to establish urban professional hereditary groups of craftsmen and artisans did not last either because a trend of social and professional mobility overcame the regulations, which were impossible to enforce.

Emperor Hung-wu was from the outset hostile to the scholar-gentry, whom he disliked and distrusted. He tended to centralize power as much as possible in his own hands and introduced within the framework of the limited state the strongest form of absolutism of any Chinese dynasty. In the central government, he dissolved the outer court's central organ, the chancellory, and ended the role of Confucian scholars as chief ministers and heads of the entire bureaucracy. Although he needed Confucian officials as regional and local administrators, he checked on them through a secret police that became the dread of the educated elite and the population at large. His confidants at the court were the eunuchs, who had to be loyal to the emperor alone and whom he entrusted with the most critical posts. They commanded the palace guard and the secret police and were appointed to key positions even in military and maritime command. This trust, unmitigated by any other loyalties or obligations on the side of these servants of the court, led inevitably to their large-scale misuse of power and corruption, earning them the hatred of the scholar-elite and resulting in a running battle between the two groups for access to the emperor and to power.

After his death, Hung-wu was at first succeeded by his grandson, then twenty-one years old. This succession was challenged by the new emperor's uncle who was commander of the northern armies at Peking. After four years of bitter civil war, the rebellious armies won, Nanking was captured, and the uncle became emperor under the ruling title Yung-lo. The child emperor probably died in the melee when Nanking fell to the usurper. In the popular imagination he escaped and led the life of a mendicant monk but never regained the throne. Yung-lo moved his capital to Peking, which remained the dynastic capital until the end of imperial times.

This was the first time that a dynasty of Chinese—not foreign—origin chose Peking as its capital. The choice has been puzzling to some historians who point to the shift of the economic development toward the Yangtze area and the South. To stay at Peking, Ming emperors had to rebuild and keep in working condition the Grand Canal that linked the Yangtze region to Peking in order to transport the tax grain for the support of the government and army as under the Mongols. This restoration of the Grand Canal took four years—from 1411 to 1415.

The intellectual center had also moved southward, and when the examinations were reinstituted, the superior success of a much greater number of southern candidates was to force the government to shift larger quotas to the North to retain regional balance within the bureaucracy. Why then keep the capital in the drier and poorer North when Central and South China had become culturally and economically so attractive?

For Emperor Yung-lo who made the move, the reason must have been that Peking was his base of power: For his successors the reason, aside from an unwillingness to leave the magnificent palace built by Yung-lo, must have been chiefly strategic. As long as the Chinese dynasty was militarily strong, Peking's proximity to the northern border made it easier to organize defenses against the invaders from the steppe and to control the steppe region beyond the Great Wall than could have been done from the far away South.

From Peking Yung-lo campaigned in Inner Asia and attempted to extend Chinese control over the tribes in Mongolia and Turkestan and as far north as the Amur River. Although this offensive venture dealing with the primary outside potential threat to the Chinese polity was only partially successful, Yung-lo and his successors also expanded Chinese influence into the maritime world of Southeast Asia and the Indian Ocean.

Maritime expeditions to the states of Indochina, the Malay archipelago, and beyond had already been undertaken in the Sung

Dynasty whose loss of North China and relocation to the lower Yangtze area provided a natural inducement to oceanic voyages to the south. These excursions strengthened the prestige of the dynasty and opened opportunities for a profitable luxury trade, a policy that was continued under the Mongols. The Ming Dynasty made a special effort to reextend the southern drive. To procure the building material for a powerful fleet the government ordered large-scale reforestation in the Nanking area in 1391, planting fifty million trees and training shipwrights to prepare for the planned naval expeditions. Altogether seven such major expeditions were sent to the South Seas during the rule of Yung-lo and his successors up to 1434. What was unique about these campaigns was that they were planned and led by a eunuch, Cheng Ho, who has become famous as one of the great navigators and commanders in history. The expeditions were composed of sizable fleets of very large junks, carrying more than 20,000 men and reaching Annam, Cambodia, Siam, Java, Sumatra, India, Ceylon, Arabia, the Somali coast, the Persian Gulf, and the Red Sea. Some of these maritime ventures resulted in short-lived Chinese intervention in local politics, but the main purpose seems to have been to exalt the prestige of the Chinese empire and simply to explore and navigate across unknown or little-known parts of the world. Cheng Ho himself came from a Moslem family, and his father had undertaken the pilgrimage to Mecca, clearly affecting his son's interest in Moslem lands.

The splendor of the Peking court attracted foreign embassies from Korea, Japan, Annam, and Malaya, confirming to the Chinese the emperor's role of holding the Mandate of Heaven for mankind. But the expense of the ventures to Central Asia and of the maritime expeditions and the fact that they were commanded by a eunuch created a reaction among a faction of officials at the court that led to an end of the policy of naval expansion. After Cheng Ho's death about 1436, plans for further expeditions were sabotaged, and the build-up of naval vessels discontinued. With the decline of the navy, piracy, which had largely disappeared, again became a major bane for Chinese coastal towns.

Almost a century later the Portuguese entered the Indian Ocean and in the sixteenth century reached Chinese cities, first Canton in 1517, then Ningpo, and when driven off there, finally established themselves in 1557 at Macao. Chinese officials had at the beginning treated the Portuguese like Arab or other foreign traders. But the Portuguese, whose history had taught them to regard all non-Christian "heathens" as fair prey, combined trade with piracy, looting, and killing when their forces seemed strong enough. The lessons thus learned by the Chinese were to regard all Europeans as uncivilized barbarians and to treat them accordingly.

The end of the sixteenth century was also a time of direct intellectual contact with Europe through the arrival of Catholic missionaries in China—the Jesuits led the way with the heroic efforts of a few prominent scholar-priests. The most famous was Matteo Ricci, who came to Canton in 1583 and made his way via Nanking to Peking, where he arrived in 1601 and subsequently died in 1610. He and the few others who came after him fully realized the problem of introducing their faith, as they were intent on doing, into a radically different cultural system. They followed two precepts: One was to reach the elite and through them the country-at-large; and the other, to work as much as possible through the existing value system into which their articles of faith were to be fitted. This posed a need to deal with Confucian scholars and to side with them against the rival religion of Buddhism and against the Taoists. In their early work the Jesuits gained a few highly placed Chinese scholar-official converts, but as a whole the worldly rational Confucian philosophers resisted and eventually turned against what appeared to them as the socially disruptive mystique of Christian beliefs.

The Jesuits had been welcomed by the Chinese for their knowledge of science, especially astronomy and mathematics, that they were able to contribute, and as transmitters of other inventions such as cannons for warfare, but their religion was at best tolerated as other religions had been. This lack of interest turned to hostility when Franciscan and Dominican missionaries who arrived later from the Philippines followed a policy of testifying for Christ at the marketplace and condemning Chinese ancestor worship as idolatry.

The modern contact between China and the West thus started on a poor footing. Yet had it come a century earlier, at the outset of the Ming Dynasty when China was a maritime power in its own right, China might have been better able to hold its own in the encounter with the West.

The retreat from maritime ventures was followed by a collapse of Chinese control over the tribal people of the steppes. A Chinese embargo on trade in arms and metals, imposed without preparation in an attempt to curb the military potential of the Oirat tribes, a successor group of the Mongols, proved counterproductive. A unified tribal force initiated raids against Chinese territory, and when Emperor Cheng-t'ung (1436–1449) led a Chinese army commanded by his favorite eunuch, a man without any military experience, in a grossly mismanaged campaign against the Oirats, the emperor himself was captured and ransomed only after several years of captivity. This major defeat in 1449 marked a further decline of Chinese power in Inner Asia and the beginning of a defensive policy based on a newly built Great Wall south of the Ordos Desert.

During the early fifteenth century, however, Ming China was immensely powerful. To display their power the Ming emperors became the greatest builders in imperial history. Their chief architectural accomplishments that survived into our time still manifest the dynastic splendor of the imperial era. The Ming palaces, tombs, city walls, and temples, the remaining sections of the Grand Canal, the sinuous lines of the Great Wall as seen today are impressive examples of the scope of architectural enterprises embarked on by Ming emperors and their architects.

The city of Peking, a creation of the Ming, was built according to a plan that had been traditionally followed by previous dynasties in the building of their capitals at Ch'ang-an, K'ai-feng, and Hangchow. The overall rectangular shape, the type of city walls, the gates, and the rectangular walled imperial palace within the city, all laid out in a south-north direction appear to have been in one form or another a Chinese tradition also copied by neighboring Asian countries. But the plan of the Ming imperial palace manifests a sense of symmetry and design of such magnificent scope that its grandeur must have awed the audience seeker of the past as much as it affects the casual visitor of the present. Entering through magnificent gates into its spacious courtyards with marble steps, balustrades, and terraces, flanked by official buildings and facing great audience halls, massive colored pillars, elaborate brackets, and sweeping, slightly curved palace roofs covered with brilliant colored glazed tiles, the visitor is struck by an exhilarating impression of symmetry, color, harmony, and grandeur. (See Plate 27.) The northern part of the palace city with its maze of courtyards, alleys, rock gardens, pine trees, and shrubs provided living quarters in which the members of the imperial family had their separate apartments. To the north, across the moat and a modern street, lies the Coal Hill Park, providing a splendid view of the palace and the city. (See Plate 28.)

The splendor of the Ming court cloaked the inherent weakness, both political and cultural, that characterized Ming rule, once its great founder and the second outstanding Ming monarch, Emperor Yung-lo had died. Rule by the emperors through their eunuchs required strong monarchical personalities to stem the corruption and exploitation that in turn would provoke unrest and revolt in the provinces. To satisfy the eunuchs' demands for bribes, provincial and local officials, to retain their positions, exacted heavy payments from the farming population. When a eunuch overplayed his hand too openly, the emperor might act, as in 1510, when the fall of the leading eunuch Liu Chin resulted in the confiscation of all his property, including over a quarter-million taels, jewels, and mansions that in their splendor surpassed the emperor's wealth. But the setback of the eunuchs' power did not last and in the early part of the seventeenth century a deadly, prolonged contest between the eunuchs and a group of scholars and scholar-officials seriously undermined government strength at a time of growing danger of rebellion and outside invasion. Major opposition to the eunuchs' rule came from members of the Tung-lin Academy at Wuhsi in Kiangsu province. These scholars had regained political influence at the court under a previous ruler but were severely persecuted under the emperor T'ien-ch'i (1621–1627) when the eunuch Wei Chung-hsien gained control of the administration and the secret police. The eunuch closed the academy, put several hundred of his scholar opponents in prison—where many were executed—while appointing his favorites to official posts and sinecures, instituting a totally corrupt system of appointments. At the death of the emperor, Wei Chung-hsien was assassinated and his clique broken up. For a while the scholar group regained some influence, but the financial and political crisis could not be stemmed and led to the downfall of the dynasty.

Under an autocratic rule, the Ming Dynasty provided no favorable climate for official pursuits in scholarship and the arts. Though the ruling house was Chinese, the scholar-elite remained much of the time in opposition to the court, the eunuchs, and their policies. As under the Mongols, the gap thus widened between the court and the scholar-gentry, and although intermittently some outstanding scholars held high office, for the literati as a whole the tradition of scholarly independence and freedom from government restraint continued, and it became a part of the scholarly creed that independence was morally superior to submission to the discipline of office and authority of the court.

The Confucianism that these scholars presented was the Neo-Confucianism of Chu Hsi of Sung time. This Neo-Confucianism had from the outset contained a cleavage between two trends, one stressing the principle of reason, the other that of intuition. Chu Hsi had distinguished between the principle of Heaven and human desire and believed that through investigation of the principles of things and the study of the classics man would overcome selfishness and partiality and by means of such self-cultivation identify with the moral mind of the universe. The school of intuition, in contrast, emphasized the unity of the human mind with the mind of the universe, a unity that had to be recognized not through prolonged and distracting study but through realization of an innate knowledge of the good. This School of the Mind or Intuition found a strong representative in Ming time in the philosopher and statesman Wang Yang-ming (1472–1529), who added to the concepts of the unity of the universal moral law a third concept of the unity of knowledge and action, which to Wang Yang-ming could not be separated. To him "knowledge is the crystallization of the will to act and action is the task of carrying out knowledge; knowledge is the beginning of action and action is the completion of knowledge."[2] Though the Ming examination system applied a rather stereotyped interpretation of Chu Hsi's principle of reason, Wang Yang-ming's teaching gained widespread response in the private academies, contributing to the division between government and scholarship. Both schools of thought joined in the fight for renewing Confucian ethics among the scholar-elite and reestablishing official integrity in government.

The division between court tradition and the scholar-elite found expression also in art and literature. The court tradition, conventional and uninspired, produced great encyclopedias rather than philosophical works, and court painters specialized in painting birds and flowers in careful detail and decorative compositions rich in color and conservative in style. The emphasis was on technique rather than on the romantic expression of the philosophical concepts—as found in the masterpieces of the great Sung artists.

More imaginative were the independent painters who flourished during the middle of the Ming period, especially in Soochow. The most famous among them was Shen Chou (1427-1509), who never held office but who became the founder of a school of painters known as the Wu school (Wu was an ancient name for Soochow) and a central figure among a group of scholars and collectors. As the philosophy of the Wang Yang-ming school stressed intuition, these scholar painters were not so concerned with portraying nature itself with its inherent spiritual meaning as the great Sung painters had been, but rather attempted to express their philosophical ideas through landscape imagery. Longer poetic and philosophical inscriptions and the imaginary scenes of the paintings indicate this new trend of Ming painters.

The different outlook of the independent scholar-painters from that of academic and court painters was well realized at the time. It was sharpened by a classification, first introduced by a poet-painter of the sixteenth-seventeenth century, Tung Ch'i-chang (1555-1636) who distinguished between a northern and southern school of painting. Tung noted that the latter was free from the control of the court and superior in its expression of philosophical concepts and its spontaneity of brushwork. This was an artistic parallel to the intuitive grasp of the meaning of life in Wang Yang-ming's philosophy. The distinction between a northern and southern school of painters, though somewhat ill defined, random, and disputed, was in various interpretations carried over into the remainder of dynastic history.

With all its autocratic restraint and bureaucratic corruption, the Ming era witnessed a long period of urban prosperity and luxury, especially in the towns of the lower Yangtze region that had become more and more the center of agricultural and commercial wealth. Here the cultural and business elites enjoyed life in an elegant and refined style. At Wuhsi and particularly at Soochow, both near the Grand Canal and close to Lake Tai and other poetic lakes, away from the court, the scholar-gentry created their famous gardens of pools, waterfalls, rockery, artificial hills, and pavilions. Painters, poets, scholars, and art critics gathered for poetry contests and philosophical debates, and renowned collections of the surviving masterworks of Sung and Yüan painters were established by connoisseurs whose seals and inscriptions confirmed and added to the value of the pieces.

This elegant life also encouraged the development of handicrafts that found a rich market not only at the court but also among the wealthy members of the scholar-gentry and the new business class. The Ming period has become famous for its love of color, so evident in its architectural monuments but also in the products of handicrafts. Ming was the period of the first appearance of cloisonné enamel, a technique of enamel designs outlined with bent wire fillets that permitted patterns of rich and strong color effects, used chiefly on various types of vessels, dishes, boxes, vases, and the like. Equally prosperous was the trade of weavers who produced robes for court officials as well as decorative tapestry—and even creating textile reproductions of scrolls of paintings and of calligraphy. Carved lacquer, preferably in a dark red color with rich designs was another Ming specialty.

The most famous of Ming crafts, however, was the manufacture of porcelain. True porcelain was already manufactured in T'ang time; and Sung porcelain had been regarded by the Chinese as the most beautiful in the simplicity of its forms and the purity of its colors and glazes. But the world renown of Chinese porcelain started in Ming time, when Chinese exports reached Europe. Indeed the Western name for porcelain, "china," indicated the importance of this product and its connection with the land of its origin. The favorite style of the time, the underglazed cobalt blue and white, has become syn-onymous with the Ming period. Of the numerous Chinese commercial kilns, the best known has been the ceramic center of Ching-te-chen near Poyang Lake in Kiangsi. There existed a seemingly inexhaustible supply of superb clay and the artistry to produce an unsurpassed luminous white porcelain.

The affluence of the towns and the new middle class of independent scholars, merchants, and manufacturers led to the advent of a new form of literature, the prose novel. Prior to that time, literature had been written by scholars for scholars. The subjects were chiefly philosophy, history, records of government, biographies, and the important issues of the economy, technical advances, and the fine arts. Through Buddhism, a vast religious literature had come in and was studied and used by the monks and priests. There had been little if any literature of entertainment.

Aside from subject matter, the limitation of the spread of the written word was due to the form of writing itself. The written language, *wen yen*, of necessity more concise and terse than the spoken word and basically pictographic rather than phonetic, came to differ more and more from the language as it was spoken in its vocabulary, its structure, and its pronunciation. The monopoly on literacy of the scholar-elite was based on the difficulty not only of memorizing the vast number of characters of the written language, but also of learning a type of expression totally different from that in common use, a language that served a scholarly and governmental purpose, but was not very suitable to express matters of daily life. A *wen-yen* text listened to by a scholar, not to mention a noneducated person, without previous knowledge of its content would not be understood.

Now, with education reaching beyond the examination candidates, a greater reading public could be found, especially if the subject matter demanded no further scholarly or technical learning. The time had come to write in *pai-hua*, the spoken language of the people, or at least close to it. Improvements in printing, not only in woodblocks, but in movable type (invented in China in the eleventh century), making books much more readily available, contributed to the popularity of reading stories simply for the enjoyment of the narrative.

The great novels of Ming time were never recognized as proper literature by the scholar-elite, which disapproved of this degrading of letters to mere storytelling; no scholar would admit to reading, let alone writing them. From Ming time on, however, the content of these novels was known to every Chinese who could read and, by retelling, to the people at large, and became a part of the cultural heritage.

Four Ming novels have become most famous. The earliest was a historical novel: *The History of the Three Kingdoms*. It dealt with the historical personalities of the period after the fall of the Han Dynasty when the struggle for power among the leaders of regional kingdoms created a time of political and military turbulence and of Machiavellianism that led eventually to the division of China during the north-south era. In the historical novel, this age of treachery and deceit was reinterpreted as a romantic epoch in which the historical figures were seen as true heroes and great villains fighting and maneuvering for their cause. The stories of their adventures, of the hero Liu Pei and his companions and the villain T'sao T'sao, have become part of Chinese folk legend.

The second of the great Ming novels, *Shui Hu Chuan* ("Water Margin"), rendered in an English translation by Pearl Buck under the title *All Men are Brothers*, was also written in its final form in the sixteenth century. It is the story of the bandit leader Sung Chiang, a historical personality at the end of the Sung Dynasty, and his fictitious 108 companions, who in the novel have all turned to banditry because of oppression by corrupt officials. In this novel the bandits are noble and upright men who fight for justice in a narrative that has been compared with the Robin Hood tale in English tradition. It is perhaps most akin to the German poet Schiller's play *Die Räuber* in its description of the individual life stories and the fates of a group of outcasts that become the fictional heroes.

Quite different in subject matter but of equal importance was a social novel, *Chin P'ing Mei*, which begins as the sequence of one of the incidents of the novel *Shui Hu Chuan*. One of its outcasts attempted to take revenge on his sister-in-law and her paramour, who had murdered her husband to prevent the discovery of her affair. The novel describes the faithless wife's new role as concubine of her lover, the intrigues between her, the first wife, and several other concubines in the household of this rich merchant. The description of life in a middle-class family in great detail, the rounded portrayals of the characters, especially the women, provide remarkable insight into Chinese social life and mores of the time. Its graphic accounts of erotic behavior, forming part though not an exaggerated aspect of its narrative of human relations, was offensive to earlier Western readers, though hardly so today.

Lastly, a romantic adventure story dealt with the legendary experiences of the Buddhist monk Hsüan-tsang who, in the first half of the seventh century A.D., travelled for sixteen years on his journey to India in search of religious texts. *Hsi-yu-chi* (*Journey to the West*), published about 1570, narrates the popular fantasies and folktales that grew around this epic tale of the perseverance and determination of a great Buddhist traveler. In the fairytale account the monk's companions were animals—a monkey and a pig—who through their ability and magic tricks assisted their master in his mission. The monkey, Sun Wu-k'ung, in particular was a well-known figure in Chinese fable, a mischief maker who could disguise himself, leap a thousand miles, do all kinds of tricks, but here was serving the cause of the indefatigable monk.

These and lesser-known novels introduced a new genre into Chinese literature. The novels were officially ignored but avidly read at the time and were in retrospect a part of the development of middle-class life and interests that began to transform Chinese society in Ming time. This new literary art remained popular during the subsequent dynastic period, the Manchu Dynasty, as the growth of an urban middle class continued. In fact, the most famous of these novels was written in the middle of the eighteenth century. *Hung Lou Meng (The Dream in the Red Chamber)*, is the story of one family and its decline, an autobiographical account of an anonymous author, a scion of a Chinese prestigious family (as determined by later research). The story recounts the childhood, adolescence, and growth to maturity of a young hero and his girl cousins under the care of a traditional family and a matriarchal grandmother. It deals with the tender growing feeling of love between a bright but capricious young boy and his delicate cousin. The romance ends in melancholy and tragedy because of the family's well-meant principles of arranged marriages—an early implied protest against the conventions of the Confucian family system. Because of its style, character portrayal, and narrative, *The Dream in the Red Chamber* has become the most famous of Chinese social novels, compared by some to the *Forsythe Saga* or *Buddenbrooks* in Western literature.

Thirteen

THE LAST OF THE IMPERIAL ORDER:

The Manchu or Ch'ing Dynasty

THE LAST CHINESE dynasty, the Ch'ing Dynasty (1644–1911), was founded by a Tungus people, the descendants of the Jurchen who had ruled North China earlier under the name of Chin. The Ch'ing founder had given his people the name of Manchu, and their homeland has since become known in international parlance as Manchuria. Their dynasty became known as the Manchu Dynasty.

The Manchus did not conquer China as other invaders had before them; they came by invitation. Theirs was a negotiated incursion, directed against an internal Chinese rebellion that had overthrown the Ming Dynasty. It ws this indirect method of power seizure with the cooperation of leading Chinese military and administrative officials that made it possible for a comparatively small frontier tribe to take over the large Chinese empire and rule it successfully for a longer span of time than any other conquest dynasty. The fact that they came in by negotiation also determined the Manchu political and social system and their cultural policy in China.

The Ming Dynasty collapsed for the same cyclical reasons that had brought about the fall of previous dynasties, Chinese or foreign: corruption and weakness at the court, famine and rebellion in the country. The autocracy of the Ming court, the eunuch system, and the prolonged contention between the entrenched eunuchs and the scholar-elite had aggravated the decline during the last century of the dynasty. The opportunity was present for founding a new dynastic rule; the question was whether it would rise from within China or from across the border.

The leader of an internal rebellion, Li Tzu-ch'eng, was a former robber band chieftain from Shensi province who had raided systematically in Shensi, Shansi, Honan, Hupeh, Szech'wan, Kansu, and Anhui provinces. His highly mobile cavalry force had at first no political aims beyond the looting and plundering of brigandage. When Li was cornered in South Shensi with a large baggage train, he ordered his men to kill their own camp followers and move on as a light cavalry force into Hupeh. There a famine brought him new followers and success as well as a base of operations in the Han River valley and in Honan. In Hupeh he enlisted the counsel of some "scholar"-advisers, gave up his marauding raids, set up a political organization with offices and ranks, appointed governors over some districts he controlled, and proclaimed himself emperor. From there Li moved through Shensi and Shansi to attack Peking, conquered the city, drove the last Ming emperor to suicide, and appeared to have conquered the empire.

Li failed to hold his conquest in the long run because of his apparent unwillingness to abandon for any length of time his looting and slaughtering and to come to terms with the scholar-elite whose support he needed to establish a workable government. According to his official biography at least, the death and destruction Li left in his path was unusual even compared with the grim record of other similar rebellions. There is little other explanation for the fact that a key Chinese commander and most Chinese officials in North China, rather than cooperate with the Chinese rebel Li, made common cause with the Manchu invaders and were willing to work for them in a system that was obviously more akin to their Chinese tradition than was the harshly destructive and socially subversive leadership that could be expected from Li.

Wu San-kuei, the Chinese commander at the border pass at Shanhaikuan, has been accused of betraying the Chinese cause when he joined the Manchus rather than defending the frontier. Wu's treason was dramatized in Chinese history as a romantic story of rage over the loss of his favorite concubine, who had been taken captive under Li and whom he regained eventually in battle. The real reason for Wu's decision to join the Manchus evidently was that in contrast to Li, who persecuted scholar-officials, the Manchus had by that time accepted the Chinese system and made use of Chinese officials in leading government positions. There had already been correspondence between the Manchu ruler and Wu San-kuei before Li's capture of Peking, and when the decisive hour came, Wu's choice, as his letters to the Manchus indicate, was between order and the protection of the system he believed in and disorder on the side of the rebel. This choice goes far to explain the quick success of a "barbarian" conqueror.

The Manchus were in an ideal position geographically to prepare for the conquest of China. Manchuria was a frontier area par excellence. Though outside the Great Wall, it included within its southern part a Chinese agricultural region, settled since Neolithic time. In the West lived Tungus forest nomads, in the steppes of the East, Mongol nomads. In conquering and incorporating these groups, the Manchus set up under their ruler Nurhaci (1559–1626) a quasi-Chinese bureaucratic government (with the help of captured Chinese officials and defectors) long before they moved into China proper.

Nurhaci had started from very modest beginnings as the head of a small clan of Tungus forest nomads in the Long White Mountains, not far from the Yalu River in Eastern Manchuria. In local contention he had become a feudal lord in one of the frontier guards that the Chinese had set up to organize adjoining clans and maintain control. When this Chinese control weakened, Nurhaci was able to defeat rival Tungus clan leaders and incorporate their clans into his growing force. In the process he captured Chinese towns, people, and officials whom he appointed as his administrators, transforming his own government more and more into a Chinese type of administration and transfering his capital to Shenyang (Mukden). By 1636 Nurhaci's successor assumed the dynastic title Ta Ch'ing, becoming a contender for rule over all China. He also gave his people the name *Manchu*, probably after the personal name of an ancestor of Nurhaci, derived from the name of the Buddhist emanation Manjusri.

When the Ming general at the frontier called in the Manchus as avengers against the rebel Li Tzu-ch'eng, the way was open to Peking. Together they defeated the rebellion, but instead of leaving, the Manchus stayed in China and moved on to destroy the last Ming contenders and eventually even the Chinese generals who had been rewarded with territories in the South and who used their new bases in a futile revolt against the new Manchu Dynasty.

From the outset, the Manchus were more traditionally Confucian than any previous alien dynasty had been. First, their numbers were

much too small to provide for an educated administrative staff for
the central government, not to mention the whole of China. They
had to rely for the major part on Chinese officials and, to gain their
services, they had to accept the entire Chinese political and social
structure—the limited state, the autonomy of the scholar-elite, the
examination system, the scholar-gentry's social and economic leadership, and even the administrative divisions, ranks, and titles with
some minor additions and changes. Only in the leading administrative
positions were Manchus appointed, to guarantee their power, but
even then the practice was followed by pairing a Manchu with a
Chinese, the former for security, the latter for expertise.

To guarantee their power the Manchus, now the Ch'ing Dynasty,
maintained their own military organization. They brought their banner
forces into China, placing them in garrisons around the capital Peking
and in strategic locations around the country. They relied, however,
on regular Chinese armies for their major military manpower. As a
matter of security the Manchu banner garrisons, though smaller in
number than the Chinese forces, were strategically disposed in such
a way as to control the more numerous Chinese units, which were
scattered in smaller garrisons. Even the Manchu banner garrisons
were made up from units of each of the eight banners so that no
leader of one banner could challenge the power of the emperor. A
new commanding officer was appointed for each campaign.

The same division of authority was applied to the civil administration. The system of bureaucratic control developed throughout
imperial history reached its greatest refinement under the Ch'ing.
In local and provincial administration no official was permitted to
hold office in his home area, and tenure in any one position was
to be no longer than three years, often shorter. The obvious purpose
was to prevent any official from establishing a local power base. For
the same reason the authority of provincial officials was curbed by
division in the chain of command. Provincial commissioners for
finance and justice, intendants for the salt tax and grain delivery,
and directors of study were to report to their superiors in Peking
directly, thus limiting the powers of provincial governors and governors-general. Such officials were also required to give secret reports
about each other. This division of authority and the political infighting
that often resulted did not contribute to admimistrative efficiency;

the purpose was rather to guarantee the security of central control and prevent defiance and independence on the part of local leaders.

All these measures were only a refinement on Chinese governmental tradition; they did not offend the sensitivities of the scholar-elite upon whose cooperation the Manchu rule depended. To maintain their support the Ch'ing rulers used every opportunity to stress their accord with the Confucian concepts of government and the social order. The Manchu emperors not only cultivated the Confucian scholars, they themselves studied Confucianism. Several emperors became famous for their calligraphy and poetry and obviously felt perfectly at home in the Confucian world. The most conspicuous sign of submission to a foreign rule imposed on the Chinese people at the time of the conquest was the Manchu hair style—the wearing of the queue. At the beginning of the twentieth century when Chinese nationalism turned against the alien ruler, cutting off the queue became a revolutionary act.

To prevent their total submergence and disappearance in the vast majority of the Chinese that surrounded them, the Manchus attempted to keep their banner people distinct from the Chinese population. They prohibited intermarriage between Manchus and Chinese, and Manchu women were forbidden to have their feet bound after the fashion of upper-class Chinese. They forbade their banner people to take up farming or any of the crafts so as to maintain their military profession. The fields allotted to the garrisons were thus cultivated by Chinese peasant farmers, and the Manchu soldiers, once peace reigned, led a dronelike existence. Their regular pay, though several times raised, was over time devalued through steady, slow inflation, and through inactivity and lack of training the banner garrisons became by the latter part of the eighteenth century militarily useless.

One of the most renowned of the Manchu emperors was the K'ang-hsi emperor, who ruled for sixty years (1662–1722) and under whose reign the empire was fully unified, at peace, and prosperous. A favorite painting of him shows the emperor as a scholar with a large, brimmed hat, relaxed in a natural setting without any attributes of imperial power. (See Plate 29.) Toward the end of his long rule, K'ang-hsi issued an edict that demonstrates both his pride as a Manchu and his basic Confucian attitude. It is worth quoting:

Having been on the throne for more than fifty years and almost at the age of eighty, I find that my country is peaceful and my people contented, though not exactly in an ideal condition of economic sufficiency and political satisfaction. I have worked all these long years carefully, patiently and faithfully, as if for a day. The word "hard" is not enough to describe the nature of my work. Some emperors of the past died young; historical critics usually attribute their early death to luxury and dissipation, even if they know the criticized monarchs were good emperors. This is academic cynicism. I want to vindicate the past emperors: in fact they died of fatigue from state affairs.

A minister can enter or retire from government service as he pleases, but the emperor has no end to his work. . . .

I am physically strong since childhood. I could bend a fifteen-strength bow and shoot long and heavy arrows. I am excellent in military tactics. But I never executed a single one of my people without justifiable cause. . . . The silver reserve in the treasury has never been used by me except for military campaigns and famine relief. Knowing that this money is the flesh and blood of my little people, I never wasted a single bit of the silver. Wherever I went, I never ordered special decorations or preparations for my visits. Each of my palaces is run with ten or twenty thousand taels of silver, which is less than one percent of the annual expenditure on reconstruction of dams and dykes.

All the above statements form a true picture of my hard work and an expression of my sincerity. Whenever I read a petition of an old official for the privilege of retirement, I wept. You all have an opportunity to retire, but when can I have mine? I am now seventy-five. A few white hairs have just appeared. Some have advised me to have them dyed, but I declined their advice with a smile, because there have not been many emperors who could live long enough to have white hair.

If I am to have both my hair and my beard snow-white, will it not be romantic? But, alas! When I look back to my old colleagues who worked with me at the beginning of my reign, none can be found.[1]

The same emperor K'ang-hsi in 1670 issued to his officials and subjects a hortatory edict that was hung up in prominent position in the government yamens of the empire. This "Sacred Edict" consisted of sixteen maxims, each containing seven words and written in the highest literary style. They invoked obedience and respect to the Confucian concepts and government authority, stressing Confucian loyalties and devotions—a sober and moralistic interpretation and political application of rigid Confucian rules of propriety.

It was thus a most orthodox Confucianism that the Manchus favored. Rather than creating new trends, they wanted to imitate the past examples of scholarship and art, which they admired, and they organized scholarly work on encyclopedias and dictionaries and based their examination system on a stereotyped interpretation of the classical texts, the "eight-legged essay," which became the object of derision for those who wanted to break through the growing limitations of official orthodoxy.

Under Emperor Ch'ien-lung (1736-1796) the Manchu Dynasty reached its greatest glory in terms of territorial expansion and domestic prosperity. Aside from China Proper, the imperial sway extended over the Chinese dependencies of Tibet, Turkestan, and Mongolia, and, of course, the Manchu homeland, Manchuria. Korea, Burma, and Annam were tributaries, and Chinese control extended, at least for some time, beyond Tibet into Nepal. For Asia and much of the world, China of the eighteenth century was the most splendid empire on the globe, equal if not superior to any European country in the minds of the foreign missionaries and other Westerners who succeeded in gaining access.

Seen through the eyes of missionaries, Chinese concepts of government and society reached Europe and had at the time more impact on European thought than had Western ideas on the Chinese elite or people. The writers of the Enlightenment, Voltaire and Leibnitz among others, applied in the formulation of their philosophical and political ideas what they had heard or read about Chinese society, believed to be ideal as it was managed by scholar-officials. The concept of a superior "Wisdom of the East" has intrigued Western philosophers and writers, and China was regarded as the greatest Eastern culture from which much could be learned. The French physiocrats, a school of political economists that emphasized the powers of nature as the source of public wealth and prosperity and the necessity of governmental noninterference with natural laws, is thought to have derived support from the Chinese example.

Chinese art and crafts were much sought after and increasingly imported, and the taste in Chinese objects led to imitations and the style of "chinoiseries" that affected Europe in late seventeenth and early eighteenth centuries.

In China Western Jesuit missionary influence remained limited to the Chinese court, where successors of Matteo Ricci, Father Adam Schall, who worked on the calendar, and Father Ferdinand Verbiest, who helped in cannon casting, contributed their knowledge to Chinese advancement. More notable still was the work of the Jesuit Giuseppe Castiglione, an accomplished painter who went to China in 1715, and, once there, adjusted his art to Chinese taste and tradition. He applied Western styles of shading and perspective with discretion and impressed with his method some Chinese painters, gaining some students. He was particularly popular because of his paintings of horses and the realistic style with which he decorated the large halls and rooms of the court. But to Chinese painters who appreciated him, Castiglione's technique was still but a craft that could not be regarded as equal to the Chinese mastery of the brush and grasp of the spirit contained in true art.

In the prosperous years of eighteenth century China, paintings were much sought after not only by officials but also by the wealthy middle class, especially of the commercial towns of the lower Yangtze area as at Yangchow (just north of the crossing point of the Yangtze and the Grand Canal) where many professional painters followed the taste of their new clientele in order to be successful. This led to imitation of the style of the classics, and painting lost much of its originality and strength. (See Plate 30.)

The same slow decline affected many of the crafts. There are still beautiful examples of ceramic ware, especially the monochromes of the Kang-hsi period, but much of Ch'ing porcelain, lacquer ware, and decorative pieces, especially those made for export, in retrospect appear to have been overloaded with decoration, insipid, and gaudy. They expressed a stagnation of the arts that reflected the socio-political landscape.

By the nineteenth century the Ch'ing Dynasty was in decline. The height of Ch'ing success under Emperor Ch'ien-lung had also marked the turning point in the dynastic cycle. Ch'ien-lung had extended Chinese power to its farthest reaches. He had destroyed Mongol power in Central Asia, had incorporated the whole of

Chinese Turkestan, extended Ch'ing control over Tibet, and forced Nepal to recognize Ch'ing superiority. Burma and North Vietnam became tributary states. He had kept the peace at home. Population had increased and so had the wealth of the urban populations.

Like his predecessors, Ch'ien-lung was himself well educated in the Confucian classics and prided himself on his scholarship and his poetry. Throughout the realm his calligraphy was displayed in tablets and inscriptions, and he worked unquestionably hard at his imperial duties. To show his devotion to the Confucian tradition, he had organized the largest collection ever of Chinese traditional writings, the *Ssu-k'u ch'üan-shu*—the "Four Treasuries."[2] Composed of 3,450 entire works, containing 36,000 volumes, this vast compilation was supposed to include the best of the scholarly writings in the classics, history, philosophy, and literature and to omit books that were thought seditious or heretical. It was a colossal effort meant to demonstrate the emperor's erudition and concern for Confucian tradition but was also keeping a large number of scholars gainfully employed in a manner that would support rather than challenge Manchu rule.

Ch'ien-lung ruled for sixty years, retiring officially at the end of this time in order not to surpass the length of rule of his famous grandfather K'ang-hsi. Ch'ien-lung died in 1799. At the end of his rule rebellions broke out and the decline began. Ch'ien-lung's campaigns had been expensive; and toward the end of his long rule, large scale corruption and bribery undermined morale at the court, worsened by the venality of the Manchu guardsman Ho Shen who had become the emperor's favorite. The emperor himself became more and more extravagant, and although his power remained unchallenged during his lifetime, soon after his death the discontent found its expression in peasant unrest and rebellion.

A rapid population increase to more than 300 million by the end of the eighteenth century and an estimated 100 million more by the middle of the nineteenth century was at first balanced by the introduction of new crops—maize, sweet potatoes, and peanuts—that could be cultivated on hilly land and increased the basic food supply, but when the population outgrew these resources, the standard of living began to decline. The increased size of the population diluted government control over local corruption and, in addition, the evolution of a city-based economy adversely affected rural conditions. In 1793, the White Lotus Sect, a Buddhist society, organized in North China a rebellion that was not suppressed until 1804. And after that all over China rebellions that the corrupt and declining Chinese and Manchu banner forces were no longer able to contain arose, and local militias and self-defense forces had to take over the protection of their home regions against bandits and rebels.

It was at this time of dynastic decline that a new, outside factor appeared on the Chinese scene that accelerated and transformed the traditional cycle of dynastic decay and fall. This was the economic, military, and intellectual impact of the West.

All Chinese dynasties had viewed the main military and political threat to their rule as coming from across the Inner Asian frontier. The Great Wall had been built to defend against this danger, and Chinese and conquest dynasties had extended their control into Inner Asia to neutralize the danger, to play barbarians against barbarians, and to prevent the emergence of any strong power in the steppe. That any danger to the Middle Kingdom could come from a few ships of strangers from faraway countries did not occur to the rulers of an empire who regarded themselves and their culture as the most civilized and powerful system on earth.

Western traders had sold their goods in East Asian countries for many centuries, but in China and also in Japan they had to accept the limitations on such trade imposed by the rulers of these countries. In the sophisticated era of T'ang time, foreign traders had lived and flourished at the capital and in the major cities of the empire. The Mongols had been equally broadminded about the foreign merchants that provided the luxuries for the ruling Mongol elite. But during the last dynasty in particular, foreign traders were severely restricted. This was at least partly due to the Chinese experiences with Portuguese and later British and other sailors from Western countries. These sailors were often an unruly lot to begin with, and in turn showed little respect for the "pagan" Chinese. By 1760 all foreign trade by sea was confined to the port of Canton, where Chinese officials collected a variety of duties and, for better control of the trade, licensed thirteen Chinese merchant houses, the so-called Thirteen Co-hong, who as a group and individually were held responsible for dealing with the foreign merchants and for the payment of all fees. The merchants confined to this contact and to a limited space in Canton where they could reside during the yearly trading season accepted this restraint and the imposition of harsh Chinese jurisdiction over the "unruly" foreigners as long as the trade was so advantageous. The ever-present Chinese threat to cut it off altogether remained an effective deterrent against any attempt to change the rules.

How one-sided the need for trade had become is apparent from the list of commodities exchanged. Tea was the chief item of export from China. Tea's importance in international trade at the time, in the fortunes of the British East India Company, and indeed in creating the wealth that went into the industrial revolution can hardly be exaggerated. Silk, porcelain, rhubarb, and Chinese art objects also formed part of the trade. But the Chinese were not interested enough in the goods the West had to offer to buy them in sufficient quantities to balance the export of Chinese goods. Furs and some Western mechanical products such as clocks were traded in China; and after the British conquest of India, Indian cotton goods found a ready market in China. But the Chinese economy was largely self sufficient and the balance of the export of Chinese goods had to be paid in cash, meaning silver, paid at first in ingots and eventually in silver coins, introduced from Central America in the form of the Mexican dollar, which became the basic currency unit for modern China. The British obtained their silver largely in India, thus connecting the exploitation of their Indian colony with the buildup of their world economic empire.

This arrangement of payment in cash, which had never been satisfactory, became offset in the second half of the eighteenth century with the arrival of the industrial revolution. In England the industrial interests in the newly important manufacturing cities such as Manchester and Liverpool clamored for overseas markets for British woolens. Under pressure from the reconstituted parliament, the British East India Company, seeking to accommodate the textile interests at home, attempted to prevail on their Chinese *co-hong* partners to sell British woolens on the Chinese market—at a loss to the British that they could well afford in view of the great profits made in the tea trade. In turn, the Chinese *co-hong* merchants, willing to please their British trading partners, sold some of these woolens—also at a loss to them, which was more than made up by *their* gains in the tea trade. Nothing more than these double losses at the import side of the China trade demonstrates the one-sidedness of the need for and interest in trade between West and East during the early part of the industrial revolution.

In 1793, the British government sent to the Chinese emperor a diplomatic mission under Lord Macartney, who was to seek a trade agreement and the opening of additional Chinese ports to British merchants and British woolens. The emperor's response clearly demonstrated the differences between the two worlds. Emperor Ch'ien-lung wrote to British King George III:

> Our Celestial Empire possesses all things in prolific
> abundance and lacks no product within its own borders.
> There was therefore no need to import the manufactures of
> outside barbarians in exchange for our own produce. But as
> the tea, silk and porcelain which the Celestial Empire
> produces, are absolute necessities to European nations and to
> yourselves, we have permitted as a signal mark of favor, that
> foreign hongs should be established at Canton, so that your
> wants might be supplied and your country thus participate in
> our beneficence.[3]

Macartney was exempted from the kowtow, the nine successive prostrations before the throne, which was the established ritual for any audience with the emperor and which the emperor himself had to practice before Heaven and before his parents. The emperor, interested in meeting the Englishman, was willing to dispense with this formality for Macartney since the "foreign tribute bearer" was obviously ignorant of proper manners. But the mission was clearly a failure. The issue of the clash of two different economic and political systems remained unresolved and might in any case have led to a confrontation, even if there had been no conflict over a commodity that the Chinese would buy in large quantities and that reversed the problem of the balance of trade: The new commodity was opium.

Opium was first produced in India and from there was imported in increasing amounts to China by individual traders, first the British and then, when it became the most profitable commodity on the Chinese market, by the traders of all nationalities. The Chinese soon realized the potential harm of this new import from not only its debilitating physical effect on individuals, but also the adverse effects it had both on corvée labor and finally on the financial balance of trade. The import of opium increased to such a degree that instead of receiving silver payments for the excess in exports, the Chinese economy had to pay a growing amount of silver for the opium import, because it far surpassed the value of Chinese exports. This negative financial balance caused a shortage of silver, a deflation, and a devaluation of the copper coins with which the Chinese farmer had to measure his tax payments.

The emperor's answer was the prohibition of opium import, resulting, as all such prohibition policies, in increased smuggling and corruption of officials and participating traders. Finally, the emperor appointed a special commissioner, Lin Tse-hsü, to enforce the prohibition of the opium trade at Canton. Under the threat of force and loss of all trade, in 1839 the commissioner obtained the surrender of all the opium that had just arrived for the seasonal trade and had it burned. Then he demanded from the foreign merchants the payment of a bond to guarantee against further smuggling. The U.S. merchants accepted; the British, claiming that they could not exert such control over the individual merchants, refused and were excluded from any further trade. After handling their seasonal business through U.S. merchants, the British decided to use force, and thus began what the British call the First Anglo-Chinese War and what the Chinese with good reason call the Opium War, a name that added a special odium to the opening of China by force.

The war lasted from November 1839 to August 1842. It consisted of a number of detached British actions, first at Canton, which the British took, and finally at the Yangtze delta region. When British ships moved up the Yangtze River, threatening the tax grain transport on the Grand Canal, the Chinese imperial government was willing to negotiate. The outcome of the negotiations was the Treaty of Nanking, August 1842, which initiated a system of foreign rights and guaranteed interests in China that eventually led to the end of the empire and helped to bring on the Chinese revolution.

The Treaty of Nanking stipulated that five Chinese ports, Shanghai, Ningpo, Foochow, Amoy, and Canton, be opened to British traders to "reside and carry on trade." British nationals were at the same time to be exempt from Chinese jurisdiction, a clause that was to protect them from the vagaries of Chinese concepts of law as it applied to barbarians, but, in practice, was to go much farther in transforming the cities in question into a particular type of status, "treaty ports," a unique political category that was to affect deeply the fortunes of China's transformation to modern nationhood.

The Treaty of Nanking also decreed the cession to Britain of the island of Hong Kong, which controlled the sea entrance to Canton and had been used as a trading depot for the Canton trade. The treaty abolished the *co-hong* system and permitted the British to trade with anyone they chose. A fixed tariff, which could only be changed by mutual consent, was set on trade. In addition, China had to pay an indemnity of 21 million taels, a sum that included the value of the opium confiscated and destroyed. It was the first of a series of indemnity payments imposed by this and later treaties that were to be guaranteed by the only reliable source of government revenue, foreign customs duties and the salt gabelle. Opium was not mentioned in the Treaty of Nanking and was not regulated until the revised treaties of 1858 and 1860, which legalized importation and imposed duties.

The Treaty of Nanking established formal equality between the rulers of China and Great Britain, ending the Chinese claim that the Mandate of Heaven was global. By so doing the treaty undermined the ideological sanction of dynastic rule, a first step in the destruction of the imperial order. In the view of the Western nations, China had to be brought into the modern world, by force if necessary, to participate in the give and take of the new economic interrelations. But the Chinese considered the Nanking treaty and the treaties that followed with other Western countries imposed "unequal treaties" that humiliated China and violated Chinese sovereignty. The role that opium played in this new relationship with the West added to the strong repugnance to the West that became a major factor in modern Chinese nationalism.

The Treaty of Nanking was an opening wedge into Chinese life for all major Western powers of the time. To secure a share in whatever advantages others might obtain in dealing with the weakening Chinese government, the British obtained through the Treaty of the Bogue in 1843 a one-sided "most favored nation clause." The treaties later concluded with the United States at Wanghsia in July 1844 and with France in October of the same year contained this most favored nation clause, which deprived China of negotiating advantages with any of the powers. The U.S. treaty spelled out in more detail than the others the right of extraterritoriality of U.S. citizens. This right provided for the privileged position of all foreigners from nations holding treaty rights in China.

How far-reaching the effect of the treaty stipulations would become was not fully realized at the time by either side. The combination of the right to "reside and carry on trade" in the treaty ports and of being exempt from Chinese territorial jurisdiction transformed the treaty ports into foreign enclaves in the Chinese body politic. And since these ports, which eventually included almost all important coastal and inland cities of China, were to become the modern economic centers of China, the political and judicial separation of this modernized section of the country from its backsliding hinterland became a most adverse factor for the formation of a modern Chinese nation-state. Here the new Chinese business class, under the protection of foreign administrations guaranteed by naval force could pursue its search for economic success without having to participate in the fight for political power in China. Though the urban business class shared in the nationalist spirit and might when the occasion arose boycott foreign goods, the battle for establishing a new polity and government was to be fought not in the cities but by military armies in the provinces.

Throughout China, foreigners resided in "national concessions," quarters set up through negotiation between a local Chinese official and a foreign consul who in practice assumed authority over the concession. The exception was Shanghai, because of its location the most important of all treaty ports, where the United States government, opposed to national concessions, insisted on transforming the British concession into an "international settlement" where all foreigners with treaty rights could reside. This Shanghai International Settlement, established in 1854, was under the nominal authority of all concerned consuls, who were required to reach unanimous decisions. In practice authority was in the hands of a municipal government of the foreign landowners to which Chinese landowners were eventually admitted. Remarkably free from practical control by any foreign government, this autonomous regime in what soon became the largest commercial and industrial city of China served community economic interests rather than showing any active concern for or even full understanding of the evolving political drama. The treaty ports, not abolished until a hundred years later, in 1943 when the cities were under Japanese occupation during World War II, had clearly an adverse effect on the course of China's transformation into a nation-state.

The gap between Westernization and a modernization within a Chinese setting was widened when modern Western education entered China, first under the auspices and institutional organization of missionaries whose well-intentioned effort was also based on treaty rights that opened the country to their work. Indeed the negative aspect of the Western impact was not so much the often touted economic exploitation as it was a total disregard, under the Westernized educational system, for the Chinese cultural setting.

The Opium War was much more than a conflict over the prohibition of the import of opium into China, as the Chinese came to regard it. It was also much more than the breakdown of Chinese barriers against Western free trade and the acceptance of Western norms of state relations and international law by a stubborn Chinese court and officialdom, as the West saw it. It was the clash of two opposed political systems: the traditional world order of imperial China and the international order of nation-states that had emerged in the West since the treaty of Westphalia in 1648. When the *cohong* system was abolished and China opened to the free flow of Western trade, when the Chinese government was forced to accept foreign nations on equal terms, and when Chinese law and sovereign judicial authority was discarded with respect to foreigners in China, the concept of the Mandate of Heaven was fatally affected. Though it survived for over half a century, the traditional Chinese imperial order was doomed. The Opium War and the Treaty of Nanking signaled the end of the imperial era.

Fourteen

FROM EMPIRE TO NATION-STATE:

The Great Rebellion, Reform, and Revolution

THE TAIPING REBELLION, 1850 to 1864, arose as a strange combination of traditional factors that had led to past rebellions with new, totalitarian concepts, derived from a fantastic interpretation of Christian doctrine. The rebellion had its origin in some of the cyclical Chinese problems marking the decline of dynastic rule, but became perverted under a strangely distorted version of Christian beliefs. It began in the South in the provinces of Kwangsi and Kwangtung, the first to feel the economic dislocations of the Opium War, swept through most of Central China, threatening the dynasty in Peking and, though defeated, heralded the end of the traditional order of central dynastic control.

The setting was a local conflict between two types of communities, the original residents and the Hakka, later immigrants from North China, a conflict that local officials could not handle and tried to resolve by siding against the Hakka. What distinguished this conflict from all earlier rebellions was that it was directed not only against the government but also against the whole social and political order.

Hung Hsiu-ch'üan (1814–1864), a Hakka from a commoner family in Kwangtung, several times had failed to pass the government examinations and had a severe mental breakdown. While recovering he read a missionary tract that he felt explained the reason for his illness. His unconsciousness and ravings had only been the outer manifestations of a religious experience during which he had ascended to Heaven, met the Heavenly Father and Jesus Christ and learned that he was himself God's son, the younger brother of Jesus, being trained to establish God's Heavenly Kingdom on earth. With the help of a few converts among relatives and friends, he preached his beliefs in localities of Kwangtung and Kwangsi provinces and organized a Society of God Worshippers.

Hung's Christian ideas were adapted to his Chinese concepts. The family system was introduced into Heaven where the Heavenly Father and Jesus each had wives and families; Hung himself had been given a heavenly wife and was only reluctantly obeying God's command to return to earth.

This strange amalgamation of Christian beliefs, Chinese concepts and institutions, and the fantastic ideas of its deranged prophet formed an extraordinarily potent ideological mixture that soon gained a growing number of fanatical adherents, but in the end collapsed amid incongruities and the absurd fantasies of its leader. The original fanaticism and strength of beliefs carried the movement beyond local skirmishes to a large-scale attempt to overthrow the Manchu Dynasty and establish a worldly kingdom to be called *T'aip'ing T'ien-kuo,* or the Heavenly Kingdom of Great Peace. Hung Hsiu-ch'üan assumed the title of Heavenly King (*T'ien Wang*) and Sovereign, and his lieutenants were appointed East King, West King, South King, and North King, plus an additional Assistant King. A hierarchical system of ranks and titles provided a combined military and administrative command over the organization that in 1850 was formed into a rebellious military movement. Eluding government troops that had been sent against them, the Taipings were joined by large numbers of discontented peasants and moved in a growing avalanche of military might, over a million strong, across South China, toward the Yangtze River, where they captured numerous boats and took the town of Nanking in 1853.

The Taiping program was based on the idea of general brotherhood and equality of men and women. Each member had to contribute all he owned to a common treasury and was in theory to be provided with all his needs from this community fund. Both the equality and the property measures were fundamentally suited for a mobile military organization. The equality of the sexes meant a separation of men and women, and women, under their own officers, were organized in camps for work, caring for children, and occasionally as combat units. At least for the duration of the campaign the Taiping attempted to enforce a complete separation of the sexes; they were brothers and sisters all, and under threat of capital punishment no sexual relations were permitted even among married couples.

In practice these rules did not apply to the leaders, who had free access to the common treasury and could live in luxury while members at times suffered great hardship. Leaders did not maintain chastity but selected harems for themselves. The power of life and death over all gave these leaders an authority that they clearly and grossly abused.

In the territory they occupied, the Taipings issued a land law for the peasants. All the land belonged to the Heavenly King but was to be distributed for use according to the number of family members, and rent was abolished—but this theoretical system was not applied in practice. The Taiping armies lived on the land and used landlords to collect taxes.

The real power and stage manager behind this bizarre and fierce uprising was the East King, Yang Hsiu-ch'ing, a former coal miner who had the ingenuous idea to represent the Holy Ghost in his trances, allegedly God's own spirit, which naturally ranked even above that of Hung himself who was only the younger brother of Jesus Christ. Yang's attempt to usurp all authority led in 1856 in Nanking to his assassination with all his family and followers. The assassin was one of the other kings, who was himself assassinated shortly thereafter. With two of the kings already killed earlier in battle, and the only survivor, the Assistant King, fleeing from Nanking in fear for his own life, the Heavenly King, who was by now totally irrational, had no central working government structure left. He was dependent on able commanders in the field, who obtained individual victories without following any promising common strategy.

In the meantime resistance against the Taiping movement had been reorganized. Two major government defeats near Nanking in 1856 and the exhaustion of the imperial treasury left the government no choice but to accept the help that came from the scholar-gentry, which rightly saw in the Taiping Rebellion not only an attack against the dynasty but also a total challenge to the social and political order, the very essence of all the scholar-gentry stood for. Tseng Kuo-fan (1811–1872), the leader of the defense against the Taipings, described the situation: The rebellion "is not only a tragedy for our Ch'ing Dynasty, but a great tragedy for the whole Chinese tradition and causes Confucius and Mencius to weep bitterly in the underworld. How could any educated person remain sitting, hands in sleeves, without doing something about it."[1] It was Confucianism, not the dynasty, that organized the only effective defense of the existing order against a crazed utopian social revolution.

Tseng's example was followed by other provincial gentry leaders, many trained and led by Tseng, among them Li Hung-chang in Anhwei. These leaders together developed a strategy that eventually led to the destruction and elimination of the Taiping movement. During the process, new provincial military leaders had to be appointed as governors and governors-general of the provinces in which their armies were gathered, disregarding the principle of dividing government functions for the sake of security. The dynasty never fully regained control.

Tseng's strategy worked: In a slow strangulation, moving down the Yangtze valley, the Taiping armies were destroyed, their base at Nanking besieged and captured in 1864, and the whole movement eliminated with the slaughter of large numbers of the original adherents.

As it was, the Taiping movement failed not only because of its insane leadership, but also because it had no grounding in Chinese social tradition and beliefs and therefore, except in its beginning, no major support from the peasants, let alone the urban population, for a social revolution. This gave the leaders of the scholar-gentry the opportunity to rally the rural population in defense of the traditional values that they all shared. Though Confucianism survived the rebellion, the dynasty was fatally weakened by the disintegration of its central control. The foundation was laid for the regionalism that led to inner division and breakdown of the old order, ending eventually in a period described as "warlordism."

There were other more traditional rebellions that punctuated the last half-century of imperial rule. Overlapping with the Taiping Rebellion and in loose contact with it, the Nien Rebellion (1853–1868) spread over Northern China from the provinces of Anhwei to Shantung. The Nien were defeated by the armies of Tseng Kuo-fan and Li Hung-chang through a strategy of blockading the Nien area and cutting off and isolating its mobile cavalry, a strategy that was later to be expanded against other forms of guerrilla warfare.

No less dangerous were the rebellions by the best organized and active religious minority group in China, the Muslims, whose insurrections in Southwest China in Yunnan province (1855–1873) and in the Northwest in Kansu, Shensi, and Chinese Turkestan (1862–1877) challenged the Chinese territorial authority until they were suppressed by regional leaders. What made these and later uprisings so dangerous to China was the opportunity they provided for foreign intervention—Russian as well as British—to gain territorial inroads into the Chinese empire.

The last decades of the nineteenth century were then a period of internal upheavals and growing foreign intervention. The imperialist powers not only obtained more and more concessions within China Proper but also began to interfere in the imperial government's control over the dependent areas of the empire—England in Burma, France in Indo-China, Russia in Turkestan—trying to extend their power at the expense of the weakening dynastic government. The acute moment of crisis in this imperial disintegration arrived when Japan joined these attacks against the empire. The Sino-Japanese war (1894–1895) was fought over the control of Korea, which had been for many centuries a Chinese dependency.

When the Japanese attacked, beginning with the same surprise tactic as they later used against the Russians at Port Arthur and the United States at Pearl Harbor, the only Chinese military force in a position to defend the peninsula was Li Hung-chang's army and navy. Its original fighting value had been vastly undercut by corruptive practices of Li's business empire, and it was no match for the modernized Japanese forces. Driven out of Korea, the government negotiated through Li a humiliating peace treaty, losing not only Korea but also the island of Taiwan. The southern part of Manchuria was saved for China only by the intervention of Russia, Germany, and France, preparing the region for Russian expansion, which was shortly to follow.

China's resounding defeat led to a general international assumption that the Chinese empire and indeed the state itself were at the point of collapse and that the time had come for all powers to secure their share of the disintegrating country's territory: the period for "the cutting of the melon"—the division of China. At this time of mortal peril for China's political survival, when the court and the country's officials began to realize the danger but proved unable to counter it, a Chinese national spirit of resistance began to manifest itself. It did not originate in the treaty ports, among the new Chinese business class, but from the ranks of the Confucian scholars who still regarded themselves as the guardians of Chinese cultural heritage and defenders of her polity.

The man who led the new national resistance and in the process became the chief spokesman for a modern transformation of Confucian society and state was K'ang Yu-wei (1858–1927), the last creative thinker in the Confucian tradition.

K'ang Yu-wei was born into a family of scholars from a district close to Canton. He had received the traditional Confucian education and went on to pass the examinations at the metropolitan level. But he had also begun to develop his own interpretation of Confucian philosophy as it related to modern times. He had studied Buddhism and became familiar with Western science and philosophical thought. His ideas eventually were formulated in a philosophical and utopian interpretation of human history, a work that he called the *Ta T'ung-Shu* ("The Common Weal"), a term with a broad connotation of common human destiny. He completed this work by 1902 but did not publish it for fear of being misunderstood and disparaged, impairing the political role that he had by that time assumed.

In his work K'ang interpreted human history as a phased advance from an age of chaotic disunion and strife, through a period of larger unity and partial peace, to a future world community and universal peace. He believed that in all human cultures there were the roots of a common humanism to which each culture would make its contribution. In China, the chief foundation of this culture was the Confucian tradition as interpreted in the light of modern conditions. He found in a section of the *Li Chi*—the *Classic of Rituals*—a reference supporting his belief in a "public-spiritedness" as the main principle on which to base the great harmony among mankind. The Confucian *jen*, which had been graded within human relations, he expanded into an all-encompassing concept of general human love.

For China, this meant a profound reform and revitalizing of Confucian concepts, beginning with a reform of the examination system, discarding the sterile form of the "eight-legged essay," which had become a symbol and contributing reason for the barrenness of the scholar-official thinking of the time. If the nation were to be saved, fundamental reforms were imperative.

In 1895, when the Japanese conditions for peace became known, K'ang organized more than 1,200 graduates in Peking to protest and sign a memorial in favor of rejecting the demands, transferring the capital, and instituting reforms to gain a popular basis for national resistance. The protest was to no avail; the government had yielded to the treaty conditions. But in 1898 when the rush by the foreign powers for spheres of interest and leased territories seemed to herald China's partition into colonial territories, the young emperor Kuang-hsü, who was governing in the shadow of his aunt, the empress dowager, called K'ang Yu-wei for lengthy audiences in which K'ang outlined his plans for reform. Pointing to the examples of the reforms in Turkey and in Japan and, earlier, by Peter the Great in Russia, K'ang suggested a wide-ranging program of institutional changes of government and laws, establishing new bureaus for all aspects of governmental and social affairs, developing a modern economy, a system of modern education, and a reorganization of the military into a modern force. Because of official opposition K'ang was given only a low position at the court, but he retained his access to the young emperor and in this position he attempted, for a period of one hundred days, to lay the foundation for a far-reaching transformation of the Confucian state and society into a constitutional monarchy, based on popular participation in government and a modern economy.

The effort failed when the traditional officialdom rallied behind the empress dowager. The leading regional military leader, Yüan Shih-k'ai, together with the Manchu commander of the guard, Jung Lu, sided with the empress dowager, who in a coup d'état arrested the emperor. K'ang escaped, but his brother and several of his supporters were arrested and executed. The emperor remained until his death a prisoner of his aunt, the empress dowager, and the reforms were undone. This was the last attempt to transform China within the Confucian dynasty framework into a modern nation-state. Whether it could have succeeded if there had been better political conditions at the court and if the effort had been approached in a more systematic and cautious way remains a matter of speculation.

K'ang Yu-wei believed that China would have a national future only if Chinese culture survived. He asked in later years, "Those who believe that one can throw away the teaching of Confucius, do they know that the whole Chinese culture is closely intertwined and linked with it, and if one abandons Confucianism, the whole Chinese culture follows it and perishes, and that all groups and clans will follow and be destroyed?"[2] After his flight K'ang Yu-wei continued his political organization abroad, but in the years that followed the abolition of the Confucian examination system in 1905, the interest in China's transformation turned from the generation of young Confucian scholars who had supported K'ang to a different social group, the overseas Chinese small businessmen and the overseas students educated in Western thought, linked to the secret society tradition in China and abroad, and, eventually, to the young cadets and officers in the regional armies.

With the failure of reform, the foreign threat remained un-answered. A spontaneous reaction against the foreign inroad occurred at the turn of the century, when a secret society movement in North China, the Society of Righteous Harmony (called by the foreign powers the "Boxers"), took on an antiforeign character. Missionary work had often disrupted village communities, and local bitterness, supported by officials, tended to blame all problems on foreign intervention. In 1899 members of the Boxers started to attack and kill isolated foreigners and Chinese converts in North China and Manchuria. They banded together and as a larger force moved on to Peking, where many foreigners had fled into the Legation Quarter. Receiving support from the empress dowager, who saw in them a means of getting rid of the foreign intervention, the Boxers besieged the foreign community until Western troops arrived and easily destroyed the Boxer forces. In 1901 the powers imposed on China the Boxer Protocol, which exacted from China a heavy indemnity and, as a matter of punishment for Chinese official support of the Boxers, ordered the suspension of the examination system in forty-five cities where the Boxers had killed or injured foreigners. In 1905, on Chinese initiative, the examination system was altogether abolished, dismantling the foundation of the Confucian social and political order.

The Boxer Rebellion, primitive and futile as it was, may have caused some hesitation on the side of the foreign powers in their plans for Chinese partition. This reticence was reinforced by the policy of the United States, which had countered the partition plans of the powers—in which it would not participate—by the Open Door Notes of September 1899. Although not effective at the time, the U.S. Open Door Notes became nonetheless the internationally accepted formula for the China policy of the powers—a policy of preserving Chinese territorial administrative integrity for the sake of equal access to the Chinese market.

China had thus gained a breather, but it soon was apparent that the imperial order was doomed. The conditions were now ripe for a breakup of the dynastic rule itself. The disaster of the Boxer Rebellion led the empress dowager's government to initiate some belated reform measures; however, the opportunity of K'ang Yu-wei's great plan had been missed. The end of the examination system in 1905 had a much more far-reaching effect than its foreign instigators may have intended. The study of Confucianism had lost its practical value, and the institution of the scholar-gentry was in fact abolished. The empress dowager's reform attempts introduced in 1907 a nine-year program for the establishment of a representative system. The program scheduled the calling of provincial assemblies within one year in preparation for a national parliament. The reform effort did not save the monarchy but only helped to prepare the ground for the final fall of the dynasty. K'ang's efforts from overseas to promote his movement for constitutional monarchy were soon outdistanced by another program for change, Sun Yat-sen's plan for revolution.

Sun Yat-sen (1866–1925) was born of peasant origin in a rural area near Canton, later named Chungshan after the official personal name of its famous son. Sun had received some education through occasional studies at a private village school. His chance came when an older brother who had emigrated earlier to Hawaii, done well in business, and owned a small plantation, sent for him and enrolled him in a British missionary school in Hawaii. Fortunately for Sun, the school had Chinese as part of its curriculum, so that Sun became literate in his mother tongue, though not well acquainted with his country's history and philosophy. Rather, he became an ardent believer in the West and a Christian. The result was that Sun Yat-sen was not entirely at home either in the West or in the world of his traditional heritage. Returning from Hawaii, Sun studied Western medicine in Hong Kong, became a medical doctor, and practiced for some time in Macao. During this time, like many of his generation, he was deeply concerned with the adversities suffered by his country

and, after a memorandum that he had sent to Li Hung-chang was
ignored, decided to work for the overthrow of the Manchu government, which he held responsible for China's humiliations. In 1894
he organized a secret society that he called *Hsing-chung-hui* ("Revive
China Society") and in 1895 attempted in Canton an uprising that
failed, costing the lives of some society members. Sun had to flee
the country and from that time traveled abroad, collecting members
and contributions for his organization.

The goal of Sun's revolution was the establishment of a republic
as in the United States, regarded by him as having the most advanced
form of government. Sun sought support among the Chinese communities in Southeast Asia, Hawaii, the continental United States,
Europe, and Japan for his cause. He had to compete first with K'ang
Yu-wei, whose program for a constitutional monarchy initially found
a greater response, particularly among the educated Chinese. With
the passing of years after the abolition of the Confucian examination
system, however, the Confucian polity lost its appeal among the
younger Chinese abroad and all who studied in missionary or foreign
schools. In 1905 Japan's victory over Russia in the Russo-Japanese
war changed altogether the attitudes among Chinese students, who
became impatient for action.

In 1905 Sun founded in Japan a new organization, the *T'ung-
meng-hui* ("Alliance Society"), fusing the *Hsing-chung-hui* and other
secret societies with a new group of members, largely recruited among
Chinese students in Japan. Among the new members were a number
of cadets from Chinese regional military academies. These academies
had sent promising students to Japan for further military training.
It was this link with the new regional military forces in China that
made possible, after some futile putsches, the uprising of October
10, 1911, that led to the collapse of the Manchu government and
the takeover of power by regional military forces in the name of
the *T'ung-meng-hui*, which elected Sun Yat-sen as first president of
the Republic of China. The Revolution of 1911, which ended the
dynastic system, brought not the new nation-state as hoped, but a
prolonged struggle for power, at first under the strongest military
leader, Yüan Shih-k'ai, who replaced Sun Yat-sen as president.

This time of transition and of military and political chaos was
also a period of intellectual ferment. Acceptance of Western forms
of international life and of the equality of sovereign states overthrew

the basic concepts of the Chinese polity, the Mandate of Heaven and the principles of the Confucian political order. It erased the role of the scholar-gentry, the organizing and controlling group in China. It destroyed the whole structure of authority and consent on which the Confucian polity had been based. To modernize China as a nation-state meant to find a new source of integration, a new social order, a new political structure, a new state.

The Revolution of 1911 had expressed a new national spirit among Western-educated students and military cadets, who aimed at overthrowing the alien Manchu dynasty and establishing a republic without any clear definition what the form of the new polity should be. In the manifesto of the *T'ung-meng-hui*, Sun Yat-sen had proclaimed his ideas, later to be formulated in the Three People's Principles: China to the Chinese, to be defined as "nationalism"; the establishment of a government chosen by the people, "democracy"; and a vague plan of equalization of landownership—derived from the U.S. urban reformer Henry George—which later was included in the third of Sun's principles, "People's Livelihood." Sun also spoke of three stages in which his system was to be realized: a first period, seizure of power by a military government and the abolition of all former "evils" (within three years); a second phase during which the military government would hand over the power to the people, starting at the local level; and a third and final stage during which the people would elect a president and parliament, in fact establishing a democratic system.

Nothing of the sort happened. After the revolution, in 1912, the *Kuomintang* ("Nationalist Party") was organized as an open political party by the amalgamation of the *T'ung-meng-hui* with other political groups. But the parliament chosen in 1913 by a limited electorate, chiefly the educated in the cities, never could assert itself against President Yüan Shih-k'ai and the regional military leaders whom Yüan had confirmed in their positions. When Yüan's attempt at reestablishing monarchy failed, and he died (1916), general chaos followed.

The disappointment of the Western-educated students who had held such high expectations for the success of the revolution led them to search for philosophical ideas and political systems that would solve China's problems and that would enable them to play a leading role in a new China. In that sense the Western-educated students saw themselves as carrying on the tradition of the scholar-gentry of the past. But in contrast to their predecessors, they had no regard for the standards and moral values of the Confucian tradition and had lost contact with the life of the large body of the rural population. They lived in the Westernized cities where they absorbed Western philosophies, Western literature, Western concepts of society, politics, and economics, without much connection with the cultural heritage of their country. In these years of political disintegration most of these urbanized intellectuals felt that Confucianism no longer suited the needs of their rapidly changing society. Many different Western schools of thought gained followers in China, the predominant trend was American Pragmatism as represented by John Dewey, who was invited to China and lectured in Peking in 1919 and 1920. As a result pragmatism and, related to it, materialism became the main schools of thought among the Westernized Chinese intellectuals. Among the scholars holding such views were leading political figures in the *Kuomintang*, such as Wu Chih-hui, a convinced believer in science as panacea for all problems, and Ts'ai Yüan-p'ei, chancellor of Peking University, who had both a classical and a Western education and who lectured that religions were impediments to human progress and should be replaced by teaching aesthetics to appreciate "the beautiful and the sublime."

The main attack against Confucianism came in 1919 with the so-called May Fourth Movement, when Chinese students, first in Peking and then throughout the country, protested the Chinese humiliation at the negotiations of the Peace Treaty of Versailles at the end of World War I and initiated a nationalist reaction that found its immediate expression in a rapidly growing nationalist press and literature. The movement was called "The New Culture Movement." One of its leading figures was Ch'en Tu-hsiu (1880–1939), the dean of the School of Letters at Peking University, then a follower of Dewey, whose essay "Call to Youth" had made a deep impression on the Chinese students. Two years later Ch'en became the chief founder of the Chinese Communist party.

The most important outcome of the May Fourth Movement, however, was the literary revolution that aimed at the abolition of the literary language of the past and its replacement by a new written language following *pai-hua*, the common spoken language. The new written language would use colloquial vocabulary and syntax but the same word characters for writing as heretofore.

The leading spokesman for the new written language was Hu Shih (1891–1962), who had studied in the United States under Dewey and became his confirmed admirer. Publishing a number of articles in the new style of writing, Hu Shih claimed that the use of the spoken language for literature was not entirely new but had been used in the popular novels of the past. He claimed that the object of the movement propagated by him was much more than a simple change in style of writing; what he promoted was no less than a "Chinese literary renaissance." The Chinese wanted:

> a new language, a new literature, a new outlook on life and
> society, and a new scholarship. They want a new language,
> not only as an effective instrumentality for popular education,
> but also as the effective medium for the development of the
> literature of a new China. They want a literature that shall
> be written in the living tongue of a living people and shall be
> capable of expressing the real feelings, thoughts, inspirations,
> and aspirations of a growing nation. They want to instill into
> the people a new outlook on life which shall free them from
> the shackles of tradition and make them feel at home in the
> new world and its new civilization. They want a new
> scholarship which shall not only enable us to understand
> intelligently the cultural heritage of the past, but also prepare
> us for active participation in the work of research in the
> modern sciences. This, as I understand it, is the mission of
> the Chinese Renaissance.[3]

The inspired statement expressed the spirit and all the hopes of the time.

The new written style was immediately accepted by the vast majority of the intellectuals. In a short time more than four hundred new newspapers and journals using the modern writing appeared and published articles on the political and intellectual problems of the time. A year later the Ministry of Education ordered that textbooks for primary schools were to be written in the colloquial form. Two years later, that order was applied to the high schools and from that time on to all Chinese education. In short order a new literature of novels, plays, essays, and poetry appeared by writers who soon became known to the reading public; and much Western literature, philosophy, and political writing was translated into the new Chinese style of writing.

Much of the new Chinese literature was critical of Chinese tradition and bitter or satirical about political and social conditions of the past and the present. The best known of the new writers was Lu Hsün (1881–1936), whose writings satirized existing society. His most famous book, *The True Story of Ah Q*, dealt with a village pauper, resigned to his fate, who symbolized the Chinese mental attitude of resignation. When the revolution finally occurred, Ah Q came late, was caught, and was simply shot, depriving the public of the excitement of a traditional execution. Lu Hsün became a hero of the Communists, although in the end he was attacked when he did not follow the party line. He would most likely have been purged had he lived. This was the dilemma of many Chinese leftist writers who had been free to write and be critical of affairs under the republic and the National Government but found themselves censored and purged when they tried to apply their critical faculties to the evils of the Communist system.

Among the best known writers of the time were Lao She (Shu Ch'ing-ch'un), a humanist concerned with the hardships of the individual, whose best-known book was translated into English under the title *Rickshaw Boy*; Kuo Mo-jo, a poet and historian who eventually turned to Communism; and Mao Tun (Shen Yen-ping), a novelist, also a convert to Communism. The group of writers divided between those who believed in "art for art's sake" and those who turned to "revolutionary literature" against "individualism" and the "bourgeoisie" and for "collectivism" and the "dialectic method." In 1930 two societies, the League of Leftist Writers, led by Kuo Mo-jo, Mao Tun, and Lu Hsün and the "contemporaries," chaired by Lao She, expressed the differing goals of the chief representatives of the new literature.

Quite another confrontation took place in an ongoing debate on philosophy and political theory. The pragmatism and materialism that had so impressed the majority of the Chinese intellectuals of the literary renaissance was opposed by some who warned against the uncritical acceptance of the so-called scientific view and argued for maintaining the ethical principles of the past. In the year of the

May Fourth Movement, Liang Ch'i-ch'ao, the foremost student of K'ang Yu-wei, argued that materialist philosophy would have to deny the free will of men and that after the carnage of World War I the European dream of the all-encompassing science had met with bankruptcy. Although intellectual problems were to be solved by science, those related to emotions transcended science. The issue came to a head in a philosophical controversy in 1923, after a lecture by Dr. Carson Chang, a follower of K'ang Yu-wei and a student of Rudolph Eucken and Henri Bergson, who asserted that metaphysics was needed to deal with those human problems that could never be solved by science alone. Carson Chang was attacked by the majority of scholars and intellectuals from several different schools of thought, including the materialist Wu Chih-hui, Ch'en Tu-hsiu, who had by now become a Marxist, and Hu Shih, who stated that Chinese rationalist tradition not only precluded metaphysics, but prepared "some of us better to appreciate the intellectual and moral significance inherent in Western civilization which the Western philosopher, because of a tremendous weight of a religious tradition, has not always been willing to recognize."[4]

This view, the Scientific Philosophy of Life, remained the accepted thinking among the dominant group of Chinese intellectuals and captured most of the younger generation to whom all metaphysics were but idolatry and superstition. The pragmatists held a naturalist view of life and believed with Dewey that truth was relative and changed with circumstances. The materialists were influenced by Ernst Haeckel's writings on the monism of substance, and both the pragmatists and the materialists were tolerant of dialectic materialism. Ch'en Tu-hsiu, at first an admirer of Dewey, had become an exponent of materialist monism before he accepted the dialectic materialism of Communist doctrine. Hu Shih, however, was later to remain steadfast in retaining his pragmatist faith against the new Marxist-Leninist doctrine that claimed to be scientific and to have all the answers.

This intellectual controversy took place in the treaty ports or abroad, removed from the life of the large number of Chinese people in the villages and the country towns. The debaters and the writers and artists lived in a Western setting, surrounded by Western art and architecture. These Chinese treaty port cities became in appearance Western, with Western-style buildings for banks, business firms, churches, or schools, in the architectural style of the turn of the century. Only later were more serious attempts made to create a new architecture out of a fusion of tradition and modernization. The same held true in painting and the crafts, where the unresolved dichotomy between the by now mostly stagnant tradition and Western experimentation widened the gulf between the Chinese cultural foundation and the impact of the Westernizers. Yet there were signs that the cultural heritage still had the potential for new growth. In painting perhaps more than in other arts a new spirit led at the latter part of the nineteenth century to greater vigor and boldness in the treatment of traditional objects, such as bamboo, flowers, trees, and rocks by masters as Jen Po-nien, Chao Chih-ch'ien, and Wu Ch'ang-shih. These painters in turn influenced a later genera-tion—which included the almost legendary Ch'i Pai-shih (1863–1957)—that returned to the tradition of expressing the essentials of the painters' objects with great strength and simplicity, preparing the ground for an altogether new phase in Chinese art.

Fifteen

THE NATIONALISTS

THE REVOLUTION OF 1911 brought a period of civil war and warlordism. A nominal central government in Peking was under the control of whichever warlord was currently predominant in the North. In Canton, Sun Yat-sen tried to establish a foothold with the help of local warlord support, but he also sought foreign support for his revolution. After failing in his overtures to the West, he accepted a helping hand from the representatives of a revolution that seemed to have succeeded; the Bolshevik revolution had overthrown Czarist rule in Russia and aroused great interest and sympathy among Chinese intellectuals, particularly when the new Bolshevik leaders offered to annul all Russian treaty rights in China. As Sun Yat-sen claimed, "a great hope was born in the heart of mankind" by the revolution in Russia. Thus, Sun accepted an offer of Soviet support extended in January 1923 by the Comintern agent Adolf A. Joffe for Chinese national unification with the reservation, stated by both sides, that conditions in China were not conducive "to carry out either Communism or even the Soviet system in China."[1]

On the basis of the Sun-Joffe agreement, Soviet advisers under Michael Borodin assisted in the reorganization of the *Kuomintang* as a one-party system, and Soviet military officers trained Chinese cadets at the Whampoa Military Academy near Canton. A Chinese Communist party had been founded in 1921 under Comintern guidance, and its members were now admitted on an individual basis to membership in the *Kuomintang*. To stress Chinese nationalist integrity, Sun Yat-sen attempted to define somewhat simplistically the ideological distinction between Chinese nationalism and communism. But under political and military cooperation, the "United

191

Front" clearly provided a perfect opportunity for Communist infiltration and takeover, which was the obvious goal of Moscow and the Chinese Communists.

That this scheme failed at the time was largely due to one man who was chiefly responsible for foiling the Communist plot and turning China onto a Nationalist course. Chiang Kai-shek (1887–1975), born in Chekiang province into a family of modest means, entered a military career as cadet in the Academy of the Northern Army at Paoting. Sent to Japan for further study, he joined Sun Yat-sen's *T'ung-Meng-Hui*, as did many of his fellow cadets. He participated in the Revolution of 1911 in Shanghai and kept in touch with Sun Yat-sen, who was impressed by Chiang's personality. When the Whampoa academy was established, Sun appointed Chiang Kai-shek as president, first sending him for a three-month visit to the Soviet Union. There Chiang learned the Soviet concept of the revolutionary army and the commissar system, which he applied at the Whampoa academy. But Chiang also had a look at conditions in the Soviet Union, which were grim, and became aware of Soviet stratagems. At the Whampoa academy he had to deal with Communist as well as Nationalist cadets, both sides organized into societies, and also with Chinese Communist commissars—headed by Zhou Enlai (Chou En-lai)—and, most of all, with the Soviet military advisers under General Galen [Wassilij K. Bluecher] who tried to dominate the academy and use it for Moscow's policy. Within the non-Communist cadet and teaching staff Chiang Kai-shek instilled a sense of loyalty and esprit de corps that became the main strength of the emerging Nationalist army.

At Canton, Soviet advisers controlled the funds and the weapons of the academy. To escape this Soviet manipulation, Chiang Kai-shek urged an early start for the northern campaign to destroy warlord armies and establish a National Government. Following the death of Sun Yat-sen of cancer in 1925, the struggle came to a head in the so-called Chungshan gunboat incident in 1926, a Communist attempt to kidnap Chiang Kai-shek. Chiang foiled the attempt by moving swiftly and placing the Soviet advisers under arrest. A compromise ended the stalemate, and the northern campaign finally got under way.

By the time the northern campaign had successfully reached the Yangtze area, the power contest again broke into the open.

Chiang Kai-shek, commanding the right wing of the campaign, destroyed the Communist base in Shanghai; when the *Kuomintang* left-wing leadership, which had moved with the remainder of the army to Wuhan, through the indiscretion of a Comintern agent learned of Stalin's plans for a Communist takeover, the *Kuomintang* expelled both the Soviets and the Chinese Communists. Eventually, the left and right factions of the *Kuomintang* became reconciled and in 1928 established a government in Nanking under the leadership of Chiang Kai-shek.

An Organic Law, promulgated in October, provided a political structure for the National Government that followed Sun Yat-sen's old plan. The government, under a state council controlled by the *Kuomintang*, was composed of five boards or *yüan*, the executive, the legislative, the judicial, the examination, and the control *yüan*, handling government functions according to Sun's five-power system. Chiang Kai-shek, chairman of the state council, was also head of the party and of the army, which gave him an authority unmatched by any other political leader. The policy now initiated was therefore in essence the policy of Chiang Kai-shek, with some interludes originating in factional struggles.

The National Government was faced with a gigantic task, a military, social, and economic revolution, to reach its goal of building a nation. The military problem was primary, with the greatest and most ominous danger being Japanese aggression. To counter this danger, it was essential to have national unity. If there were to be a chance of effective resistance in the decisive battle for national survival, the internal foe had to be removed; the warlords first had to be overcome and the Communists' civil war brought to a successful end. "Unity before resistance" became the slogan and the basic concept behind Chiang Kai-shek's policy.

This military strategy was the protective frame for a policy that was to create a new social cohesion, economic advancement, and the ideological determination as foundation for the new nation. Even though the National Government on the mainland eventually fell, it was clearly this policy of Chiang Kai-shek that made it possible for China to survive the onslaught of Japanese aggression and eight years of a devastating war.

To prepare for the impending Japanese invasion, Chiang Kai-shek regarded the creation of a modern army as paramount. After the split with Moscow and the expulsion of the Soviet advisers, Chiang turned to Weimar Germany and enlisted retired officers as advisers who reorganized and trained the Chinese army into a professional military force. A new military academy was set up at Nanking where Chiang, as president, had his residence.

Until the final Japanese attack in the summer of 1937, the military plan of the National Government was largely successful. The National Government resumed the northern campaign, took Peking, and when the Manchurian warlord Chang Hsueh-liang joined the government and the *Kuomintang* in 1928, China became at least nominally united. But in 1931 the Japanese army created the so-called Manchurian incident—leading to Japanese military occupation of Manchuria and the establishment of the puppet state of Manchukuo. A subsequent Japanese attack on Shanghai led to strong Chinese resistance, but unable as yet to regain Manchuria, the National Government was forced to conclude a truce that left Japan in control of Manchuria and in a position to prepare for further advance into North China.

Despite loss of territory, Chiang Kai-shek's National Government emerged from the Manchurian incident more unified than before. The warlord opposition had been largely eliminated, and rival *Kuomintang* leaders had lost most of their influence. The next task was the removal of the Communist military force entrenched in Kiangsi and an end to the civil war that kept China disunited.

Contrary to an often repeated myth, the Chinese Communist rural strategy was not a deviation from Soviet policy, but was Moscow directed. As Stalin declared in 1926: "The peasant question is the most important question of the Chinese national liberation movement. . . . The most important task of the Chinese communist party is to win the peasant masses for active struggle on behalf of fighting slogans which link up political and economic demands comprehensible to and important to the peasantry."[2]

After some blunders, the Chinese Communists established several rural bases, the principal one a Soviet government in Kiangsi where the Communist leadership took refuge after the defeat in Shanghai. The National Government had to design a strategy to deal with the evolving guerrilla warfare. After five traditional campaigns that brought no success, Chiang Kai-shek finally devised a strategy that successfully countered the Communist mobile warfare—a strategy of blockades that strangled a shrinking guerrilla base. The Communists finally broke out of the blockade and went on the "Long March" that took them through Western China to Shensi province. There a greatly reduced force eventually settled in Yenan (Yanan).

The Communist Long March has become a legendary triumph of determination to survive against heavy odds. The political reality behind this propaganda image was a government policy that harassed and decimated the retreating Communist troops, forcing them into an area of meager supply where they had the possibility of retreat into Soviet territory.

Like the earlier warlord problem, the Communist problem had thus been greatly reduced when the increasing Japanese pressure changed both the international and the Chinese scene. The program set up by the German advisers called for two additional years in order to complete the training of new divisions in the army and the buildup of a navy and air force. The Japanese did not wait for this timetable.

Soviet policy had changed as well. In 1935 while the Chinese Communists were on the Long March, the Soviet Union switched from the policy of attacking "Western imperialism" to a United Front line against the mounting threat of Nazi Germany, aggravated by the rapprochement between Nazi Germany and Japan. The Soviet Union had joined the League of Nations to work with the "Western democracies," and needed to strengthen Chinese resistance against Japan as a security measure for the Eastern border of the USSR. This resistance could only be led by Chiang Kai-shek. The slogan of a United Front in China was suddenly heard in an abrupt change of Chinese Communist propaganda, shifting from demanding the death of the archcriminal Chiang Kai-shek to pressuring him to lead an anti-Japanese United Front.

An intense propaganda barrage was directed primarily at students and professors, most of whom lived under treaty port protection. The propaganda led to their protests against Chiang's policy of unifying the country first under the National Government. In turn, the propaganda was used to affect some of the troops engaged in the civil war against the Communists.

The turning point came at the so-called Sian incident in December 1936 when mutinous Manchurian troops, under the influence of United Front slogans, captured Chiang Kai-shek. Under Stalin's orders, Zhou Enlai negotiated Chiang's release in exchange for a cessation of the civil war and a promise of cooperation in the resistance against Japan. Japan's attack at the Marco Polo Bridge in July 1937 finally ended the phase of Unity before Resistance. China was only half-prepared for the conflagration that was to overrun the country.

The military unification was merely a framework within which an intrinsic transformation of the Chinese polity into a modern nation-state was to take place. The old social and ethical order of Confucian society was under attack; a new social cohesion had to be formed to replace the social system that had disappeared with the end of the monarchy and the effacement of the scholar-gentry.

The greatest accomplishment of the National Government during this decade of establishing a new national identity was the introduction of a system of law to regulate social, economic, and ethical relationships. In the period between 1929 and 1935 more than one hundred laws were passed and promulgated by the legislative *yüan*. These laws included a civil code of five books; criminal laws; commercial legislation relating to banking, copyright, stock exchanges, chambers of commerce, and commercial companies; labor laws; laws of mining, forestry, and fisheries; and codes of procedure that set up a system of courts—local district courts, courts of appeal, and the Supreme Court at Nanking, which had final authority on interpreting the new legal system. The creation of this new legal order was an enormous legislative task based primarily on Western legal tradition. The civil code was basically related to the Swiss and German *Bürgerliche Gesetzbuch*, which in turn led back to the *Code Napoléon* that had revolutionized the social order in Europe. Family law in particular and laws of procedure, both in formulation and in practice, respected Chinese heritage and tradition. For the student of law, Chinese Supreme Court decisions have been an interesting lesson in the problems of introducing modern law into a non-Western cultural setting.

In the decade between 1929 and the outbreak of the Sino-Japanese War this legal structure was effective primarily in urban centers rather than in the rural areas, where tradition and the obvious shortage of legally trained officials and staff delayed the transition from old to new legal practices. There remained wide areas where no courts functioned, and in the regions beset by civil war, military force often prevailed.

To assert its international integrity, the Chinese government sought to abolish the "unequal treaties" and regain full jurisdictional control. The humiliation resulting from foreign rights and interests, as well as racial disparagement and insults, created a Chinese reaction erupting in protests, strikes, and boycotts of foreign goods. These protests, together with the reality of an established National Government, led to a change in foreign attitude and a new willingness to compromise. When Nationalist troops occupied British port concessions in Hankow and Kiukiang in 1927, the British negotiated a surrender. By 1928, all Western powers had concluded treaties with the National Government. These treaties restored Chinese tariff autonomy, thus enabling Chinese entrepreneurs to compete against foreign enterprises, which no longer enjoyed the protection of treaty rights and fixed low custom fees. In 1930 the British returned the concessions of Kiukiang and Amoy and the leased territory of Weihaiwei; however, other treaty ports remained, including the Shanghai International Settlement. A Chinese attempt to force the surrender of all extraterritoriality was abandoned when the growing threat of Japanese aggression required the concentration of all government efforts against this immediate danger.

The weakest part of the Nationalist program was an absence of agricultural policy. The Ministry of Agriculture and the agricultural departments of universities concentrated on technical improvements, better seeds, chemical fertilizer, and other technological reforms but did not carry through the original *Kuomintang* land program to alleviate the burdens of tenancy and taxes imposed by local authorities.

Two other areas of government policy were, however, of vital importance to economic growth: a sound financial policy and a rapid extension of the communication system. The person chiefly responsible for this government policy was T. V. Soong, who played a key role in the handling of economic policy for the National Government.

The task of building a modern educational system was clearly of major importance. The literary renaissance of 1919 had intensified interest in modern educational methods in a popular language in contrast to the traditional Confucian system, but the urban background of many of the new leaders caused them to be more concerned with a rapid growth of higher learning than with expanding primary education to the rural areas of the vast Chinese hinterland. The immense financial problem of providing trained teachers and schools for hundreds of millions of potential school children accentuated this inclination to a vertical rather than a horizontal educational growth.

Even before the National Government came to power, national colleges and universities had sprung up in all major regions of the country. At first they followed the general model established by missionary institutions that had pioneered modern higher education in China after the pattern of the home country. Because a majority of missionary educators were from the United States, it was the U.S. college tradition, credits, textbooks, and all that became widely accepted in China. When the National Government came to power, there already existed more than fifty national and private universities and colleges, which were reorganized and classified by the Ministry of Education. The leading Chinese national university was Peking University, originally established by K'ang Yu-wei as the apex of the educational pyramid that he envisaged and the only part of his reform program to survive his political failure. Under the National Government, the quality of the program of the national universities vastly improved until their standards surpassed the level of the missionary institutions and were recognized internationally.

A practical effort was also made by the National Government to expand primary and secondary education and vocational training for badly needed teachers. In 1935 a five-year educational plan was accepted in the hope of eventually accomplishing a substantial decrease in illiteracy, but this long-range program had not yet started when the war interrupted all further efforts to intensify educational progress.

More successful was the government policy of aid for higher education through support of the national universities and the organization of research in Chinese history as well as in the modern sciences. The work on the oracle-bone inscriptions of the Shang Dynasty, the excavations of the Shang tombs at Anyang, and other archaeological work by leading Chinese scholars achieved world-renowned results. To undertake such research and to provide academic training for it, the National Government established in 1928 the National Central Research Academy, which became known as the Academia Sinica.

Development in the field of fine arts, especially in painting, continued on a Chinese path. During periods of traumatic political events, when traditional values were no longer adhered to, the artistic past of T'ang and Sung art became a refuge and inspiration for a form of art that, rooted in Chinese tradition, found new expression in the artists' individual feelings. The objects remained the same: notably flowers, birds, and landscapes, or animals and persons; but a vigorous new style and interpretation characterized the spirit of the times. The technique of the brush, the minimum use of media of expression, the renewed study of nature, and the spontaneity all were parts of Chinese tradition that continued to appeal to a large circle of patrons as did, in a related field of art, Chinese theater. This attachment to a great tradition of Chinese culture was something of a counterweight to the inroad of Western literature and its impact on Chinese writers.

Ch'i Pai-shih, the most widely recognized among modern Chinese painters, reached maturity in the late 1920s, when he painted literally hundreds of monumental landscapes, and his pictures of fish, shrimp, birds, plants, and flowers covered the spectrum of life in nature, and in their synthesis of the concrete and the spiritual, expressed the essence of the painter's objects. His work, recognized by the Chinese as well as by the foreign public, now received official recognition by his appointment as professor to the Art Academy at Peking. His contemporary, Huang Pin-hung (1863–1954), regarded by some as the most important Chinese landscape painter of the twentieth century, also became a member of the Peking academy.

Among other well-known painters of academic standing was Lin Feng-mien (b. 1901), who had studied in Paris and was appointed director of the Art Academy at Hangchow. Lin, who was influenced by European Postimpressionists, earlier had painted in their style but then adopted some European principles to traditional Chinese techniques and subject matter, fusing the two into a new form of Chinese painting. There were many others who, influenced by Western styles, used them to add to and develop new techniques and expression in Chinese painting. (See Plate 31.)

This flourishing development was interrupted by Japanese military aggression. Ch'i Pai-shih refused to cooperate in any form with the foreign military conqueror. He continued to paint at home, depicting Japanese soldiers as voracious crabs. Lin Feng-mien retreated inland with the Hangchow academy; most Chinese higher educational institutions did likewise.

The war was the turning point in modern Chinese history. The Japanese invasion and occupation of many modern cities deprived the National Government of the very bases that had been the mainstay of its modern development and political strength. In the wartime capital of Chungking the government was isolated and cut off from Western supplies except through the long and precarious link over the Burma Road and, when this was closed by the Japanese conquest of Burma, through an airlift over "the hump."

At the outset of the war Chiang Kai-shek had broad national support as the only possible leader behind whom all resistance could be united. When his life seemed in danger during the Sian kidnapping attempt, there was countrywide anguish, and the news of his release brought spontaneous torchlight processions in many cities. This spirit of national unity grew with the actual outbreak of the war. At Moscow's behest the Communists worked together with the government, nominally abolishing their Soviet government and placing their armies under government command. A People's Political Council, which had advisory functions, was organized with Communist participation. The atrocities committed by the Japanese army after the capture of Nanking and other cities only served to strengthen the Chinese will to resistance. When the Japanese failed to destroy the National Government and the Chinese armies at Nanking and were unable to prevent the government and the armies' escape and retreat into the Western hinterland and the wartime capital of Chungking, Japan in effect lost the war. Chiang Kai-shek's statement of the time, "Let them come in, the farther they go, the better for us," initiated his strategy of trading territory for time.[3]

As a result, a war of attrition developed. To recover some of their costs, the Japanese had to exploit their conquest of cities and territory economically. To do that they established puppet governments in North, Central, and South China, but they never succeeded in breaking Chinese resistance.

To deny the Japanese control of the country surrounding the cities that they occupied required that the Chinese organize rural guerrilla warfare. It was in this area that Chinese unity and Nationalist-Communist cooperation broke down. From the outset, the Communists had a clear advantage in gaining control of the countryside.

The civil war strategy of rural-based military organization had given them the experience and the structure for expanding their political control. From their headquarters at Yenan, the Communists soon extended their organization throughout much of North China by setting up in provincial border areas a number of local governments— so-called border governments—that provided great flexibility in the movement of military forces. In line with the United Front policy of cooperating with Nationalists, the Communists abandoned for a time the killing of landlords and distribution of their land. Instead the Communists introduced an agrarian reform policy taken from the original program of the National Government. The reform reduced rent payments to 37.5 percent of the main crop; local governments with one-third participation by cooperative landlords (selected and approved by the party—which retained control) were set up.

This policy was constantly advertised by Communist propaganda and led to the Western misconception of the Chinese Communists as agrarian reformers, a misconception widely held at the time and included in some Western academic studies.

The National Government was much less prepared than the Communists for organizing rural resistance behind the Japanese lines. The neglect of agrarian policy during the decade before the war now came back to haunt the Nationalists. In Szech'wan province where they had retreated, the conservative element, the landlords, were more numerous than in most of the other provinces. The National Government, which had to depend on income from land tax, was in no position to risk political and economic upheaval through sudden drastic reforms. It was by then too late for an agrarian policy that might have strengthened the government's hold over the rural hinterland. Nonetheless, the National Government attempted to establish guerrilla organizations but failed—largely because of Communist opposition.

Communist policy itself had changed with the Hitler/Stalin pact that removed the two-front danger for Moscow and ended the conciliatory posture of the Chinese Communists. Behind the Japanese lines the Nationalist-Communist conflict for power intensified, and Communist acceptance of Nationalist authority came to an end.

The first major clash between the sides occurred in January 1941. The Communists had organized guerrilla bases in the lower Yangtze region, the area between Nanking, Shanghai, and Hangchow, the previous stronghold of the National Government. Unwilling to accept the loss of this region, the National Government ordered the Communist forces to move north across the Yangtze, and when they delayed, attacked the rear guard of the Communist troops. From that time on, an uneasy truce prevailed between both sides.

During this time the Nationalist forces bore the brunt of the fighting against the Japanese. After one major clash in 1938, the so-called one-hundred-regiments battle, in which their forces suffered heavy losses, the Communists no longer risked major military confrontations with the Japanese armies. Instead, the Communists concentrated on expanding their territorial control and building up their forces. The burden of the war rested chiefly on the National Government.

It proved to be a long, drawn out trial: from 1937 to 1941, four years of constant fighting with little and uncertain outside support and after Pearl Harbor, four more years with allies that had decided to concentrate on Europe first, while China had to wait in an increasingly desperate situation. During these years, the National Government lost its economic, political, and moral force and credibility within the country. Having sacrificed most of its best officer corps and trained troops in the first years of a heroically fought resistance and retreat, the army had to throw raw recruits into battle; great loss of life resulted. Economically strangled by the Japanese blockade and without income from traditional sources, the government had to live on borrowed money, and a serious and accelerating inflation undermined standards of personal integrity and honesty within the administration. Industries that had been able to move inland were taken over by the government for the war effort. Faculty members and university students who had retreated suffered most from the inflation and hardships and became increasingly alienated from the government. The very core of the government's support became disillusioned and critical.

At the end of the war a major effort was made to avoid a new outbreak of the civil war. The effort focused on a negotiated political solution between the National Government and the Communists. Both sides claimed to be in favor of a negotiated settlement but held contrary views on the desired outcome. The Communists wanted to replace the National Government with a new coalition government in which they obviously would have played a quasi-equal role in a new reinstatement of a United Front. The National Government offered to have the Communists join its existing government, pointing out that both parties represented a small minority of the Chinese people who should, through general elections, determine the political power in a coming parliamentary system.

The deadlock was broken when Moscow concluded a Sino-Soviet treaty in August 1945, promising to recognize only the National Government—having apparently concluded that the Communists at this point could not prevail; and in the People's Political Conference Agreements of January and February 1946 three political and military settlements were made that, for the time, stopped the clashes that had broken out over control of the territories now surrendered by Japan. It was a hopeful moment, all the more so since the victory gave Chiang Kai-shek's National Government new prestige. But the agreements broke down over local apportionment of power and military moves. The main issue was control of Manchuria, where the Communists broke the accord by moving in and trying to keep the Nationalist armies out.

Manchuria was occupied by Soviet troops in the final days of the war. They not only facilitated the entrance of Chinese Communist troops under Lin Biao (Lin Piao) but also helped to equip them with arms, including artillery and heavy equipment, which the Soviets had taken from the surrendering Japanese armies. When Nationalist armies arrived in U.S. transports, the Soviets prevented their landing at Soviet-held ports, so that they had to fight their way in overland against Chinese Communist resistance.

Disregarding the advice of the U.S. special ambassador, General George Marshall, Chiang Kai-shek sent about half his best trained and equipped troops to Manchuria to retain control over this most valuable industrial and strategic area. Even though the Soviets had by that time looted much of the machinery, China's future development seemed to depend on the potential and resources of this area, which in Communist hands would also remain a constant threat, as it had been as a Japanese puppet state.

At first the Nationalist troops were victorious. After defeating the Communist troops that interdicted their entrance, they defeated Lin Piao's armies of 300,000 men at Ssup'ingchieh, in a major battle that lasted more than two months and ended in a complete rout of the Communist armies. The Communists retreated north across the Sungari River.

At this point fortune turned because of a change of strategy by the Nationalists from offensive to defensive warfare. This disastrous reversion was caused by a U.S. policy that opted for negotiations and imposed an embargo on the deliveries to the Nationalists of military supplies—without which further pursuit of Communist armies was impossible. While negotiating, the Communists with Soviet assistance rebuilt their armies and their infrastructure in the Manchurian countryside that they controlled. When the Communists resumed the attack, the Nationalist armies, on the defensive and cut off from supplies, were destroyed or forced to surrender. Their equipment fell into Communist hands.

This Manchurian defeat of the Nationalist armies was not merely a military disaster of the first order; it decided the fate of China. Peking, indefensible, fell to the Communists. The National Government made another attempt, in December 1948, to stop the Communist advance at the battle of Hsüchow—in which a million men on each side fought for many weeks over a vast area along the crucial east-west and north-south railroad lines. Demoralization, however, leading to important defections, resulted in another disastrous defeat for the Nationalists and, in effect, sealed the Communist military conquest of the country.

The National Government was overthrown on the mainland not by popular revolution, but by military defeat. More than a million civilians, together with more than half a million army troops, fled to Taiwan, where Chiang Kai-shek and the National Government reestablished themselves. Millions more went to Hong Kong.

The survival of the National Government on Taiwan after such a disastrous defeat is truly remarkable. On Taiwan, the Nationalists not only survived but also built a viable economic, social, and political order on the island, which prospered under their rule.

The foundation for economic growth on Taiwan was laid by an agrarian reform program that was initiated with U.S. aid under the Joint Committee for Rural Reconstruction. The National Government was not to repeat the mistake made on the mainland, where the absence of an agrarian policy had aided the Communists' rural strategy. In three stages completed in 1953, the reform largely abolished landlordism and the government took over land and sold it on easy terms to the former tenants. More than half a million peasants became owners; production rapidly increased and so did the purchasing power and living standard of the peasantry. Landlords were not, however, expropriated, but reimbursed in industrial shares; thus the former landlords participated in the capitalization of the developing private industry. The long-range impact of this reform was that Taiwan continued to have the smallest income differential between rural and urban population of any industrialized or developing country.

In 1965 when the economy of Taiwan had reached the level of growth to become independent, U.S. aid was discontinued, and the rapid economic advancement that followed was the result of Chinese private initiative, ably supported by government policy. The astounding growth rate—averaging over 9 percent annually except for the oil crisis year of 1974—has been equaled by only very few other countries, such as Korea, Japan, and Singapore, though by none of them at such a steady pace.

Taiwan's economic growth was export related. Like Japan, Taiwan did not have enough raw material for industrial development and had to trade to survive. According to economists, foreign trade has always played a major role in the development of industrial countries, the more so for smaller countries, and Taiwan is no exception. In the years between 1960 and 1980 foreign trade rapidly advanced and far surpassed the growth of the national product. The production of export commodities began with labor-intensive industries, but with the accumulation of savings, capital-intensive industries began to be established. In the 1980s the shift to service and communications industries followed the example of the leading industrial nations.

The government's policy that relied upon the market and private initiative facilitated economic growth. Ten and later twelve major industrial government projects strengthened the infrastructure of the basic industries. But the most important government policy for this as for all other areas of development was the heavy emphasis on raising the educational level of the population.

Under Japanese rule the foundation had been laid for a literacy rate comparable to that of Europe and the United States. Japan, however, admitted only a handful of Taiwanese Chinese to higher education—in Japan. All that was changed under the National Government. Primary education provided not only literacy for almost

100 percent of the young, but trained them also in the standard national language—*kuo yü*—to unify the different dialect groups. Higher education by universities and colleges received major attention and support, and quality and standards again reached the level of the West. An important result of this educational policy was the rising number of overseas Chinese students, who made up about a third of the student body enrolled at the universities in Taiwan, while the number of overseas Chinese students going to the mainland declined correspondingly. A growing number of Chinese students from Taiwan continued their studies abroad, mostly in the United States. At first many did not return, creating the problem of a brain drain, which, however, was eased when conditions and opportunities on Taiwan improved.

There was little formal change in the structure of government. The constitution of 1947 was brought over from the mainland. Governmental institutions remained intact, but the substance, amplified, transformed the government into a more participatory system. In essence, control of the government remained in the hands of the *Kuomintang*, though the character of the party was affected by the increase in its membership by younger and especially by Taiwanese Chinese, as well as by the independence of the free enterprise system and by the new professionalism of the bureaucracy.

A distinction had to be drawn between the National Government that had come over from the mainland and the provincial government, more and more based on local elections and in the hands of Taiwanese Chinese. In these elections non-*Kuomintang* candidates were elected in increasing numbers. The latter filled about a third of the representatives' positions as "independents," though not permitted to form any opposition party of their own. It was this absence of a true multiparty system that was on occasion criticized abroad.

The National Government had to face the problem of an aging leadership. Executive power remained in the hands of the president but was shared by the prime minister. Chiang Kai-shek was reelected president until his death in 1975. He was succeeded eventually by his son, Chiang Ching-kuo, who filled the executive positions with many younger, often Taiwanese Chinese, professionals. The important legislative *yüan*, fulfilling the role of a parliament, was dwindling in size as many of its members who had been elected in 1947 on the mainland and who had made it to Taiwan aged and died. Twice, in 1971 and 1980, local elections were held to increase the membership through representatives elected in Taiwan.

One issue that has paled over the years was the Taiwan independence movement. Originally an offspring of the antimainlander revolt of 1947, it was continued by a few individuals chiefly in the United States and Japan and supported by anti-Nationalist opinion. Internationally it lost some of its appeal to leftists when it ran clearly counter to Peking's policy of regaining control of Taiwan; for Peking's policy, a "one China" concept was a prerequisite. On Taiwan, the totally changed social and economic conditions, the coming to age of a new generation all born on Taiwan, educated together, and intermarrying has gone far to dispel old antagonisms. For them the Communist offensive, political or military, presents a common danger.

In literature and art, however, the early conservatism of Nationalist bureaucracy, apprehensive and intolerant of any avant-garde tendencies, has given way to a greater acceptance of freedom of expression. In the long run Taiwan alone can guarantee the viability of a free Chinese tradition. Taiwan remained the cultural refuge for the great heritage that was being assaulted and greatly endangered on the mainland. For the past, this heritage is demonstrated by the greatest collection of Chinese art and ancient texts, which was saved by the National Government during the war from Japanese capture or destruction, brought to Taiwan, to be exhibited at the newly built National Palace Museum. For the present and the future this heritage will have to be expanded, enriched, and transformed if it is to survive.

All this prosperous and industrious life remains constantly under the shadow of the forces across the narrow Taiwan Strait. The necessities of defense of this island against the ever-real danger of military attack or strangulation remain a heavy burden, militarily, financially, and psychologically. It has been faced with calm determination, even though the republic's chief ally, the United States, has derecognized the Republic of China and cancelled its defense treaty with the National Government. What has remained is the Taiwan Relations Act that binds the United States "to provide Taiwan with arms of a defensive character and . . . to resist any resort to force or other forms of coercion that would jeopardize the security, or the social and economic system, of the people of Taiwan."

The drift of Peking's future course is uncertain. If Taiwan can remain free from conquest, then the tradition preserved there and its path of Chinese modernization may still play a part in the future of all China, because in ideological and cultural confrontation the size and political power of the antagonists does not, after all, really matter.

Sixteen

COMMUNISM UNDER MAO

FOUNDED IN 1921 under the guidance of the Comintern, the Chinese Communist party had as its goal a Marxist-Leninist revolution and world order. Marxism advocates a revolution by the proletariat to establish a class dictatorship and create an idealized social order, and Leninism conceives of the Communist party as the vanguard of the proletariat, a disciplined body of professional revolutionaries who presumably would understand and be able to execute policies for and in the name of the proletariat.

By separating the professional revolutionary organization from the alleged revolutionary class, it became possible to start "Communist" revolutionary movements in countries like China where there was little industrialization or proletariat. This extension of Communism to the nonindustrial world became imperative for Lenin when after World War I, Germany, the highly industrialized center of Europe, did not turn to the hoped for Communist revolution but established the democratic Weimar Republic. Disappointed, Lenin turned East to promote the Communist revolution in the nonindustrial countries of Asia, and China became the focus of Moscow's revolutionary Communist strategy.

Two elements were needed for this strategy: One, a doctrinal justification, and two, the promotion of a peasant policy for these largely agricultural countries. As for the latter, to the surprise of his colleagues, Lenin had already used peasants in the Bolshevik revolution and established his Soviets of workers and peasants in the Soviet Union. In Asia, this strategy was to be expanded. Doctrinally, Lenin declared that imperialism, the final stage of monopoly capitalism, had shifted from exploitation of the proletariat inside each industrial country to the exploitation of the colonial countries by the imperialist powers. The liberation of these countries from the colonial yoke was therefore a struggle against capitalism and doctrinally a part of the socialist world revolution.

In practice, Communism would make common cause with the aspirations of the nationalist parties emerging in the colonial world and use them as allies in a strategy whose final Communist goal was left more or less unstated. For this purpose China was described as a "quasi colony," exploited not by one but by all imperialist powers. Its nationalist struggle was to be supported in a United Front with Sun Yat-sen for an eventual Communist takeover from within. This first attempted power seizure in China failed, however, and a National Government was established, excluding the Communists.

The Communist strategy then changed from United Front to civil war and rural-based military organizations, with the Soviets again providing the formula. The Chinese Communists established the Kiangsi (Jiangsi) Soviet, survived the hardships of the Long March, and eventually arrived at Yenan, maintaining, albeit precariously, a Communist political structure that was constant in its compliance with Moscow's directives. The man who emerged as the Communist leader, Mao Zedong (Mao Tse-tung), who lived from 1893 to 1976, was a discerning student not only of Soviet strategy, but equally important, of the Soviet system of gaining and retaining power in the rough game of struggle for leadership and survival among the Communist elite.

Mao, of "middle peasant" origin according to Communist classification, received both traditional and modern schooling, became a political activist, and joined, as a junior member, the small group that founded the Chinese Communist party. Dismissed from his provincial party committee and the politburo for his tactical failure in not carrying out the proper peasant organization at the Autumn Harvest Uprising (January 1927), Mao nonetheless remained a member of the Kiangsi Soviet. At the outset of the Long March at a leadership conference held at Tsunyi (Zunyi) in 1936, Mao seized control of the Communist party-army with the help of the majority of commanders, replacing Zhou Enlai, who yielded without a fight. Mao's first move was to inform Joseph Stalin, who approved and henceforth provided Mao with direction, advice, and doctrinal education.

Communist power struggles, especially in Stalin's time, ended usually not only with the physical purge of any potential rival to the established leader, but also with the condemnation of the opponent as a "deviationist" from the right doctrinal line, which the leader claimed to possess. This doctrinal authority was therefore crucial for the head of the Communist system, and in Yenan Stalin provided Mao the Soviet leader's writings, textbooks, and encyclopedias that enabled Mao to assert the "correct" political line in his speeches and writings. The so-called Thought of Mao Tse-tung followed Stalin's explication of Marxist-Leninist doctrine, and Mao used Stalin's line of reasoning for the first purges of competitors, many of them as "Trotskyites." This was the beginning of the Mao cult that was to reach such an extraordinary degree in later decades.

In Yenan, Mao had thus become the paramount, authoritative Communist leader, largely responsible for the tenacity of the policy that led through the four years of renewed civil war to the Communist victory. The establishment of the People's Republic of China on October 1, 1949, meant a complete break with the Chinese past. Although nominally a United Front was maintained, in practice the Communist party, or rather its leadership, was in sole control.

As in other Communist countries, "the revolution" came after victory. One year after Communist entrenchment in power and restoration of the economy from the ravages of the Japanese war and the civil war, Mao Zedong set out to destroy the social and economic order and replace it with a Communist totalitarian system.

Immediately after the founding of the People's Republic, the existing legal order was abolished. All law codes and the court structure were abrogated; they were not replaced. As long as he lived, Mao did not accept the introduction of legal norms, even Communist law as developed in the Soviet Union and other Communist states. The only exception were codes that prescribed the new political structure and, in the sphere of social life, the marriage law, to regulate one aspect of private life for which legal norms were necessary.

In place of law, Mao's new regime used mass drives against presumed opposing groups to destroy the social order and create a totalitarian system. The chief method was terror, applied on a national scale to target groups and classes. This first violent phase of the

Communist program coincided with Chinese participation in the Korean War, which was used for its propaganda appeal.

Between 1950 and 1953 there were five major drives, for which Mao often set quotas for those who should be found very guilty, less guilty, or not guilty of the crimes that the respective drive claimed to prosecute. During the period of the drives the Chinese people were terrorized into acceptance of the Communist policies and order. There are no exact figures for the cost in human lives, but careful estimates range between ten to twenty million who lost their lives in these massive liquidations.

As drastic as these drives were in destroying the social order and establishing compliance with Communist totalitarian rule, the most insidious drive was an attack against all freedom of thought: The Study Campaign for Ideological Reform. It began in September 1951 with a five-hour lecture by Zhou Enlai to a large group of educators. The goal was acceptance of Communist doctrine by all, and the means to accomplish this was the "reform of the teacher's mind." The teachers had to learn the "ideology of the progressive elements of the working class, that is to say the revolutionary theories of Mao Tse-tung, a product of Marxism-Leninism, and the actual practice of the Chinese revolution."[1]

This thought reform, also called "brainwashing," was conducted by the use of a special, psychologically programmed method, so-called criticism, self-criticism, and confession in struggle meetings in which one individual at a time was criticized by his or her colleagues, themselves under pressure, and impelled to self-criticism and confession, all under the direction of Communist cadres. These struggle meetings became a general practice for all groups, often applied physical abuse, and sometimes led to the death of the victims. The method combined physical and psychological terror to assure acceptance of Communist doctrine and policies and eliminate any independence of thought; there was no "freedom of silence." This "Orwellian" method of terror, the destruction of all existing social bonds and loyalties and their replacement by the party's command accepted as a matter of survival, can be seen as the chief factor in creating the uniformity of expression—the repetition of the official line of the moment—by a totally cowed population, a uniformity that so disturbed observant visitors during the years of Mao's rule.

Once this Communist order was established, the People's Republic followed the example and guidance of the Soviet "older brother," complete with five-year plans, emphasis on heavy industrial development assisted by a swarm of Soviet advisers, blueprints, and material, and the study of Russian language throughout the school system. The regime succeeded in reestablishing order and beginning a program of industrialization that reflected the Soviet model.

The art and literature of the time reflected Communist concepts. In painting, socialist realism meant that museums showed the accomplishments of heroic fighters and workers on landscapes that contained red flags and work teams of collectives. Socialist romanticism painted a new happy life under Communism in total disregard of actual conditions. In the cities massive new structures built in the Stalinist wedding-cake style demonstrated a new architectural era. As for China's past, a book on Chinese literature (published in 1954) characterized the great philosophers of the past as "progressive" or "reactionary." Confucianism was in general condemned as idealist and reactionary, but some Taoists supposedly had been Marxist and dialectic. All Chinese history had to be forced into the Procrustean bed of the doctrine, and thus ancient China was a society of slavery transformed to feudalism by the first emperor. As a consequence Confucius was depicted as having been reactionary in defending slavery against the feudalism introduced by the first emperor—demonstrating how far doctrine could be made to prevail over historical realities.

The model of the Soviet Union was to be followed in agriculture. Collectivization was to be introduced in stages, but then Mao, as Stalin had been, was determined to rush the completion of collectivization without waiting for the production of agricultural implements and machinery. The so-called mutual aid teams and peasant cooperatives, the first stage of agricultural organization, in which the peasants were to pool labor without the abolition of private ownership of land, was changed immediately to full collectivization—from which Mao hoped to gain the increased income necessary for industrialization. The time span in China was even shorter than in the Soviet case. Stalin had waited until 1930, thirteen years, before forcing his brutal drive for collectivization at a loss of millions of lives; Mao, however, demanded in 1953 that full collectivization had to be completed at the end of the first Five-Year Plan. He ridiculed the slow stride of his number two man, Liu Shaoqi (Liu Shao-chi), as "walking on bound feet," like old women of traditional China. The process of collectivization was accomplished in China with less resistance than in Russia, largely because the upper level in rural China had already been liquidated in the Agrarian Reform Drive four years earlier. But in 1956 some resistance occurred. Peasants engaged in wanton slaughter of animals that were to be collectivized, and a spring famine forced the government to relax some of the rules of collectivization of small animals and to permit private plots. But the chief result of collec-tivization, the general decline in agricultural production, was in the long run the same in China as in all Communist countries.

This phase of Chinese Communism ended shortly after the death of Stalin. Under Stalin, Moscow had supported Chinese Communism from the beginning. Stalin had helped Mao, though with some hesitation, in establishing his primary role in the Chinese party leadership. Despite occasional reluctance in carrying out Stalin's orders, Mao never challenged Stalin's position in the Communist world. Stalin had been proclaimed as the "red sun in the people's heart," a title later assumed by Mao himself. After the death of Stalin in 1953, Mao published an essay, "The Greatest Friendship," in which he glorified Stalin in the grandiloquent Communist rhetoric of the time.

Khrushchev's de-Stalinization campaign of 1956 took the Chinese leadership completely by surprise. As a Chinese Stalinist, Mao was vulnerable to an attack that affected Communist leaders throughout the Communist world. The Chinese leadership, itself divided over some of Mao's policies, joined after some delay in the downgrading of Stalin, but with noticeable moderation. Stalin had made mistakes, but those were outweighed by his great merits in leading the Communist world movement. As for China, mistakes in the death of innocent victims were admitted but ascribed to overzealous lower cadres, because Mao could hardly "de-Mao" himself. Most significantly, the Eighth Communist Party Congress, which met in September 1956, stressed collective leadership and omitted from a new consti-tution any reference to the Thought of Mao Zedong, who himself did not give any major speech at the congress.

The Soviet so-called Thaw, the time of literary protest against Stalinism, was paralleled in China in 1957 by the period of the Hundred Flowers. Alluding to the old Chinese slogans, "let a hundred flowers bloom" and "let the hundred schools of thought contend," which referred to the early era of competing philosophical schools, the Communist leadership signaled a new policy of intellectual tolerance as long as criticism remained within the Marxist-Leninist framework. Mao quickly took the lead, speaking in February 1957 "On the Correct Handling of Contradictions Among The People." Mao admitted past mistakes, promised rehabilitation and exoneration of innocent victims, and invited criticism of the Communist party and its policies.

The Hundred Flowers policy was designed to control and deflect any potential opposition by permitting well-supervised criticism. The result, unforeseen by Mao and the party, was an explosion of criticism, riots, strikes, protest meetings, and attacks on the party, on officials, and on Communism itself. Quickly the Hundred Flowers became "poisonous weeds" that had to be destroyed, and an antirightist campaign led to hundreds of thousands of arrests and purges. Millions of young people were sent to the countryside to work with and learn from the peasants.

To reestablish his role in the world movement, Mao went to the interparty conference in Moscow in 1957 to demand a role in the overall Communist policy making. At the conference the Soviets officially recognized the "equality, independence, sovereignty, non-interference and mutual cooperation" of all Communist parties of the bloc countries. With the establishment of Communist governments in other countries, Moscow held no longer the monopoly on policy making for the movement; but in practice, the Soviet leaders meant to retain control. There was still only "formal but no real consultation," as Mao had complained. The Soviet party, because of its greater experience and the advanced stage of Soviet development, claimed to be the vanguard of the Communist movement and as such was leading the way to Communism that all other parties had to follow. Mao, who gave a lengthy speech for a stronger policy against the capitalist world, was ignored.

When Mao returned from Moscow, he must have realized that if he were to remain free from Moscow's decisions, he would have to become independent economically from the whole Soviet-directed and supported program of five-year development plans. China, so he thought, had to go it alone and lift itself up by its own bootstraps. This was the basic reasoning behind Mao's fantastic plan of the Great

Leap Forward. Mao went further; his Great Leap Forward was to challenge this Soviet leadership by "bypassing the Soviet Union on the way to communism," as the Chinese press proclaimed at the time.

Mao's Great Leap Forward of 1958 served a number of purposes. Because China had no adequate capital reserves, massive labor organizations would have to replace them. Mao's rapid collectivization policy had resulted in resistance and a decline of agricultural production; therefore, he had to attempt complete control and organization of all agricultural production. He also had to speed up industrialization without outside aid. The result was the first demonstration on a grand scale of Mao's utopian mysticism and his belief in his ability to drive people by means of his direct leadership to the envisaged revolutionary future. Although Mao still worked through the party, it was military organization of the masses that was to lead to instant Communism.

The original plan, as announced in May 1958 at the second session of the Eighth Communist Party Congress and spelled out by the directives of August of the same year, was formulated under the slogans of the Three Red Banners: "The General Line," "The Great Leap Forward," and "The People's Communes." It became known popularly as the Great Leap Forward, consisting of a massive organization of human labor in quasi-military fashion for work and life. The communes were to group rural collectives and local towns into a centralized system of human labor that could be applied alternately, wherever wanted, in agriculture, industry, or any other human effort. The communes consisted of several tens of thousands of people each, with a total of 26,000 communes for the whole of China.

Under the original plan all life was to be collective. Family houses were to be torn down and the material used for barracks where people were to live. They would eat in mess halls. The commune was to replace family life. Husband and wife could be assigned to different teams, children placed in dormitories, old people in "old people's happy homes." Private plots and animals were to be taken away. Payment was in kind and for "need."

Society was to be totally restructured. People were to be organized into squadrons, companies, battalions, regiments, and divisions, marched to and from work, and in addition, receive military training in local militias. In some cases the commune administration was taken over directly by the local party organization, thus abolishing government— a Maoist form of "withering away of the state." Indeed, the idea of using everybody alternately for agricultural, industrial, or any other kind of labor was apparently related to the utopian Marxist view of socialist man as an all-around person, no longer confined to one field of endeavor. China was advancing from socialism to Communism.

The world was fascinated by the attempt to decentralize and multiply steel production with so-called backyard steel furnaces. More than 600,000 of them, all over China, using scrap metal as raw material, would be tended by fifty million people in their off hours and were to double and multiply Chinese steel production in a few years.

It was not long before the disastrous results of this plan became obvious. Misuse of soil, wrongly applied agricultural techniques, senseless deforestation leading to destruction of natural resources resulted in a catastrophic decline in agricultural production, and during the next two years an unprecedented famine caused the death of millions. The disarray in the industrial development meant that only a third of the industrial plants were able to work, and those, at reduced speed.

In December of 1958 in a central committee meeting, new directives greatly modified this program. The name of the communes was maintained, but real management was transferred back to the village work teams. Payment was again in money and for work done, rather than "need." Private plots were again permitted, family life was restored, so that "old and young could live together." Nothing much remained of the program except the slogans. But the damage was done, and the famine took an increasing toll. This time Mao could not altogether escape responsibility. He resigned from the chairmanship of the republic, which was taken over by Liu Shaoqi, who abandoned the Great Leap policy and attempted to restore economic production to its previous level.

When the Great Leap ended in disaster Zhou Enlai journeyed to Moscow, and for a short time relations with Moscow improved. But at the Lushan conference in 1959, Mao countered a personal letter of criticism of his policy, written by Minister of Defense Peng Dehuai (P'eng Te-huai), by threatening civil war. In a heated confrontation Mao obtained the purge of his accusers. Mao did not regain full control, however, and after half a decade of a see-saw struggle between Mao and the party leadership under Liu Shaoqi, Mao decided to break through the Marxist-Leninist framework itself and destroy the party whose loyalty he could no longer command. For this extraordinary move Mao organized the so-called Great Proletarian Cultural Revolution (1966–1969).

To attack the party Mao needed a Maoist force. Backed by the new defense minister, Lin Biao (Lin Piao), and using Lin's troops as a supporting force, Mao had the brilliant idea of organizing the wild enthusiasm and radicalism of the malcontents among the high school and college students to create the Red Guards, the "little generals" of the revolution. Hardened first by their assault on the "four olds"— old customs, old habits, old thoughts, and old culture—and by the atrocities they were induced to commit against the "five black elements"—landlords, rich peasants, counterrevolutionaries, rightists, and bad elements—and having learned to rampage in the cities, breaking into houses, assailing and beating to death people in the streets and in the struggle meetings, the Red Guards were called to Peking to hail their chief, Chairman Mao. They were then sent out to the provinces and localities in the hinterland to attack and destroy the provincial and local party and government administration. When some of these local cadres resisted, army and air force units were sent by Lin Biao to support the Left and quash any local opposition to the Red Guards.

To destroy the party, Mao had to place himself above the Marxist-Leninist concept that the party was the vehicle of the historical truth of the moment. For Mao, it was no longer the party that held the truth, but Mao himself. The cult of Stalin had been used in the USSR to manipulate policy at least formally within the framework of the party structure. Mao was to go a step further; like the *Führerkult* of Hitler, the Mao cult resulted in a quasi deification of Mao and of the Thought of Mao, which supposedly could be used (if "rightly interpreted") to answer all problems. Mao's homilies were collected by Lin Biao in the *Little Red Book*, which everyone had to memorize, quote from, cite in unison, and be seen with at all times. Mao's image in offices, factories, and homes was given quasi-religious reverence, "consulted" in the morning on problems of the day, and in the evening given "reports" on affairs of the day. Three songs, "The East is Red," "Sailing the Seas Depends on the Helmsman," and "Father and Mother are Dear but Mao Zedong is Dearer" were constantly to remind all of Mao's fatherly role.

The Cultural Revolution was, however, more than Mao's attempt to give his utopian fantasies an institutional framework. He intended to remain the prophet of this new order: He had envisaged it, and he appears to have believed it was not only China's but mankind's destiny. The quasi-religious aspects of the Mao cult, the catechism of the *Little Red Book*, the pictures, and Mao's quasi-philosophical ramblings indicated that Mao believed in his own role as founder of a new phase of Marxism-Leninism, a belief stated not only by the Maoist generation in China but also by radical revolutionary groups worldwide.

The claim of Mao's infallibility, which was used to stir up and galvanize his adolescent followers, could not be accepted either doctrinally or politically by the party leaders, depriving them as it did of any authority and even defense against Mao's arbitrary rule. Some, like Zhou Enlai, yielded; others ridiculed and challenged the concept of Mao's omniscience. The battle over the cult of Mao in the media, literature, the arts, and the theatre formed the "cultural" issue of this so-called Cultural Revolution.

It was in this field of culture where Mao used the service and support of Jiang Qing (Chiang Ch'ing) and her friends, who became leading figures in the Maoist movement. Jiang Qing, Mao's fourth wife, was a former actress from Shanghai who gained Mao's favor in Yanan days (when he bundled off his former wife to Moscow). Mao married Jiang Qing over the protest of his comrades, who strongly suggested that Mao's new marriage partner should not play any public role in the party or government. She was to take revenge during the Cultural Revolution for these old restrictions.

From her Shanghai days, Madame Mao knew two leftist writers, Zhang Chunqiao (Chang Ch'un-ch'iao) and Yao Wenyuan (Yao Wen-yuan), who had already proven themselves by their ability to denounce writers out of step with the party line of the moment. These two were now leading the literary inculcation of those who tried to deflect the Mao cult and its political consequences. Together with Madame Mao they were to form the core of Mao's Cultural Revolution group. The conflict now moved into the educational institutions where young People's Liberation Army (PLA) soldiers had been enrolled and helped to organize Maoist student groups, later called the Red Guards, to propagate the cult and attack party organizations. Many students came from worker and peasant families, admitted because of their proper background but without adequate educational preparation, and were jealous of their better-qualified fellow students, hated their teachers, and feared examinations. These malcontents formed the core of the Red Guards, joined, however, by others mostly out of fear or simply carried away by the enthusiasm of the moment.

On June 2, 1966, Mao unleashed these juveniles by a directive that closed the schools for six months—later to be extended for an indefinite period—and promised a further proletarianization of education. At the same time a new form of political attack, outside the regular media, was initiated by Mao: the use of wall posters to express and inflame the furor of the masses in condemning the bourgeois reactionaries and glorifying their idol, Chairman Mao. In August Mao called a central committee meeting under protection of Lin Biao's troops. The meeting accepted a sixteen-point declaration that officially initiated the Cultural Revolution.

Now the rampage of the students commenced, millions of them going throughout the country. For the majority it was a great holiday, boys and girls together traveling all over the country at the army's expense, feeling the glamour of their new importance as the young leaders of the country. But behind the adventure of the journey was the grim reality of their licensed destruction of culture—"destroying the old" at Mao's command. They destroyed temples, statues, books, and old art all over China, including the Confucian halls and tomb at Chüfu (Qufu) in Shantung province, and they dynamited all but a few of more than three thousand temples and monasteries in Tibet. In talking to his trusted police and intelligence chief, Kang Sheng (K'ang Sheng), Mao recalled an old Chinese folktale, the story of the monkey Sun Wu-k'ung, who used magic for his many deeds of wickedness, leaping a thousand miles and traveling to the end of the world, breaking into Hell and Paradise and even trying to overthrow the Heavenly Emperor. For help in his many fights, the monkey pulled out some hairs, spat on them, called out his magic word, and threw the hairs into the air where they changed into hundreds of little monkeys—an army of monkeys that fought his battle and then returned to the body of their master. This tale was in Mao's mind when he called out the Red Guards to destroy the party for him.

When they eventually moved into the factories and communes, the Red Guards were supplemented by discontented local dissidents, "revolutionary rebels," and accompanied where necessary by military personnel. They were to attack, abuse, and in some cases kill and remove the party and government authorities.

The Red Guards, by now a mass movement of tens of millions of students, were to gain "the victory of the proletarian revolution over the open and hidden representatives of the bourgeoisie, the reactionaries and capitalist reactionaries and capitalist roaders, as represented by the leadership of the Party." In January 1967 the call went out by radio and newspapers over the country to all these revolutionaries to "seize power."[2]

Mao wanted not only to destroy the present leadership of the party but to replace it altogether by a new institutional framework, more akin to the Führer-principle than to Communism. Trying to find a Marxist justification for his venture, he declared it was modeled after the Paris Commune of 1871, the seizure of power by workers in Paris during a siege by the Prussian army, which Karl Marx himself had called a "proletarian" force. This was Mao's attempt to describe the relationship between the leader and the masses with himself as the absolute leader and the masses following him, the proletarian masses.

A few attempts were made by Mao to establish such a Paris Commune, mainly in Shanghai, but the whole utopian plan had to be abandoned when it went out of control. More and more the Red Guards split into opposing factions that fought each other. There was great loss of life and general chaos. In a night session in his home in July 1968, Mao in an emotional scene accused five of the Red Guard leaders of having betrayed him. He had to abandon his scheme. Its failure demonstrated the need for organized authority. In Zhang Chun-qiao's words: "We still need a party," but it was to be a reconstructed Maoist party, supported by military force—the PLA. A new structure, the revolutionary committees, were established to take over government. They were formed by three elements: the military as the power leverage; "liberated" cadres who accepted Maoism, to provide expertise; and the Maoist revolutionaries—the Red Guards. On this basis at least a working administrative system could be established, with the military suppressing the anarchy of Red Guard infighting that had quickly spread throughout the country.

The Red Guards were almost completely excluded from any influence or leadership, and Mao gave the PLA authority to shoot and kill armed Red Guards and to smash "like flies on the wall" those who resisted. Then he sent teams of workers and poor peasants into colleges and high schools to propagate the Thought of Mao Tse-tung, and to break the defiance of the Red Guards on their home ground. These teams, consisting of uneducated, often illiterate, loyal Maoists, many of whom had never been to an educational institution before, confronted the students, teachers, and also the administrators with strong-arm tactics. They were forced through "struggle, criticism, and transformation" into an acceptance of Mao's revolutionary order. Not only were the Red Guard factions eliminated, but also the rule over educated or at least quasi-educated people in universities, middle schools, in literature and art, science, legal work, propaganda, medicine, and public health was now in the hands of these workers and peasants who were to be the teachers, providing, together with the Thought of Mao Tse-tung, the "world outlook of the working class."[3]

The whole program of the reopened universities and schools was reformed. In his directive of July 22, 1968, Mao admitted that it was still necessary to have universities but they should constitute mainly colleges of science and engineering, and their schedules should be shortened and revolutionized. Students should be selected from workers and peasants with practical experience and would return to their work after a few years of study. This frontal attack against education terrorized the Red Guards as well as all teachers and educators now open to constant supervision and harassment. They were panic stricken and afraid to continue their dangerous profession. Most of the students were sent to the countryside for indefinite periods to join the peasants in carrying on Mao's revolution. In truth, the Cultural Revolution destroyed education and cost the country the loss of a generation of educated people.

For the Soviets, Mao's fantastic usurpation of all power and especially his doctrinal assumption of monopoly authority was a clear threat to the Communist system in China, let alone to Moscow's leading role in the world movement. While the destruction of the Communist party organization in China continued, Moscow began to concentrate some forty fully equipped Soviet divisions along the Chinese border in Manchuria and the Mongol People's Republic. In August 1968, at the time of the Soviet invasion of Czechoslovakia, Leonid Brezhnev proclaimed the so-called Brezhnev doctrine, according to which socialist countries had the right, indeed the duty, to interfere in any country where socialism was threatened from within or from the outside, a principle clearly applicable in Moscow's eyes to China. And when the fanaticism of Maoist frontier guards provoked some incidents along the Amur River and in Turkestan, the Soviets retaliated in force.

The clear danger of Soviet intervention on the side of the Chinese Communist party leadership appears to have been one reason for ending the Cultural Revolution turmoil short of Mao's goal. In April of 1969 at the Ninth Communist Party Congress, the "congress of unity," the results of the Cultural Revolution were legitimized in a new constitution and the turmoil was declared ended. In August of that year, Soviet Premier Aleksey Kosygin and Zhou Enlai met at the Peking airport for discussions. From time to time there have been further discussions, and in effect the acute tension between the two Communist countries has ended.

The new draft constitution of 1969 provided originally that Mao should again become chairman of the republic, a position that Mao had lost to Liu Shaoqi, who was purged and killed in the Cultural Revolution. Mao did not want to reoccupy that position. For Chairman Mao the chair of the party was all; he disdained regaining what he had been forced to surrender. But Lin Biao, who assumed the position of vice chairman and proclaimed successor, had introduced the clause without consulting Mao. This Mao could not tolerate: The man who had organized the Cultural Revolution for Mao and had backed its success with the PLA had come too close to power, and Mao would destroy him.

How Mao accomplished Lin's purge is still a matter of speculation. The official version is that Lin plotted Mao's death and, when discovered, attempted to flee to the Soviet Union in a plane that crashed in Mongolia—a highly unlikely scenario. Wherever and however, Lin died or was killed in September 1971, and the commanding officers of his Fourth Field Army were purged together with a few party leaders.

The fall of Lin Biao, however, weakened Mao's military support. To fortify his position, Mao reorganized the people's militia, making it independent of army control. Young militia leader Wang Hongwen (Wang Hung-wen), a worker from Shanghai, entered the close circle of Mao's confidants, to participate later as one of the "gang of four" in the power struggle that erupted for Mao's succession.

For the country to recover from the chaos of the Cultural Revolution, Mao faced the necessity of political reorganization, particularly in view of the destruction of government authority on all levels. The man he turned to was Zhou Enlai, who reorganized the administration and charted a new course in foreign policy. Domestically, to reestablish production and economic stability, the eccentricities of the Cultural Revolution were discontinued. To reintroduce incentive, payment was again made by work points according to labor performed and private plots were again permitted in agriculture. In foreign policy, the most astounding shift was the normalization of relations with the United States, a complete change for both sides. For China, this breakout from self-imposed isolation strengthened its position in the face of the Soviet menace. It also led to the People's Republic's admission to the United Nations and, as Peking had demanded, the expulsion of the Republic of China on Taiwan.

Zhou Enlai played an ambiguous role during the Cultural Revolution. Apparently he had tolerated the frenzies of Mao's movement, the *Little Red Book*, the songs, the fraternization with the Red Guards, Mao's assault on the party and government establishment and on culture and tradition, only protecting a few of the most valuable military scientists, the foreign service, and a few cultural treasures. To rebuild the government and make it work again, he now initiated a policy of widespread rehabilitation of purged cadres to staff the administrative departments, to bring the ship of state back on an even keel.

Soon, however, it became clear that Zhou was being used only to recover from immediate dangers, that the shift to order was only a tactical move, and that Mao had not given up his utopian goal. In the latter part of 1973 a campaign was instituted that began with an attack on Confucius (for his reactionary role in Chinese history two thousand years ago). Confucius was accused of attempting during his lifetime to "turn back the wheel of history" and was called a reactionary and a counterrevolutionist. Since it was Mao's practice to use historical allegories as opening moves in the purge of his potential opponents, it soon became apparent that the attack was intended against new policies in the economy, in education, and in the rehabilitation of cadres, and its chief target was no other than Zhou Enlai. To make the identification even clearer, the condemnation began to single out the Duke of Chou of the Chou Dynasty, who had been so highly praised by Confucius and whose family name happened to be the same as that of Zhou Enlai. The Mao cult was reemphasized at the same time by the appearance in Shanghai of a journal, "Study and Criticism," carrying a Mao masthead and a quotation from Mao at the head of each number.

When the Tenth Communist Party Congress was convened August 24 to 28 (1973), Zhou Enlai gave one of the two main speeches; the other was by the new Maoist leader, Wang Hongwen. The sole purpose of the session was to read Lin Biao out of the party constitution. But Zhou, the moderate in the view of the time, did not use his speech to report on the considerable progress in recovering from the economic disaster made by his changes in policies, which he hardly mentioned. Instead, he glorified the Cultural Revolution, praised Mao, whom he quoted extensively, singled out especially the revolution in literature, art, education, and public health, and predicted the continuing "struggle between the socialist and the capitalist road" and the necessity of perpetual revolutions. His main target, however, was Lin Biao, whom he reviled with all the vituperation of a Maoist harangue. The anti-Confucius drive became fused with the anti–Lin Biao drive, and Zhou continued in his role of rebuilding the government and the economy. But the veiled argument against him, with other historical allegories, continued.

Then Zhou fell ill and his role was more and more taken over by Deng Xiaoping (Teng Hsiao-p'ing) who was the number two target of the Cultural Revolution but who had been rehabilitated by Zhou, seemingly with Mao's approval. As Zhou had done, Deng also made his obeisance to Mao's vagaries, though his speech before the United Nations in Paris in 1974 giving Mao's interpretation of the advance of world revolution may have been identical with Deng's own view. Because by that time Mao had given up the challenge to Moscow's leadership of the socialist camp, Deng declared simply, "As a result of the emergence of social imperialism, the socialist camp which existed for a time after World War II, is no longer in existence."[4]

Instead, there was a division into three worlds: the two superpowers, the secondary capitalist countries, and the third world. The third world was the developing world of Asia, Africa, Latin America, and other regions, the chief revolutionary force of the time, to which China as a developing socialist country belonged and where it assumed its new leadership role.

When Zhou Enlai died of cancer in January 1976, Deng delivered the eulogy. Mao neither appeared nor expressed any sorrow at the death of his longtime comrade and chief supporter. On April 4, at the Ch'ing Ming festival—the Chinese All Souls Day—mountains of wreaths were piled on T'ienanmen Square in memory of Zhou Enlai by tens of thousands of mourners. When the wreaths were removed overnight by the police, a massive spontaneous demonstration erupted on the square, where over 100,000 people shouted slogans and composed poems against Mao and Madame Mao. The Maoist militia eventually suppressed, with great loss of life, the demonstration as a counterrevolutionary movement. Deng Xiaoping, who was accused of fomenting it, was ousted. Mao appointed Hua Guofong (Hua Kuo-feng), his police chief, as acting premier. Later, after Mao's death and Deng's return to power, the T'ienanmen protest was proclaimed a revolutionary event, although the anti-Mao slogans were no longer mentioned. In retrospect, this incident marked the end of Maoism.

Seventeen

THE POST-MAO EXPERIMENT

MAO ZEDONG DIED on September 9, 1976. The funeral committee listed the names of all Chinese Communist leaders, giving the impression of unity among a collective leadership. But less than a month later, on October 7, the power struggle for succession came into the open in what the East German Communists in a rare display of dry humor called the "Chinese October Revolution." In a coup d'état Hua Guofeng, who claimed to have been appointed as successor by Mao himself, arrested the four leading Maoists, Madame Mao, Zhang Chunqiao, Yao Wenyuan and Wang Hongwen, accusing them of attempting a coup of their own. These four, from now on vilified as the "gang of four," became, as representatives of Mao's radical policies, the scapegoats for everything that went wrong under Mao's regime, in particular the Great Proletarian Cultural Revolution, soon to be recognized as the unmitigated disaster it actually was.

By this coup, apparently supported by the military leadership, Hua obviously thought to deflect and dispel the anti-Maoist emotions that had so vehemently exploded at the T'ienanmen demonstrations in April. Hua needed Mao's unspoiled image to sanction his own authority, not based on any party procedure, but solely on a statement allegedly made by Mao to Hua in the opaque words, "With you in charge I am at ease." In large posters, showing a seated Mao placing his hand on Hua, who was seated next to him, and supposedly delivering these words, Hua spread his claim to power countrywide. For a time, Hua assumed the status of Chairman Hua, had his hair cut like Mao's, uttered Maoist pronouncements, proclaimed "The Thought of Chairman Hua" and built in a great hurry a colossal mausoleum—sixty times the size of Lenin's tomb—for Mao on

227

T'ienanmen Square, where Mao's embalmed body was enshrined in a crystal sarcophagus.

The rank and file of party members, however, wanted more than the arrest of the most radical Maoists. They pressed Hua to rehabilitate for the second time Deng Xiaoping as the man to be trusted to restore an orderly Communist government. Hua first resisted, but in July 1977 Deng was rehabilitated and restored to all his former positions. A new party congress, the eleventh, elected a new central committee, a new politburo and a new standing committee. Many rehabilitated cadres and the military were included. Under Deng, the process of rehabilitation of more than a million cadres went on, in many cases replacing Maoists and eventually leading to the removal of Hua Guofeng from all power.

On Deng's return to power hopes were raised that an orderly administration would replace the drives of the past and that, as promised, the special excesses of the Cultural Revolution would never be repeated. In addition it was hoped that a freer political order with legal guarantees to protect the individual and manage human relations would be introduced. For a short four months, from November 1978 to March 1979, there was indeed an opportunity to express political views of almost any kind. This was the time when large numbers of young, discontented workers and students expressed their feelings and ideas in posters, pamphlets, poems, and whole essays plastered on a wall at Xidan, a main thoroughfare of Peking, a place that became known as "democracy wall." Simultaneously a large number of journals with articles raising demands for freedom and human rights made their appearance.

The use of wall posters for political demands had begun under Mao during the Cultural Revolution, when the Red Guards all over China covered every free space of wall with slogans, demands, and accusations against individual party members, the victims of the Cultural Revolution. The practice continued, and in 1975 Mao's last constitution guaranteed the right of putting up wall posters as one of the so-called four big freedoms to express views freely—in support of Mao. The new constitution of 1978 restated these four freedoms— now to be used in an attack against the Maoist past.

The views proclaimed on democracy wall and in the articles of dissident underground journals voiced a whole scale of demands from reform of the present party system to a multiparty system modeled after Western democracy. Some of the writers showed a surprising familiarity with Western literature on development of and ideas of democratic institutions, from Montesquieu's *L'Ésprit des lois* to Robert Owen's *A New View of Society*. They demanded laws, a new constitution, freedom of speech, and freedom of religion—all religions. They described the constant fear under the oppressive system of the past and the hope that "a new epoch had come."

The best known of Chinese dissidents was Wei Jingsheng, a worker and the editor of *Tan Suo* ("Exploration"), who in an article, "Real Death," described the cruelties and mental and physical tortures in a prison near Peking and in another essay deplored China's backwardness, condemned Communism as utopian and demanded political modernization—"The Fifth Modernization: Democracy." In January 1979, the China Human Rights League was founded.

This outbreak of dissidence was at first tolerated by the regime; indeed it appeared to be patronized as long as the attack against Maoism was useful to Deng Xiaoping in the demotion and replacement of Hua Guofeng. In March 1979, however, when the dissidence got out of hand, the government clamped down. Deng declared that demands had gone too far, and an editorial in the *People's Daily* claimed that "the worn out weapon of 'human rights' which has long been reactionary bourgeois dictatorship's window-dressing" was "no remedy for the problems of a socialist society."[1] Wei Jingsheng, when he criticized Deng personally, was arrested and condemned to fifteen years in prison. Democracy wall was first transferred to an out-of-the-way location and then permanently closed down. The journals were shut down, their editors—arrested—disappeared, and a new constitution, promulgated in 1984, eliminated the guarantee of the four big freedoms after Deng had already disapproved of them. Thus died the hope that the end of Maoism might bring a new, freer and more democratic epoch in China. The Peking Spring was over.

The first priority of Deng Xiaoping's regime was the realization of the "four modernizations." The slogan of the four modernizations in industry, agriculture, science and technology, and defense had first been proclaimed by Zhou Enlai in 1964 and again in 1975. On this basis Hua Guofeng announced at the Fifth National People's Congress in 1978 a program of major construction goals and grand plans. Deng used the same slogan thereafter to initiate his new policy that aimed at a complete shift from Mao's previous course. Deng's goal was to lift China out of the depths of decline into which thirty years of Communism and Maoist utopianism had thrust it. In so doing, he would disregard to a heretofore unknown degree Communist doctrinal rigidity. Deng's well-known saying that it did not matter whether the cat was black or white so long as it caught mice may be regarded as a true, if simplified, characterization of his approach to the problems he faced.

Responding to Hua's call in 1978, Peking went all out in planning a rapid industrial development with the aid of foreign know-how, funds, and equipment. Soon it became clear, however, that many of the plans had been overambitious or poorly conceived and that the planners had seriously misjudged China's limited capacity to fund or repay capital investment. Plans had to be reduced under a new program in 1979 of "Readjustment, Restructuring, Consolidation, and Improvement," under which the emphasis was shifted from new ventures to renovation of the existing industrial plant structure.

Although Hua's grandiose projects were reduced, deferred, or suspended, the course toward economic regeneration was sustained by Deng, who initiated one after another the basic changes that would lift China's economy out of the Maoist morass.

From a Communist viewpoint, Deng's measures were revolutionary. The first turnabout came in agriculture with the introduction of the responsibility system under which each farming family was allotted land under contract for delivery of a fixed amount of product to the state. Beyond that the family was free to sell on the market and to use its land for specialization in any kind of produce, to be in fact independent farmers. This agricultural emancipation was combined with the evolution of free markets for agricultural and other products that sprang up in towns throughout the country.

The agricultural responsibility system first introduced for three years was soon extended to fifteen years; thus ended the collectivization of agriculture. The result of this policy of land to the tiller was an immediate and continuing substantial increase in agricultural production, which in turn raised considerably the living standard of the farming population. The sight of individual farmers, instead of teams, at work in the countryside demonstrated the change that meant the end of a Communist system in agriculture. Peasants could now become rich again; and the official approval of newly rich peasants was explained by the inference that one person's affluence would lift and benefit all others.

The chief economic problem, however, was not in agriculture, as critical as agricultural decline under Communism had become, but rather in the main industrial part of the economy, the policy of public ownership and of central planning in the industrial sector. A partial answer to the problem was sought in a variety of ways. The twin problem in the cities was the growing unemployment and the shortage of consumer goods and services that had been created under bureaucratic planning. To handle this critical deficiency the regime introduced a policy of licensing private entrepreneurs. By 1984 more than two million licenses had been granted to carpenters, bicycle repair shops, barbers, beauty shops, restaurateurs, food producers, eateries, textile manufacturers, doctors, small-scale workshops, and many others, permitting them not only to work for profit, but also to hire up to seven employees, called "assistants." In many cases these private entrepreneurs and their assistants earned considerably more than state workers, although they had to forego the guarantee of the "iron rice bowl" and the insurance benefits for health and old age.

This partial solution of problems in the main economic sector did not affect the deep malaise caused by the bureaucratic stultification of industry, faulty planning, incompetent management, slackening and loafing of the work force, corruption, waste, poor quality of products, and the resulting cost inefficiency requiring heavy state subsidy to industrial plants. The plants remained unaccountable for costs as long as they manufactured goods and quantities as ordered. Nothing exemplified the irrationality of the system better than the backyard furnaces of the Cultural Revolution. Additional steel production of eight million tons was claimed but the products proved to be totally useless and a great waste of time and material. Of course, this steel production example was out of the ordinary; however, the whole central planning system of industrial development was faulty, magnifying all the failures of bureaucracy and the lack of incentive for the work force. The question for Deng's reformers was how to reverse this economic debacle without giving up the system of a socialist planned economy.

A first experiment was made by introducing elements of a free market economy, to relate production in at least some degree to consumer demand. In certain consumer industries, notably textiles, managers of factories were encouraged to study the market by themselves, produce goods on the basis of demand rather than solely as dictated by the planners, and to manufacture goods above the allotted state quotas for sale at profit, such profit to be used for new investment or bonuses as incentive to the work force. Funds for operation were no longer to be simply defrayed by the government, but by government banks that were to advance money at interest rates, so that there would be some way to measure the profitability of production. This policy was first and with some success applied by the governor of Szech'wan, Zhao Ziyang, who as a result of his successful performance was called by Deng Xiaoping to Peking to become premier and introduce this policy nationwide.

This limited introduction of free market elements was clearly not enough to provide a viable industrial development. In essence, the basic problem could only be solved by turning to Western economies, beginning with the authorization of joint enterprises in major industries and businesses (some 600 by 1984) in which foreign and overseas Chinese partners invested capital, technology, and administrative expertise in exchange for some promised freedom in hiring and technical decision making, tax advantages, and permission to take profits out of the country. Next came the establishment of four "special zones" where foreign firms were invited to settle. These firms would have substantial tax advantages and some freedom to plan their product and its marketing. The special zones, which soon developed a life of their own, introducing blocks of high-rise sky-scrapers and a Western life-style, were in many ways reminiscent of the treaty ports of the past in which foreigners had the right to reside and carry on trade, albeit without the rights of extraterritoriality of the former treaty ports, because the zones remained under special Chinese jurisdiction. This system of "Westernization" of the economy was extended in 1984 through the creation of fourteen special regions for foreign economic development, with Shanghai as the most important region.

Where this "Westernization" of a section of Chinese modern industry would lead remained a matter of speculation—officially this market economy remained only a part of a socialist economic system. The basic industries, mining, most of steel, energy—coal and oil— and indeed all heavy industry, remained firmly in the hands of the planners; and all intimations by untutored outside commentators that China was turning toward capitalism were indignantly denied. In fact, the policy appeared to lead to a dual system under which the basic, heavy industry section of the economy formed the core of socialist central planning, while the remainder turned at least in name toward a so-called market economy.

To express this dichotomy in foreign policy terms, Chinese economy was apparently to be divided into a market section, to be promoted with Western help, and a socialist section, for which the new Chinese leadership turned again to the Soviet Union to reestablish a Soviet share in Chinese modernization. During October and November 1984, the fifth round of Sino-Soviet talks on normalization of relations was held in Peking and differed from former talks both in form and result. The Chinese no longer stressed the three obstacles that previously prevented agreement: Soviet refusal to withdraw from Vietnam, Afghanistan, and the Chinese northwestern border. Consequently, the fifth session concluded with a joint communiqué expressing the resolve by both sides to improve economic, trade, scientific, technological, cultural, and sport relations and to continue the talks in April in Moscow. In December 1984, Soviet Vice Premier Ivan Arkhipov, the highest Soviet official to visit China since the meeting of Kosygin and Zhou Enlai at the Peking airport in 1969, came to Peking to sign three agreements on economic, technological, and scientific cooperation plus a five-year trade pact seeking to boost Sino-Soviet trade from the $1.6 billion of 1984 to $6 billion annually.

Aside from the political aspects of this renewed cooperation— a Soviet check on China's new Western orientation and a Chinese playing of the Soviet card in relations with the West—it appears only reasonable and of mutual Sino-Soviet interest that the Soviets should cooperate in the upkeep and modernization of the heavy industrial plants in China, which they originally helped to build and which under the new policy were to remain the core of the socialist centrally planned and dominant sector of the economy. How the market economy would function and how it would relate to the socialist sector of the economy remained uncertain. By 1985 the problem of determining price was left in a twilight zone in which upper and lower limits were to be set by government fiat, while the various managers would bargain with each other for deals more determined by their political relationship than by the freely working factors of price setting in a free enterprise economy. As examples of Eastern Europe have shown, an economy half-socialist and half-free enterprise contains irreconcilable contradictions. Leaving aside all doctrinal incongruities, monopoly party rule and independent management are inherently irreconcilable. Moreover, China still must overcome its serious and worrisome shortage of trained managers and engineers.

This shortage was but one of the adverse results of the educational calamity bequeathed by Mao to his successors. The prolonged closing of the schools during the Cultural Revolution, the abolition of examinations, the priority given to political fanaticism over knowledge had resulted in an abysmal ignorance among what many Chinese regarded as a lost generation. The new regime immediately launched an effort to reestablish a stable educational system. According to Deng, the main task of the student was "to study, to learn book knowledge." Examinations were reintroduced with a vengeance, eliminating many political radicals from the student body. Standards of teaching were restored, and an emphasis on science and technology led to the decision to send large numbers of young students and older academics overseas to enroll in Western universities; by 1984 there were 15,000 Chinese students in the United States alone.

The post-Mao era appeared at first to permit greater tolerance for writers and artists. In some areas the newly gained freedom seemed to bear fruit, as in painting and music. A number of renowned Western orchestras were admitted to China and Chinese modern musicians and composers were reappearing in China and abroad. In the field of painting, the fusion of Chinese and Western—especially French impressionist—traditions of the twenties was revived and regained preeminence in China and abroad. (See Plate 31.) In the field of literature novels with critical themes appeared, but the trend was soon to be curbed. The Fourth National Congress of Chinese Writers and Artists, held in 1979, acclaimed the new policy, which also led to the "return from silence" of the most noted leftist writers who had fallen prey to Maoist purges. Among them was Zhou Yang (Chou Yang), formerly Mao's cultural czar who, having himself been purged in the end by the Maoists, was rehabilitated and reappointed to the party central committee and again to the chairmanship of the Chinese Federation of Literature and Art Workers. New works critical not only of Mao but also of the socialist system soon came under attack. Zhou Yang, as new chairman of the federation, rebuffed the claim of some writers of the right to follow their conscience; there was no individual freedom outside the party—the policy seemed to have come full circle.

For a modern economy, socialist or quasi–free enterprise, Mao's policy of rule by political drives was manifestly impracticable. The new regime attempted to end the arbitrariness and unpredictability of government policies by proclaiming the need for rule by law, albeit Communist law. Previously the introduction of legal codes, proposed on several occasions by leaders like Liu Shaoqi or Zhou Enlai, had always been prevented by Mao, who objected to any restraint of his wanton drives against sections of the population and his arbitrary use of power. After Mao's death legal norms were to be established for an orderly progress of modernization and protection against outrages such as those of the Cultural Revolution. In 1979 a number of laws were promulgated, the procurates were reestablished and the profession of lawyers—though only as state employees—was recognized. The new laws included a criminal code, but in the main they dealt with regulations for foreign businesses in China and their legal rights and status. This part of the economy, rebuilt with Western participation, had indeed to be treated in an internationally acceptable way.

The new criminal code received a great deal of publicity, but in the few cases that became well known (such as the trial of the "gang of four"), the new rules of procedures were arbitrarily disregarded. What was most disturbing from the point of view of a true legal order was the large remaining area of extralegal disposal of defendants of whose actions or attitudes the government disapproved. The large majority of arrests did not lead to legal criminal proceedings but to administrative sentencing to "reform through labor," in the Chinese gulags, which have been refilled with opponents of the regime as well as with ordinary culprits. The death penalty, soon to cover forty-four different criminal actions, was applied in anti-crime drives in which people were arrested for political crimes and, immediately after the verdicts in their cases, were executed, with no regard for the procedural regulations for appeal. Show trials before large audiences in public arenas dramatized the undiminished harshness of authority.

The most totalitarian aspect of the new regime was related to its population policy. The race between growth of production and the size of population was a problem faced by every Chinese government. Under Mao, any argument in favor of control of population growth was decried as "Malthusian bourgeois" schemes and "wicked imperialist plots" to weaken the country. Propagators were purged. Even the term for population, *jen k'ou,*—mouths—was changed to *jen shou*—hands—to indicate that under socialism increased population meant an increased labor force that would produce more and thus invalidate any argument for population limitation. This policy contributed greatly to the problem. The new regime realized quickly that unchecked growth would undo all economic advance of the modernization program.

The method applied constituted the worst interference into the realm of individual freedom that any totalitarian regime had yet attempted. The target of the new policy was to permit each married couple only one child, a target to be reached "principally through education," but, when necessary, "through administrative and organizational measures." The "educational" measures consisted of the promise of advancement for one-child couples in promotion and pay, and educational privileges for the child, advantages that of course would become self-defeating if the rule were generally accepted.[2] For those who attempted to disregard the rule, there has been a ruthless interference in the most private aspects of a woman's life, regular checks by women group wardens on the periods of menstruation and, in case of second pregnancies, enforced abortion even at the most advanced stage. The local communities drew up waiting lists for young couples for permission to give birth to their first and only child so that the community would not exceed its yearly quota of permissible births. This appears to be the first time that a totalitarian regime assumed the right to decide individual rights of procreation for the whole population.

The continuing ruthless interference in all personal life by the police and the local communities called in question the very purpose of the Communist order. A disillusionment had set in when the absurd exaggerations of the cult of Mao had to be disclaimed. It was of little avail that the Mao cult was now condemned as "theology," a fanatical aberration of true Marxism, and that there was to be a return to "scientific Marxism." After all, the party also admitted having made mistakes and could no longer be regarded as the infallible vehicle of Truth. A favorite phrase used by Deng: "Seek truth from facts," now often repeated, left all major questions unanswered. The Communists faced, in their own words, "a crisis of confidence."

Neither Marxism nor Maoism in particular provided any answer to the great ethical questions about life, let alone the religious issue of life after death. Formerly, all Chinese Communist constitutions had contained articles on the people's right of freedom of religion, but as so many stipulations of these constitutions, these articles remained meaningless. Churches and temples were destroyed or used for government purposes, priests and monks were imprisoned and many lost their lives. Worship was interdicted and became dangerous if carried on clandestinely. The persecution reached its climax during the Cultural Revolution, when all religion became a special target for Red Guard malevolence.

The worst cases of persecution occurred in Tibet, a country invaded in 1950 by the Chinese. In 1959 the Chinese bloodily suppressed a rebellion that led to the flight of the Dalai Lama and a hundred thousand Tibetans to India, with many more perishing on the way. The subsequent Chinese policy instituted in Tibet must be regarded as one of the worst cases of genocide of the century. Besides exterminating barbarically at least one million of an estimated six million Tibetans, the Chinese systematically dynamited and destroyed (with the exception of fewer than twenty of the most prestigious structures such as the Potala in Lhasa) more than three thousand Tibetan temples and monasteries, after looting them of their treasures. After Mao's death there followed a period of relaxation, but the goal of the Communist policy remained unchanged. It will remain a dark spot on the Chinese name.

As so often in history, however, religious convictions were strengthened by adversity. Tibetan Buddhism continued under the Dalai Lama in the Indian diaspora and retained its hold over the Tibetan people in their homeland, hampered as it was not only by continued persecution but even more by the destruction of Tibetan education. Islam survived in part because the knowledge of the militancy of its believers restrained the Red Guard's fervor. Christianity went largely underground. Though always a small minority of the population, it is believed to have increased during these years in which it was clandestinely practiced in home churches by families and groups. There were believed to be from six to twenty million practicing Christians in China at the end of the Cultural Revolution, when official policy began to change.

The new policy of toleration introduced by the Deng regime was based on the assumption that it was better to permit religious services in public under licensed organizations that could be held responsible. Under government control eight religious associations had been established at the time of the founding of the People's Republic—three Catholic, two Protestant and one each for Buddhism, Islam, and Taoism; these were now revived. These associations must have no allegiance to any non-Chinese authority, a restriction that forced Chinese Roman Catholics to give up their loyalty to the Vatican and accept government policies that ran counter to Catholic teachings, causing opposition by and imprisonment of some high-ranking clergymen. Though hampered by harassment and especially restrictions in education of youth and the training of novices, religious life in China apparently has survived a period of extreme suppression.

For the majority of the Chinese people, however, there remained, after the bitter disillusionment of the Mao years, the problem of the lack of a faith that would give meaning to life. Hu Yaobang (Hu Yao-pang), Deng's appointee as chairman of the party, tried to provide an answer. In a speech in September 1982 he introduced the concept of "spiritual socialism"[3]—for the traditional Marxist clearly a con-tradiction of terms. According to Hu, the spirituality of socialism was made up of such ingredients as education, science, art, literature, the media, recreation, libraries, museums, and public health. Ideo-logically the spiritualism was embodied in the "Weltanschauung of the working class," scientific Marxism, Communist ideals, beliefs, and moral values, and "most of all revolutionary ideals, morality, and discipline." This conceptual potpourri of institutions, ideas, and ideals appeared to be a crude form of what Marxists call "idealism," the superstructure of Marxist materialism that in this version would become the determining element, "standing Marx on his head." To define further this spiritualism, Hu listed "five stresses (decorum, manners, hygiene, discipline, and morals), . . . four beauties (mind, language, behavior, and environment) and three loves (party, moth-erland, and socialism)," in a recurrence of the Maoist numbers game.

The problem of the spiritual void of this doctrine, however, cannot be dealt with by slogans. With the introduction of Western economic methods it would become as difficult to separate new forms of economic and social life from their intellectual foundation as it was to find within the Marxist framework the justification for rich peasants, millionaires, and the trickle-down theory. This ideological danger to Communist rule was apparently realized by the Communist leadership, when with the import of Western technology and economic management and the continuing contact of Chinese on all levels in China and abroad with Western concepts of life and value systems, it became clearly more and more difficult to keep out the ideas so intricately connected with this economic and social order in the West.

To counter this conceived threat, the party initiated in late 1983 a nationwide drive against "spiritual pollution," defined by Deng Xiaoping as the "dissemination of all varieties of corrupt and decadent ideologies of the bourgeoisie and other exploiting classes" and the spreading "sentiments of distrust towards the socialist and communist cause and the Communist Party leadership."[4] For the traditional wing of the party, those opposed to the economic changes and the loosening of restrictions and party control that went with them, this condemnation of spiritual pollution was a signal for a general attack against all aspects of the new spirit in politics and economics, as well as in literature and art. The new life-style of the young in the cities, the use of cosmetics, fashionable clothing, and entertainment, and the existence of newly rich peasants and successful entrepreneurs all came under attack by radical party members. The drive, so reminiscent of aspects of the Cultural Revolution with its attack against ideological deviation, life-styles, and intellectual freedom, threatened to interfere with the policy of the four modernizations. It had to be curbed. Premier Zhao declared that "the people's demand for a better cultural and material life is justified and should be encouraged and . . . in no circumstances be confused with spiritual contamination on the ideological front."[5]

However, whatever new activity was to be permitted would have to stay within the parameter of what Deng Xiaoping called the Four Basics: The Socialist Way; Marxism-Leninism Mao Tse-tung Thought; Dictatorship of the Proletariat; and Leadership by the Chinese Communist Party. It was left to the cadres and indeed to the people to find the fine line between control and freedom of behavior and of the mind. As under Mao, the line remained vague and flexible and was to be determined by whatever the government decreed at the time.

In spite of current economic transformations and political loosening of control, the question of an emerging new social and political order remains unresolved in the China of the mid-eighties. Clearly though, enough of the traditional ethics and values of a great cultural tradition will survive the onslaught of Mao and Communism to provide a strong humanist foundation for whatever Chinese order—under whatever name—may evolve from the debacle of Maoist Chinese Communism.

Eighteen

CONCLUSION

THE MOST REMARKABLE aspect of Chinese imperial history has been the contrast between the ever-recurring hiatus in the political process with its rise and fall of dynasties on the one hand and the steadily evolving continuum of the social order on the other. On this social continuity a unified political structure was always rebuilt. This converse interrelationship in imperial time between a constant society and an ever-reestablished dynastic state emanated from the acceptance of Confucianism as the social and political foundation for Chinese polity.

Confucianism propagated a government by suasion. The emperor's wisdom would, so it was claimed, attract people near and far to his sway. In practice this concept resulted in a limitation of government functions, leaving many concerns regarded as government's responsibility in modern nation-states to the free interrelationship and autonomous management of society. The comparatively small number of imperial officials testifies to this limitation of the state, so diametrically opposed to the twentieth-century totalitarian state, with which some have mistakenly linked it.

In imperial China, the Confucian scholar-gentry were leaders of society who at the same time held a monopoly on the positions of officialdom in the state of the emperor, thus forming a vital link between society and state, essential to maintain the unity of the polity. Not limited by Confucianism, the scholar-gentry learned and gained from other philosophies and faiths. Taoism sought an understanding of the riddle of reality and led to an appreciation of nature, without which Chinese art would be unthinkable. Mahayana Buddhism added its philosophical interpretation of the mystery of

241

existence and provided religious faith and compassion and a great sculptural art. Taoist philosophical and Buddhist religious speculations about the problem of reality have been regarded by some modern astrophysicists as a conceptual parallelism in the most basic sense to their scientific findings. Whatever their importance in general may be, without these religious and philosophical elements, the rational ethics of the Confucian order in China could well have remained tedious and prosaic. Together these three tenets provided the intellectual panorama of a rich and versatile civilization.

No strict line was drawn for scholars between these varying intellectual and spiritual currents. Profiting from them all, the scholars were the carriers of the cultural tradition, the teachers, historians, artists, writers, as well as the social models and leaders of this civilization; the Confucian prototype of the *Chün'tzu* became the ideal. Even if, as in all civilizations, reality remained a far cry from the ideal goal, the aspiration itself was as high as any sought by common human endeavor.

The role of the scholar-gentry as the custodians of Confucian teachings allowed them to assume an ideological authority over both society and state that matched the emperor's power over the government, resulting in a dualism of authority and providing a realm of freedom for social and economic life, for art, and for belief and thought that guaranteed the multiformity and long endurance of Chinese civilization.

In the twentieth century, the problem for this civilization has been its transformation from a universal empire into a modern state and society. The attempt to transform the imperial order into a constitutional monarchy, undertaken at the end of the nineteenth century by K'ang Yu-wei, the last Confucian scholar-statesman, failed altogether. Instead, the Revolution of 1911 led by Sun Yat-sen brought a break with the past but no immediate viable political and social order. At last a National Government under Chiang Kai-shek, established in 1928, initiated a serious program to build a modern nation, a new social order under law, modern education, economic development, and the beginnings of political participation. The latter participation was handicapped by the survival of the treaty ports where the growing Chinese middle class, living under the protection of foreign rights, was prevented from assuming a logical place in the fight for a share of political power. It fell to the army to fight for the new national interests until war and civil war took the place of politics.

Japan's aggression and invasion destroyed the great chance for a true Chinese nation-state and provided the conditions and the opportunity for the Chinese Communists to take power. The Nationalist Chinese tradition has been carried on in Taiwan where China has become modernized and where tradition and new freedom may yet make their contribution to a future Chinese nation-state.

In its origin, Chinese Communism was a child of Moscow, founded and directed under the guidance of the Comintern throughout its early period until the beginnings of the Sino-Soviet conflict in the late 1950s. The myth of the "other Communism" still abounds, fostered as it was by many Western writers. The Communist strategy of national liberation movements and wars of national liberation was Lenin's invention, followed by Stalin, both of whom fully understood the importance of gaining peasant support in the preindustrial world of Asia and other analogous countries.

In economic terms, Communism has failed everywhere; but in China Maoist utopianism added its fantasies and costly chimeras to create a human and economic crisis. A drastic shift in policy after Mao's death has been required to lift the country out of the deep hole into which thirty years of mismanagement had thrust it.

The regime of Deng Xiaoping is trying to restore a working economy, improve the miserable living standards and undo the damage of the past decades without giving up the claim to proceed within Marxism-Leninism and the framework of a socialist order. With Western help, a limited market economy is being introduced in a system that is to remain basically Communist. Other modifications include: a freer life-style; to get rich is no longer a capitalist sin because eventually one person's wealth should benefit all; legal codes and judicial procedure are being introduced for criminal law and handling foreign economic enterprises, but criminal laws are applied selectively, procedures are disregarded at will, and the large majority of cases, especially political, are dealt with administratively through "labor reform" camps. Movement and work assignment remain restricted, and the worst form of totalitarian control was introduced in demographic policy with the one-child-per-couple system, enforced by detailed supervision, forced abortion at any stage of pregnancy, infanticide, and sterilization. The danger that with Western economic methods Western ideas and beliefs might take hold was countered by anti-spiritual pollution drives meant to intimidate a population that remembered only too well the ruthlessness of the past.

This complex admixture of limited freedoms within a continuing Communist totalitarian order constituted a new departure from orthodox Marxism-Leninism and an experiment whose outcome appears uncertain. For anyone to whom social existence without basic freedoms remains intolerable it appears unlikely that a system half-Communist and half-free will long endure. Whatever trials may lie ahead in China, the great humanist tradition of the past may still provide the moral strength on which to base a freer order for a people who have suffered so much in our time.

NOTES

Chapter 1

1. Recent excavations have uncovered neolithic sites in southeastern China that may be earlier than those in the Northwest, but it was in the Northwest where Neolithic settlements became the foundation of the emerging Chinese civilization.

Chapter 2

1. J. Li Dun, *The Ageless Chinese: A History*. Charles Scribners Sons, New York, 1985, p. 35.

2. Chi Ts'ui, *A Short History of Chinese Civilization*, Putnam, New York, 1943, p. 13.

3. The identity of these findings with the Hsia Dynasty is, however, still controversial. See among others Chang Kwang-chih, *The Archeology of Ancient China*, 3d ed., Yale University Press, New Haven, 1978, and Chang's chapter 16 on "Sandai Archeology and the Foundation of States in Ancient China; Processual Aspects of the Origins of Chinese Civilization," in David N. Keightley, *The Origins of Chinese Civilization*, University of California Press, Berkeley, 1983. Chang's theory that the three early political entities, the Hsia, the Shang and the Chou were "parallel"—or at least overlapping—political groups (p. 497) "with different geographic centers" (p. 500) is probably correct but in no way contradicts the now generally accepted assumption that the Shang and the Chou ruled the China of the time in succession. Indeed, Chang's beliefs about the Hsia geographic center in the Loyang area seem to support the interpretation of the new excavations as Hsia centers.

4. J. Gunnar Andersson, *Children of the Yellow Earth*, London, 1934.

5. Franz Weidenreich, "The Sinantropous Populations of Choukoutien (Locality 1) with a Preliminary Report on New Discoveries," *Bulletin of the Geological Survey of China* (1935), 14.4, referred to by Herrlee G. Creel,

The Birth of China, Frederick Ungar Publishing Co., New York, 1979, p. 41.

6. The question of the linkage between the Peking Man population of Chou-k'ou-t'ien and Neolithic and modern Chinese is still a matter of speculation. Although Peking Man shows clearly Mongoloid characteristics, some specialists have regarded the three restorable crania found as akin more to other Mongoloid branches, the American Indians, Eskimoid, and Melanesoid respectively, rather than the later Chinese Mongoloid branch. Two possibilities have been considered: a Chinese direct descent from these early humans through special evolution, or a replacement of this early type by the Neolithic Chinese coming from somewhere else, though not likely from far away. In any case, early Mongoloid life existed in Paleolithic China. See W. W. Howells, "Origins of the Chinese People: Interpretations of the Recent Evidence," chap. 11 in Keightley, *The Origins of Chinese Civilization*, pp. 297–319.

7. This interpretation has been challenged by some recent writings but is retained by others (see bibliography for Chapter 2) and is, in this author's view, still basically acceptable.

8. The relationship between Yangshao and Lungshan cultures is still a matter of speculation. One view now suggests that the Lungshan culture was "developed out of the Yangshao culture." See Chang Kwang-chih, *The Archeology of Ancient China*, chap. 3. Another theory maintains the view expressed here, that Yangshao and Lungshan represent two independent traditions, the latter of entirely Chinese origin, which both affected the Chinese polity of Hsia and Shang with the later Lungshan culture predominant. See Louisa G. Fitzgerald Huber, "The Relationship of the Painted Pottery and Lungshan cultures," in Keightley, ed., *The Origins of Chinese Civilization*, chap. 7.

Chapter 3

1. B. Karlgren, "Some Fecundity Symbols in Ancient China," *Bulletin of the Museum for Far Eastern Antiquity*, Stockholm, 1930, no. 2.

Chapter 4

1. The victory of the Chou over the Shang ruler at the battle of Mu-yeh was obviously regarded as of primary importance in the Confucian tradition, and the record has been clearly embellished in the annals. Thus it was stated that King Wu attacked Shang with only 50,000 men who were opposed by 700,000 Shang troops. These figures were to explain the Shang forces' unwillingness to defend their corrupt ruler. See Ssu-ma Ch'ien,

Shi-chi 4.2-27, referred to in Herrlee G. Creel, *The Origins of Statecraft in China*, vol. 1, *The Western Chou Empire*, University of Chicago Press, Chicago, 1970, p. 57.

2. Ch'i Ssu-ho, as quoted in Ibid., p. 85.

3. From the Shu king, Shao kao, as quoted in William Theodore de Bary, et al., comps., *Sources of Chinese Tradition*, Columbia University Press, New York, 1960, pp. 12–14.

4. Creel, *The Origins of Statecraft in China*, pp. 98–100.

5. From the *Shih Ching*, as translated by de Bary, *Sources of Chinese Tradition*, p. 14.

6. Creel, *The Origins of Statecraft in China*, p. 101.

7. Again and again the annals record the bloody victories of Ch'in, adding "a hundred thousand heads were cut off." When the Ch'ao army surrendered in 259 B.C., the Ch'in generals are supposed to have slaughtered 400,000 men. See Charles Patrick Fitzgerald, *China, A Short Cultural History*, 4th ed., Praeger, New York, 1961, p. 72.

Chapter 5

1. *Confucian Analects*, de Bary, *Sources of Chinese Tradition*, pp. 22–35.

2. *Meng-tzu*, Ibid., p. 110.

3. *Confucian Analects*, Ibid., p. 60.

4. Ibid., p. 53

5. Ibid., p. 75.

6. Ibid., p. 39.

7. Ibid., p. 147.

Chapter 6

1. J. L. Duyvendak, *The Book of Lord Shang*, London, 1928.

2. For Lü Pu-wei, *Lü-shih Ch'un-ch'iu*, see de Bary, *Sources of Chinese Tradition*, p. 223 f.

3. Werner Eichhorn, *Chinese Civilization, An Introduction*, Praeger, New York, 1969, p. 126.

4. de Bary, *Sources of Chinese Tradition*, p. 154.

5. Ibid.

6. Eichhorn, *Chinese Civilization*, p. 127, quoted from *Shih Chi*, chap. 6.

7. de Bary, *Sources of Chinese Tradition*, pp. 154–155, quoted from *Shih-ching*.

Chapter 7

1. For a discussion see Franz Michael, Introduction to Chang Chung-li, *The Chinese Gentry*, University of Washington Press, Seattle, 1958, pp. xviii ff.

2. From Tung Chung-shu's memorial on land reform, see de Bary, *Sources of Chinese Tradition*, p. 233.

Chapter 8

1. The author, Juan Chi, was one of the "Seven Sages of the Bamboo Grove" discussed in Chapter 8. See among others de Bary, *Sources of Chinese Tradition*, p. 287. (Juan Chi, *Biography of a Great Sage* [in Chinese]). For a somewhat different translation see K. C. Hsiao, *History of Chinese Political Thought*, University of Washington Press, Seattle, vol. 1, p. 621, trans. by Fritz Mote.

2. Tsung Ping, A.D. 375–443, de Bary, *Sources of Chinese Tradition*, p. 294 ff.

3. Wang Wei, A.D. 415–443, Ibid., p. 295.

4. The Eightfold Path prescribes a middle course between ascetic self-castigation and indulgence in sensual delights. It consists of:

1. The right view and understanding of the Four Noble Truths.
2. The right aspiration and thought, an attitude of equanimity toward life, renouncing the craving for existence.
3. The right speech, avoiding lying and slander.
4. The right conduct and action, no stealing or acquiring anything to which one is not entitled.
5. The right mode of life; no violence or drunkenness.
6. The right endeavor, not to think evil but to control one's mental state. ,
7. The right mindfulness, to control one's body and feelings.
8. The right concentration to awaken one's mind through meditation.

5. These aggregates are material properties, feelings, or sensations, perception of sense objects, mental formations, and consciousness, which interrelate and combine to form any being during the time of its existence.

6. Theravada is called by the Mahayana followers "Hinayana," the "smaller vessel," a designation that the Theravada Buddhists do not accept.

7. de Bary, *Sources of Chinese Tradition*, p. 378.

Chapter 9

   1. Fitzgerald, *China*, p. 294.

Chapter 10

   1. Fitzgerald, *China*, p. 384.
   2. Franz Michael, "From the Fall of T'ang to the Fall of Ch'ing," chap. 7 in *China*, Harley Farnsworth MacNair, ed., University of California Press, Berkeley, 1946, p. 91.

Chapter 11

   1. Marco Polo, *The Travels*, Penguin Books, New York, 1958.
   2. Michael Sullivan, *The Arts of China*, rev. ed., University of California Press, Berkeley, 1979, pp. 196–197.

Chapter 12

   1. For Ming and Ch'ing emperors most writers use reign titles rather than the emperor's posthumous names. The author follows this general practice.
   2. de Bary, *Sources of Chinese Tradition*, p. 570.

Chapter 13

   1. Hsieh Pao-chao, *Chinese Government, 1644–1911*, Johns Hopkins Press, Baltimore, 1935, pp. 33–34.
   2. Literally: The Complete Works of the Four Divisions of the Imperial Library.
   3. Harley Farnsworth MacNair, *Modern Chinese History: Selected Readings*, Shanghai, 1933, pp. 4–5.

Chapter 14

   1. Franz Michael, *Taiping Rebellion*, Vol. 1, *History*, University of Washington Press, Seattle, 1966, p. 101.
   2. Franz Michael and George E. Taylor, *The Far East in the Modern World*, 3d ed., Dryden Press, Hinsdale, Ill., 1975, p. 201.
   3. Hu Shih, *The Chinese Renaissance*, University of Illinois Press, Chicago, 1934, p. 46.
   4. Ibid., p. 93.

Chapter 15

1. See also Milton J. T. Hsieh, *The Kuomintang: Selected Historical Documents 1894–1969*, St. John's University Press, New York, 1961, p. 71.

2. See Jane Degras, ed. *The Communist International, 1919–1943, Documents*, Praeger, New York, 1964, vol. 2, p. 279.

3. Radio speech heard by author in rural China at the time.

Chapter 16

1. For this campaign see Robert T. Lifton, *Thought Reform and the Psychology of Totalism: A Study of "Brainwashing" in China*, Norton, New York, 1961.

2. Franz Michael, *Mao and The Perpetual Revolution*, Barron Educational Press, Woodbury, New York, 1977, pp. 159 ff.

3. For references on the Cultural Revolution see Ibid., pp. 155–182.

4. Zhou had first used this phrase in 1968 after the Soviet invasion of Czechoslovakia.

Chapter 17

1. *People's Daily* [hereafter, P.D.], March 22, 1979.

2. *Sixth Five-Year Plan*, chap. 29.

3. See *Beijing Review*, no. 18, May 2, 1983, pp. 18–19.

4. P.D., Nov. 16, 1983.

5. *Beijing Review*, no. 24., June 11, 1984, p. 11.

BIBLIOGRAPHY

General Histories

de Bary, William Theodore, Wing-tsit Chan, Burton Watson, comps. *Sources of Chinese Tradition.* Columbia University Press, New York, 1960.

Eichhorn, Werner. *Chinese Civilization, An Introduction.* Praeger, New York, 1969.

Fitzgerald, C. P. *China, A Short Cultural History.* 4th ed., rev. Praeger, New York, London, 1976.

Gernet, Jacques. *A History of Chinese Civilization.* Trans. by J. R. Foster. Cambridge University Press, Cambridge, 1982.

Goodrich, L. Carrington. *A Short History of the Chinese People.* Harper & Row, New York, 1957.

Michael, Franz, and George Taylor. *The Far East in the Modern World.* 3d ed. Dryden Press, Hinsdale, Ill., 1975, Chap. 1, 2, 7, 12, 13.

Chapter 1

Cressey, George B. *China's Geographic Foundations.* McGraw-Hill, New York, 1933, p. 134.

Chapter 2

Chang Kwang-chih. *The Archeology of Ancient China.* 3d ed., Yale University Press, New Haven, 1978.

Cheng Te-k'un. *Archaeology in China.* Vol. 3, *Chou China,* Cambridge, England, 1963.

Keightley, David N. *The Origins of Chinese Civilization,* University of California Press, Berkeley, 1983.

Whitehouse, Ruth D., ed. *The Macmillan Dictionary of Archeology.* Macmillan, London, 1983. (Articles on oracle bones, Yang Shao, and Longshan.)

Chapter 3

Chang Kwang-chih. *Shang Civilization*. Yale University Press, New Haven, 1980.

Cheng Te-k'un. *Archaeology in China*. Vol. 3, *Chou China*, Cambridge, England, 1963.

Keightley, David N. *The Origins of Chinese Civilization*, University of California Press, Berkeley, 1983.

Li Chi. *The Beginnings of Chinese Civilization*. University of Washington Press, Seattle, 1957.

Chapter 4

Cheng Te-k'un. *Archaeology in China*. Vol. 3, *Chou China*, Cambridge, England, 1963.

Keightley, David N. *The Origins of Chinese Civilization*, University of California Press, Berkeley, 1983.

Creel, Herrlee G. *The Origins of Statecraft in China*. Vol. 1, *The Western Chou Empire*. University of Chicago Press, Chicago, 1970.

Waley, Arthur. *The Book of Songs*. Grove Press, New York, 1960.

Chapter 5

Chan, Wing-tsit. *A Sourcebook in Chinese Philosophy*. Princeton University Press, Princeton, 1963.

———. *The Story of Chinese Philosophy*, "Philosophy: East and West." Ed. by Charles A Moore. Princeton University Press, Princeton, 1944.

Fung Yu-lan. *A History of Chinese Philosophy*. Trans. by Derk Bodde. Princeton University Press, Princeton, 1952. (See also Special Topics)

Hsu Cho-yun. *China in Transition, An Analysis of Social Mobility, 722–222 B.C.*, Stanford University Press, Stanford, 1965.

Lau, D. C., trans. *Confucius: The Analects*, Penguin Books, New York, 1979.

———. *Mencius*. Penguin Books, New York, 1970.

Legge, James. *The Chinese Classics*. 5 vols. Oxford University Press, Oxford, 1883–1895. Reprint. Hong Kong University Press, 1960.

Mote, Frederick W. *Intellectual Foundations of China*, Alfred A. Knopf, New York, 1971.

Waley, Arthur. *Three Ways of Thought in Ancient China*, Doubleday Anchor, New York, 1956.

Watson, Burton, trans. *Han Fei Tzu*, Columbia University Press, New York, 1967.

———. *Hsun Tzu*, Columbia University Press, New York, 1967.

————. *Mo Tzu*, Columbia University Press, New York, 1967.

————. *Chuang Tzu*, Columbia University Press, New York, 1967.

Weber, Max. *The Religion of China: Confucianism and Taoism*, Trans. by Hans H. Gerth. Free Press, Glencoe, Ill., 1951.

Chapter 6

Bodde, Derk. *China's First Unifier, A Study of the Ch'in Dynasty as Seen in the Life of Li Szu.* F. J. Brill Ltd., Leiden, 1938.

Chapter 7

Bielenstein, Hans. *The Bureaucracy of Han Times.* Cambridge University Press, New York, 1980.

Chang Kwang-chih. *Han Civilization.* Yale University Press, New Haven, 1980.

Dubs, Homer. *The History of the Former Han by Pan Ku.* 3 vols. Waverly Press, Baltimore, 1955.

Watson, Burton. *Records of the Grand Historian of China,* Columbia University Press, New York, 1961.

————. *Ssu-ma Ch'ien, Grand Historian of China,* Columbia University Press, New York, 1958.

Chapter 8

Ch'en, Kenneth Kuan-sheng. *The Chinese Transformation of Buddhism.* Princeton University Press, Princeton, 1973.

Thompson, Laurence G. "Chinese Buddhism," part 2 in *Studies of Chinese Religion.* Dickenson, Encino, Calif., 1976.

Wright, Arthur F. *Buddhism in China.* Atheneum Paperback, Stanford University Press, 1970.

Zürcher, Eric. *The Buddhist Conquest of China.* 2 vols. E. J. Barth, Leiden, 1959.

Chapter 9

Twitchett, Denis, ed. *Sui and T'ang China.* Vol. 3, part 1, *The Cambridge History of China.* Ed. by Denis Twitchett and John King Fairbank. Cambridge University Press, Cambridge, 1979.

Wright, Arthur F. *The Sui Dynasty.* Alfred A. Knopf, New York, 1978.

Chapter 10

Bruce, J. P. *Chu Hsi and His Masters; An Introduction to Chu Hsi and the Sung School of Chinese Philosophy*, A. Probsthain, London, 1923.

Kracke, E. A., Jr. *Civil Service in Early Sung China, 960–1067*, Harvard University Press, Cambridge, Mass., 1953.

_____. "Sung Society; Change Within Tradition." *Far Eastern Quarterly* 14, 4, 1955, pp. 479–488.

Liu, James T. C. *Reform in Sung China: Wang An-shih and His New Policies*. Harvard University Press, Cambridge, Mass., 1959.

Williamson, H. R. *Wang An Shih, A Chinese Statesman and Educationalist of the Sung Dynasty*. 2 vols. A. Probsthain, London, 1937.

Chapter 11

Langlois, John D. *China Under Mongol Rule*, Princeton University Press, Princeton, 1981.

Polo, Marco. *The Travels*, Penguin Books, New York, 1958.

Zucker, Adolph E. *The Chinese Theater*, Little Brown & Co., Boston, 1925.

Chapter 12

Goodrich, L. Carrington, and Fang Chao-ying. *A Dictionary of Ming Biography*. 2 vols. Columbia University Press, New York, 1976.

Hucker, Charles O. *Chinese Government in Ming Times*, Columbia University Press, New York, 1969.

_____. *The Ming Dynasty, Its Origins and Evolving Institutions*. University of Michigan, Center for Chinese Studies, Ann Arbor, 1978.

Chapter 13

Fairbank, John K. *Trade and Diplomacy on the China Coast: The Opening of the Treaty Ports 1842–1854*. Harvard University Press, Cambridge, Mass., 1953.

Feuerwerker, Albert. *State and Society in 18th Century China; the Ch'ing Empire in Its Glory*. University of Michigan Press, Ann Arbor, 1976.

Hsiao Kung-ch'uan. *Rural China*. University of Washington Press, Seattle, 1960. (See also books listed for Chap. 14)

Hsieh Pao-chao. *Chinese Government, 1644–1911*. Johns Hopkins Press, Baltimore, 1935.

Hummel, Arthur W., ed. *Eminent Chinese of the Ch'ing Period, 1644–1912*. 2 vols., Government Printing Office, Washington, D.C., 1944.

Michael, Franz H. *The Origin of Manchu Rule in China*, Johns Hopkins Press, Baltimore, 1942. Reprint. Octagon Books, Inc., New York, 1965.
————. Introduction to *The Chinese Gentry*, by Chang Chung-li. University of Washington Press, Seattle, 1955.
————. Introduction to *The Income of the Chinese Gentry*, by Chang Chung-li. University of Washington Press, Seattle, 1962.

Chapter 14

Cameron, M. E. *The Reform Movement in China*. Stanford University Press, Stanford, 1931.
Chou Tse-tsung. *The May Fourth Movement*. Harvard University Press, Cambridge, Mass., 1960.
Hsia Chih-tsing. *A History of Modern Chinese Fiction, 1917–1957.* Yale University Press, New Haven, 1961.
Hu Shih. *The Chinese Renaissance*. University of Chicago Press, Chicago, 1934.
Hsiao Kung-ch'uan. *A Modern China and A New World: K'ang Yu-wei, Reformer and Utopian*. University of Washington Press, Seattle, 1975.
————. *Rural China*, University of Washington Press, Seattle, 1960.
K'ang Yu-wei. *The One World Philosophy of K'ang Yu-wei*. Trans. by L. Thompson. Allen & Unwin, London, 1958.
Michael, Franz, and George E. Taylor. *The Far East in the Modern World*. 3d ed. Dryden Press, Hinsdale, Ill., 1975.
Michael, Franz. *The Taiping Rebellion*. 3 vols. University of Washington Press, Seattle, 1966–1971.
Sharman, Lyon. *Sun Yat-sen, His Life and Its Meaning*. John Day Co., New York, 1934.

Chapter 15

Cavendish, Patrick. "The Rise of the Chinese Nationalist Party and the Foundation of the Nanking Regime, 1924–1929," Ph.D. diss., Cambridge University, England, 1968.
Ch'i Hsi-sheng. *Nationalist China at War; Military Defeat and Political Collapse, 1937–1945.* University of Michigan Press, Ann Arbor, 1982.
Chiang Kai-shek. *China's Destiny*. Trans. by Wang Chung-hui, with introduction by Lin Yu-tang, Macmillan, New York, 1947.
Hsu, Leonard Shihhen (Shih-lien). *Sun Yat-sen, His Political and Social Ideals*. Los Angeles, 1933.
Linebarger, Paul M. A. *The China of Chiang K'ai-shek*. Norton, Boston, 1941. Reprint. Greenwood Press, Westport, Conn., 1973.

Liu, F. F. A Military History of Modern China, 1924–1949. Princeton University Press, Princeton, 1957.

Schiffrin, Harold Z. Sun Yat-sen and the Origins of the Chinese Revolution. University of California Press, Berkeley, 1968.

Sharman, Lyon. Sun Yat-sen: His Life and Its Meaning. John Day Co., New York, 1934.

Thornton, Richard C. China, the Struggle for Power, 1917–1972. Indiana University Press, Bloomington, 1973. (See also books listed for Chap. 16)

Chapter 16

Chen, Theodore H. E. Thought Reform of the Chinese Intellectuals. Hong Kong University Press, Hong Kong, 1960.

Cohen, Arthur A. The Communism of Mao Tse-tung. University of Chicago Press, Chicago, 1964.

Degras, Jane, ed. The Communist International, 1919–1943, Documents, Vol. 1 (1919–22), 1956; Vol. 2 (1923–28), 1964; Vol. 3 (1929–43), Praeger, New York, 1965.

Lifton, Robert J. Thought Reform and the Psychology of Totalism: A Study of "Brainwashing" in China. Norton, New York, 1961.

MacFarquhar, Roderick. The Hundred Flowers Campaign and the Chinese Intellectuals. Praeger, New York, 1960.

Mao Tse-tung. Selected Works. Vols. 1–5. Peking Foreign Language Press, Peking, 1961–65.

Michael, Franz. Mao and the Perpetual Revolution. Barron Educational Press, Woodbury, N.Y., 1977.

Rice, Edward E. Mao's Way. University of California Press, Berkeley, 1972.

Schwartz, Benjamin. Chinese Communism and the Rise of Mao. Harvard University Press, Cambridge, Mass., 1964.

Snow, Edgar. Red Star Over China. Random House, New York, 1938.

Thornton, Richard C. China, The Struggle for Power, 1917–1972. Indiana University Press, Bloomington, 1973.

Walker, Richard L. The Human Cost of Communism in China. Prepared at the request of the late Senator Thomas J. Dodd, Subcommittee to Investigate the Administration of the Internal Security Act and Other Internal Security Laws of the Committee on the Judiciary, U.S. Senate, Washington, D.C., n.d.

Chapter 17

Bonavia, David. *Verdict in Peking*. Putnam, New York, 1984.

Butterfield, Fox. *China Alive in the Bitter Sea*. Bantam Books, New York, 1983.

Copper, John F., Franz Michael, and Yuan-li Wu. *Human Rights in Post-Mao China*. Westview Special Studies on East Asia, Boulder and London, 1985.

Domes, Jürgen. *The Government and Politics of the PRC: A Time of Transition*, Westview Press, Boulder, 1985.

Moser, Steven W. *Broken Earth: The Rural Chinese*. Free Press, New York, 1983.

Special Topics

Fung Yu-lan. *A History of Chinese Philosophy*. Trans. by Derk Bodde, Princeton University Press, Princeton, 1952.

Hsia, C. T. *The Classic Chinese Novel*. Columbia University Press, New York, 1968.

Hsiao Kung-ch'uan. *A History of Chinese Political Thought*. 2 vols. Trans. by Frederick Mote. Princeton University Press, Princeton, 1979.

Lattimore, Owen. *Inner Asian Frontiers of China*. American Geographical Society, New York, 1951.

Sickman, Laurence, and Alexander Soper. *The Art and Architecture of China*. Penguin Books, New York, 1971.

Siren, Osvald. *Chinese Sculpture from the Fifth to the Fourteenth Century*. 4 vols. London, 1925.

Sullivan, Michael. *The Arts of China*. Rev. ed. University of California Press, Berkeley, 1979.

Weber, Max. *The Religion of China. Confucianism and Taoism*. Free Press, Glencoe, Ill., 1951.

Wittfogel, Karl August. *Oriental Despotism; A Comparative Study of Total Power*. Yale University Press, New Haven, 1957.

Wright, Arthur, ed. *The Confucian Persuasion*, Stanford University Press, Stanford, 1960.

INDEX